WHAT GETS THEM TO READ LIKE THAT?

The Story of the Woman Who
Got Millions of Children to Read

What Gets Them to Read Like That?

The Story of the Woman Who Got Millions of Children to Read

Geneviève Patte

Translated by Tegan Raleigh

LIBRARY JUICE PRESS
SACRAMENTO, CA

© Editions les Arènes/L'Ecole des Loisirs, Paris, 2015.

English translation copyright 2022

Published in 2022 by Library Juice Press

Library Juice Press
PO Box 188784
Sacramento, CA 95822

http://libraryjuicepress.com/

This book is printed on acid-free paper.

Library of Congress Cataloging-in-Publication Data

Names: Patte, Geneviève, author.
Title: What gets them to read like that? : the story of the woman who got millions of children to read / Geneviève Patte ; translated by Tegan Raleigh.
Other titles: Mais qu'est-ce qui les fait lire comme ça? English
Description: Sacramento, CA : Library Juice Press, 2022. | Includes bibliographical references and index. | Summary: "The story of Geneviève Patte's life and her social engagement as a librarian, which originated with her appreciation of stories told by Parisian refugees her family hosted during the period of the Nazi occupation"-- Provided by publisher.
Identifiers: LCCN 2022014831 | ISBN 9781634001328 (paperback)
Subjects: LCSH: Patte, Geneviève. | Bibliothèque d'enfants (Clamart, France) | Children's librarians--France--Biography. | Children--Books and reading--France.
Classification: LCC Z720.P38 A3 2022 | DDC 020.92 [B]--dc23/eng/20220520
LC record available at https://lccn.loc.gov/2022014831

Contents

Introduction—*Leonard S. Marcus*	vii
Author Dedications—*Geneviève Patte*	1
What Gets Them to Read Like That?—*Geneviève Patte*	5
List of Titles Mentioned in Text	211
Index	215

Introduction

As visionaries go, French librarian and literacy advocate Geneviève Patte has had a most fortunate life. She has not only led the way as a thinker about the importance of books and libraries for young people regardless of their economic circumstances or nationality, but has also had many chances to road test and implement her ideas and to encourage and train others to build on her foundational work. In this wide-ranging and moving memoir, Patte tells her remarkable story and continues her pathfinding work as a guide and inspiration for librarians everywhere.

Patte grew up in Poitiers, a historic provincial city in west-central France, in a house filled with books. The German invasion of France occurred when she was just three and greatly disrupted the life of her large, cultured, close-knit family: her older brother was jailed for his participation in the French Resistance, her paleontologist father was forced into hiding, and her mother was left to cope with the knowledge of being constantly watched by the occupying authorities. Patte emerged from this frightful time as a serious reader and a student of the German language and German literature. Following her undergraduate studies at Poitiers, she headed to Paris to see more of the world and explore career options. Soon after her arrival in the French capital, she discovered children's librarianship as a vocation, enrolled in a library training program, and found ideal mentors in the small staff of L'Heure Joyeuse (The Happy Hour), an experimental children's library where she was offered an internship. This special library had been established after the First World War as a friendship gesture by visiting librarians associated with the American Committee for Devastated Regions, an initiative led by Annie Morgan, daughter of New York banker Pierpont Morgan. France had no prior tradition of specialized library service for children, and as Patte explains, L'Heure Joyeuse developed along idiosyncratic lines suggested by contemporary progressive educators' ideas about children as full collaborators in their education. She was struck by the combination of seriousness and informality with which the librarians welcomed the children and engaged with them as valued members of what felt like a kind of utopian community. Equally important for Patte, it seems, was the realization that the women who oversaw L'Heure Joyeuse had elevated library work with children to the level of art. Through their example, her own future became clear.

She could hardly have asked for a better beginning and after several months at the Paris library, another opportunity to expand her professional horizons came her way. Creative initiatives for the benefit of children tend to proliferate in the wake of war, and Patte next headed to Munich for several months (1959-1960) as a visiting researcher at the most ambitious of all post-Second World War experiments dedicated to children's literacy and cross-cultural understanding: the Internationale Jugendbibliothek (International Youth Library).

This unique repository and study center for children's literature from around the world had opened its doors in 1949 through the determined efforts of a German Jewish journalist named Jella Lepman, who believed that a world center for the study of children's books might play a positive role in building a more peaceful future. Lepman won support for her idealistic vision among publishers and librarians in the United States and across Europe. Four years later, her work inspired the creation of a second institution, the International Board on Books for Young People (IBBY), which continues to serve not only as a clearing house for the dissemination of information about children's books, but as a generator of exhibitions, publisher of lists of books recommended for translation, sponsor of conferences and awards, and more.

In Munich, Patte met librarians and book advocates from across the globe in a series of encounters that laid the groundwork for her vast circle of professional colleagues. She found that researchers came to the library with a wide range of objectives. A young woman from Sri Lanka, for example, had come to learn how to introduce high-quality literature to her country's children. Visitors from the Soviet Union and other East Bloc countries had come to refine their understanding of the nation-building—or propaganda—function that books for young readers have traditionally served. They did so while also making clear their high standards for illustration art and showing a degree of seriousness about children's literature as a cultural enterprise that far surpassed what Patte knew to be the prevailing sentiment in France. Each of Patte's Munich conversations gave her much to reflect on.

The next stop on her professional odyssey was the United States—the wellspring, as Patte knew, of nearly all modern efforts to extend free library service to young people. A Fulbright Fellowship provided her with two years' living expenses, and a job offer from the New York Public Library assured her the opportunity to learn from professionals who were only one step removed from the field's American pioneers.

The assumption, now widely taken for granted, that public libraries ought to serve young people and engage trained specialists to meet their needs first took root in the United States during the early years of the twentieth century. Librarians had vigorously debated the issues—Are children too noisy? Are there too many books that the young should *not* have access to?—before finally concluding that libraries did, indeed, have a contribution to make to young people's well-being. At the time, America was a cauldron of economic growth and societal transformation and the needs of millions of children, especially those living in cities, were not being met. The new children's librarians took up their work in tandem with those social reformers who dedicated themselves to improving pediatric care, housing conditions, and public schooling, and to regulating food safety and child labor. While many American libraries still barred children under the age of twelve, New York Public chose to admit any child able to write his or her name in a registration book and present a clean set of hands. Because the library served a city that was home to the lion's share of the nation's publishers, its senior children's librarians seized the chance to become industry standard-setters, not only by purchasing large numbers of books for the library's collection but also by advising publishers on editorial matters, joining with them in launching Children's Book Week and other literacy initiatives, reviewing children's books in newspapers and journals, and issuing authoritative best books lists that raised the visibility of the genre.

Patte arrived in New York in 1961, soon after the death of Anne Carroll Moore, the legendary founder of the library's children's division. But she was not too late to observe and—selectively—absorb Moore's outsized influence as mentor, critic, and standard setter for the culturally ambitious activities she deemed appropriate to a children's library. Patte was stirred and impressed by the New York Public Library's democratizing influence on the city's vast and heterogeneous population; in particular, its commitment to serve as a safe harbor for people of all ages with little or no formal education or money who looked to the library for a chance to better themselves and to feel connected to a community of learners. She witnessed this philosophy in action, not just in the library's grand marble Beaux-Arts central building at Fifth Avenue and Forty-Second Street, but even more so at its far-flung neighborhood branch outposts scattered around the city. At L'Heure Joyeuse, Patte had already seen living proof of the benefits, for children and librarians alike, of hewing to the principle that "small is beautiful"; now, in the city's branch libraries—and, within them, in their intimately proportioned, charmingly crafted and furnished children's reading rooms—she again realized the wisdom of always keeping a human scale in mind when approaching children as readers.

Anne Carroll Moore had been a dynamic institution builder under whose leadership the children's division developed a rigorous book selection process and a training program for storytellers, and nurtured the careers of countless authors and illustrators. But Moore had a dogmatic, imperious streak, and such was her iron grip on her library colleagues' loyalty that those who later wrote about her tenure rarely dared to question the efficacy of any of her ideas and practices. As a dispassionate outsider, Patte avoided getting caught up in the worshipful side of

Moore's legacy, and her balanced appraisal in these pages of the library's highly ritualized style of storytelling contributes a useful corrective to the great librarian's legend.

Moore had always placed storytelling at the center of her department's offerings and enforced strict guidelines as to how it should be done. After observing the library's Story Hours, Patte found she was of two minds about them. She appreciated the librarians' skill at conjuring up an atmosphere of magic and mystery around the sharing of make-believe tales. But she also noted with some sadness the passive good behavior that the librarians clearly expected of their young listeners and concluded that "respect for the traditions the librarians were so proud of" could, in practice, be "a little stifling." (44)

Patte is equally clear-eyed in her assessment of the comparative state of children's book publishing in the United States and France during the 1960s. In recent years, French publishing for young people has enjoyed a well-deserved reputation for boldness and freedom from prudish inhibition. (The example typically cited is that of the willingness of French publishers, in contrast to their American counterparts, to allow depictions of a mother breast-feeding her baby in a park scene from a picture book. Those puritanical Americans!—sigh French publishers and their European colleagues.) Readers of this memoir may be surprised to learn, then, that the situation was almost the reverse during the 1960s, when an outpouring of conceptually daring picture books by Maurice Sendak, Arnold Lobel, Charlotte Zolotow, Tomi Ungerer, Remy Charlip, and others flowed from the American houses in stark contrast to the mostly lackluster offerings of that period's French publishers. In those days, for example, the title of Margaret Wise Brown and Remy Charlip's tender, forthright picture book, *The Dead Bird*, could not be translated literally for the French market but instead had to be softened into *Un Chanson pour l'oiseau* (*A Song for the Bird*). Patte's comments not only set the historical record straight but also serve as a reminder that no one group has had a monopoly on the creativity required to give young people their best possible start as readers and learners. By turning supposedly unpromising children into life-long readers, Patte and her colleagues have doubtless also inspired some of the artists and writers of the future who will take children's literature in meaningful new directions. As an impassioned librarian working to advance the cause of literacy in an economically struggling region of Peru once told her, "It is not enough to learn to read. We must also produce our own books." (170)

Throughout this memoir, Patte sides with children as individuals over the institutions ostensibly designed to serve their collective needs. Her New York experience confirmed her preference for the philosophy of L'Heure Joyeuse, which emphasized the importance of children's collaborative participation and a spontaneous approach aligned with the spirit of street theater. Patte makes no mention of having actually done so, but had she wished during her New York sojourn to meet storytellers in greater sympathy with her own ideals, she might have looked in on the progressive Bank Street School in Greenwich Village, where the focus on the child as an experiential learner and independent thinker had inspired the creation of ground-breaking "participatory" picture books by Margaret Wise Brown, Dorothy Kunhardt, Crockett Johnson, Ruth Krauss, and Maurice Sendak, as well as a complete re-imagining of children's relationships to their books. Patte does introduce us to Janet Hill, an English activist librarian and author of *Children Are People: The Librarian in the Community* (1974), who also advocated for a less buttoned-down approach to storytelling with children. From her rugged base in working-class Lambeth, London, Patte reports, Hill "would tell stories anywhere" (42), often for an all-ages audience she happened upon in a local park. The effect was to upend the perception of stories and books as pedestalled artifacts reserved for the privileged few and, in effect, to put the life-changing question "What if?" at the forefront of everyone's consideration. It is striking that while L'Heure Joyeuse owed its beginnings to the generosity of the American Committee for Devastated Regions (a group composed in part of librarians trained by Anne Carroll Moore), the women who breathed life into that idiosyncratic Parisian sanctuary for young people were much closer in their views to progressive educators like France's Roger Cousinet and to Janet Hill and the founders of New York's Bank Street School, than to Moore herself.

Patte might have remained in New York and enjoyed a rewarding career at the New York Public Library—or, who knows, perhaps the Bank Street School—but chose instead to return to Paris, where she soon realized that she would have to navigate around the library establishment's institutionalized structures and practices if she wished to remain true to her professional ideals. Her chance came when, thanks to a sustained act of enlightened philanthropy, she was given the opportunity to help launch an experimental children's library—a kind of mini-International Youth Library that would feature a collection of books from around the world and be located, not in picture postcard Paris, but rather in an underserved, low-income neighborhood of Clamart, one of the city's neglected suburbs.

Spearheading the venture was Anne Gruner Schlumberger, who was from a family of French industrialists and recognized the potential to create a small but artfully conceived free library as a pilot project that would expand literacy skills and nurture community life and a sense of hope among people, many of whom were immigrants cut off from mainstream French society. If the plan worked, there would be no shortage of opportunities to replicate the model elsewhere. Schlumberger, who formed a private association called La Joie par les livres (The Joy of Books) to undertake this and other literacy initiatives, hired Patte to be one of three full-time librarians.

When Schlumberger expressed her wish for a library that was "open to the world," (191) she was not speaking metaphorically. She engaged the services of a first-rate team of architects to design a distinctive structure that children would be excited to explore. When it opened in the fall of 1965, the Clamart library attracted international media attention, including a photo essay in *Life*. Predictably, the French library establishment regarded the privately-funded experiment with suspicion, but it was embraced by local residents, many of whom had no prior experience of libraries, as well as by literacy advocates and children's book people from pretty much everywhere. First-time visitors were surprised to find children manning the check-out desk (79), conscientiously washing their hands before handling a book, and generally acting as if the library belonged to them which, in a very real sense, it did. While all this was going on, Patte also took the lead in another Joie par les livres project: the founding of the journal of children's literature studies that is today called *La Revue des Livres pour Enfants*. The world's first such publication, dating back to the 1920s, was the *Horn Book* magazine, another American innovation. France was now playing cultural catch-up, and the advent of this new bimonthly review journal meant that its librarians and publishers would have a forum, not only for sharing information about new books for children and teens, but also, and perhaps more importantly, for developing a language for thinking critically about them.

In one realization of Schlumberger's call for a library open to the world, Clamart became a magnet for visiting book creators and literacy advocates from abroad. Among the artists and writers who made the trip were Maurice Sendak, Ezra Jack Keats, and Arnold Lobel (all from the United States); Josef Wilkon (Poland), and Katsumi Komagata (Japan). Emperor Akihito and Empress Michiko of Japan, the latter a longtime supporter of IBBY, made a pilgrimage to Clamart, too. Those who did so admired the library building's elegant modernist design, its honeycomb cluster of rounded white forms framed by a circular patio set within a park-like space. Even more than that, they marveled at the deep affection the library's young patrons felt for a cultural enterprise that cynics had predicted would hold no interest for them as children from the ranks of the uneducated.

By the 1970s and 1980s, Patte had found another way to fulfill Schlumberger's mandate—by taking to the road and putting her Clamart insights and experiences to use as a catalyzing agent for literacy efforts in far-flung locales across the globe. During this period she assumed leadership positions in IBBY and collaborated on projects with the French Ministry of Culture, the International Federation of Library Associations and Institutions, and UNESCO, among other organizations. In Leipzig, Caen, and Bangkok, she led three international conferences focused on literacy initiatives for developing countries. The extent of

Patte's travels is breathtaking. Before long, the reader ceases to be surprised by such casual segues as: "I received an invitation to the Algiers Book Fair..." (162); "After the meeting in Cajamarca [Peru]..." (171); "While I was in Sweden for a conference..." (142); "During a training week in Mali..." (188).

Central to Patte's vision of the role of children's books in our time is the conviction—amply borne out in her account of the Clamart library and by numerous other examples—that children's literature need not be thought of as a solely middle-class phenomenon—a cultural enhancement to the educational and recreational lives of the segment of society that is most intensely concerned with its own upward economic and social mobility. Historically, Western publishers have tended to define their market in terms of this subset of the population. But Patte repeatedly demonstrates that the real potential audience for high-quality books is much broader than that. It is because market forces do not, on their own, generally favor efforts to reach that larger group that her work has been so important and—it is no exaggeration to say—revolutionary.

In the best French literary tradition, Patte has a gift for the *mot juste* and well-turned phrase. Her narrative is liberally salted with aphorisms both of her own making and gleaned from the writings of others. In a gentle rebuke to the tendency of libraries, especially the most venerable ones, to become weighted down, even hobbled at times, by their own traditions, she writes: "The library is always in a state of flux because at its center it is human." (150) To those who would dismiss as old-fashioned or otherwise irrelevant a concern for the place of books and reading in a twenty-first-century child's life, she offers a succinct rejoinder that is as powerful a statement of first principles and common sense as any essay on the subject one could wish for: "Reading," Patte says, "serves no other purpose except to live better, to know oneself, to encounter the other, and to discover the world in all its beauty and complexity." (150)

She cites French psychoanalyst Colette Chiland's evocative characterization of the experience of reading with curiosity and passion as an act of "fill[ing] up one's inner theater" with memorable avatars and role models who, from then onward, will inhabit the reader's imagination and thereby enlarge their consciousness of life's possibilities. (131) In response to the naysayers who sometimes dismiss fairy tales and other make-believe stories as inconsequential or even harmful, she quotes the wise remark of nineteenth-century French mathematician Charles Hermite: "Cultivate the imagination, Gentlemen, everything is there. If you want mathematicians, give your children fairy tales to read." (130) She shares French child psychiatrist René Diatkine's eloquent definition of reading as "an essential psychological activity, allowing the [child] to become the narrator of his own story, thus allowing him greater inner freedom." (143-4)

Of all the mentors Patte introduces in these pages, Diatkine looms largest as the one who furnished her with a rigorous theoretical validation of her own on-the-ground experiences, a framework rooted in the work of Freud, Piaget, and others for explaining the urgency of introducing the young children of underserved populations to the best possible books. She sums up Diatkine's contribution to her thinking as the revelation that "under the age of five, in the period when their language is being structured, children all have the same appetite, the same interest in stories, the same taste for books, no matter what their environment might be." (144) It follows for Patte that, "When all very young children have access to books while also getting the attentive and discreet guidance that is so very vital, inequalities in reading may no longer be inevitable. This," she writes, "is what moved me to action." (148)

Patte took Diakine's mantra—"Go where you are not expected" (149)—as her marching orders. Even while in residence at Clamart, she did not always wait for the last local child to find his or her way through the library doors. Instead, she and her colleagues made a habit of frequenting the waiting rooms of health clinics, day care centers, and other heavily trafficked locales where parents and children congregated with time on their hands, and set out baskets of books for them to discover. At one time, the Clamart library staff would even take books door-to-door in the apartment blocks of the local residents.

Perhaps what is most remarkable about Geneviève Patte's career is the combination of audacity and humility that has characterized her efforts and her steadfast openness to learning from the examples of others as she has continued to build on her own vast reserve of experience. Recalling the Leipzig conference, which she organized in 1981 as a forum for the exchange of ideas by literacy activists from across the developing world, she notes that it was as much a learning experience for her as it was for any of the less formally trained or well-traveled participants. "Here and there," she writes, "we'd discover…seemingly modest initiatives that got us to rethink the very notion of reading services for children and adolescents and to imagine new strategies." (173) A professor of library science from Bangkok, for example, described what was then a novel approach to community outreach: the introduction of portable libraries consisting of small batches of books strapped to her university students' motorbikes to share with the children of the Thai countryside. "The idea for these libraries traveled," Patte reports with typical understatement, "and today they can be found in Egypt, Lebanon, and Albania, as well as in refugee camps, where people gather around them to read and talk." (176) Mention of this inventive, low-budget project and its successful adaption in a range of culturally diverse settings leads to a similar consideration of the phenomenon of grassroots home libraries, typically organized by activist mothers for their neighbors; Patte describes examples from Zimbabwe and Japan that she has observed firsthand. Her memoir doubles as a kind of well-stocked library of models and maps for use in considering how best to bring children and books together—even in the most challenging circumstances. Yet, for all the accumulated wisdom recorded here, *What Gets Them to Read Like That?* is not so much a how-to book as it is a why-to book. Patte's response to the "why" of library work with children is deeply felt and deeply imagined: "Giving children the opportunity to wonder is a magnificent gift!" she reminds us. (161) Giving *all* children that opportunity is only fair.

—*Leonard S. Marcus*

To my father and my mother.
To Anne Gruner Schlumberger.

A big thanks to my friend Mijo. Without her encouragement, this book would never have seen the light of day.

Some days, the magic of our childhood games transformed our garden into a village. One of my brothers would run the grocery store, the other would oversee the post office, my little sister would look over the café, and I would take charge of the library. I'd arrange the books, each with their own number, on a stone bench and then lend them out. My source of inspiration was a tiny library located behind a bookshop in Poitiers that I often visited as a little girl.

How could I have imagined back then that decades later I'd be engaged in these same activities, long since forgotten, when I became a librarian in Clamart? For many years, I'd set up a "for real" library every Wednesday in a disadvantaged neighborhood. This library was near a sandbox, and I made use of a low wall to arrange the storybooks we were going to share with the neighborhood children.

A House Full of Books

I was born and raised in a house full of books. My parents were avid readers and liked to read to us and to tell us stories. All I had to do was knock on the door to my father's office and he'd take a break from his paleontological research to make some time for me. He'd pull some exquisite picture books from the drawer of his worktable and read them aloud, then encourage me to explore them to my heart's content. Those books made a strong impression on me. They gave me access to a meticulous world inhabited by friendly mice, but that wasn't all: One of the books was shaped like a boot and told of an old woman who lived in a shoe. An English tale, as I was to later discover. On the cover there was a little door that opened. To gain entry into the cozy, cluttered home, all I had to do was knock.

I cherished these moments I spent with my father, the two of us looking at those picture books that brought us such joy. For a child from such a large family—I was one of nine siblings—it was a real honor that he would set some time aside for me alone.

I've sometimes wondered what must have gone through the Germans' minds when they ransacked his office looking for something incriminating, only to find, amidst the scholarly books and skulls, those children's picture books hidden away in the drawers of his desk.

My mother was a natural storyteller with a great sense of humor; she was also an artist. She had fond memories of her studies at the École des Arts Décoratifs. She took pleasure in the beauty of simple things and knew how to get us to appreciate them. With interests in education and pedagogy, she'd collect reading recommendations from magazines. She admired the quality of the books' images and stories and because she loved them, she got us to love them, too. Her passion for storytelling was a source of great joy for us, and the most commonplace event could give rise to a story. At the dinner table, she would sometimes tell us about the books she was reading or movies she'd enjoyed. She'd keep us informed about what she was reading. For example, she took us into the world of Pearl Buck's *The Good Earth*, chapter by chapter. She would get inspired and liked to share her discoveries. She would draw my attention, for example, to simple and beautiful things such as a ray of sunshine on a bouquet of tulips.

What she loved most of all was reading to us aloud. I remember when she read to us from the works of the Comtesse de Ségur. My brother Dominique, who was four years older than me, would join us furtively. He'd tell me how much he loved these moments, even though he was too old to listen to such stories. I loved to savor the words and descriptions, and it seemed that my mother did, too. She'd read to us with feeling, and even a touch of sensuality: "A round straw hat with a little white feather and black velvet ribbons; a green parasol with an ivory handle, four pairs of ankle boots; a black taffeta dress." These were just some of the many items that we discovered together with Marguerite, one of the Comtesse de Ségur's exemplary little heroines, in her doll's hope chest. All I had during this era of war and deprivation was a single rag doll, so this was the stuff of dreams for me.

With her wonderful sense of humor, my mother also shared our enthusiasm for works by the French author Christophe. She knew *The Fenouillard Family, Cosinus the Scholar,* and *The Sapper Camember* (*La Famille Fenouillard, Le savant Cosinus, Le sapeur Camember*)[1] from front to back. She'd quote these works at just the right moments. Sometimes she would announce her arrival by simply stating, "I've come like Themistocles." These few words were all it took to evoke the grandiloquence of Monsieur Fenouillard, who maintains his dignity even though he's drenched to the bone and looks like a dog that's just come out of the water. Addressing Captain Asdrubal Mac Haron, he declares: "I've come, like Themistocles and Napoleon, to sit at the hearth of perfidious

---

1. Translator's note: For the reader's reference, original French titles of works that are not available in English translation are provided in parentheses. For French works that have already been published in English, the titles of those published English versions are used. Translations of citations are my own, unless specified as otherwise.

Albion." It was in this way that the Athenian general found his way into our everyday lives.

Over dinner, our father would sometimes treat us with stories he'd chosen from Sara Cone Bryant's collection, *How to Tell Stories to Children*. He would also share tales from the Poitou region, including those collected by his friend Léon Pineau, who is well-known today among lovers of folk tales. We were all fans of *The Rooster's Little Share* (*La petite moitié de Geau*), which he would usually recite in a comedic tone. We delighted in how crude it was. How we loved hearing the little phrase that the rooster would repeat like a refrain when inviting the animals to accompany him on his frantic quest: "Pack yourselves in my butt, I'll take you!"

My father would take a break from his research on Sundays and, to give us a taste for the natural sciences, would show us books by Cuvier and Buffon.

When I was growing up, childhood was very different from what it is today. We were left to our own devices. There were no recreation programs for our parents to choose from and schedule for us, meaning we had a lot of free time. Our summer vacations also seemed to go on endlessly. There would be one week when we'd join our father at his field research sites to scratch around in the dirt, but apart from that we would stay at home. It was up to us to decide what to do! We had our magic lantern, and we'd go on walks through the surrounding woods in search of insects or try catching little freshwater fish in the Boivre. There was, of course, no television and no Internet. The radio, however, was a real presence. I remember listening to Pierre Dac, whose wordplay would make us laugh out loud, and a very grumpy Paul Léautaud being interviewed by an extremely patient Robert Mallet. One of my older sisters closely followed the series about the Duraton family, featuring the actor Noël-Noël. Words and stories flowed into the house, and we had plenty of time to imagine, to dream, and to read.

But those times were also troubled ones. In July 1941, my older brother was arrested and sentenced to two years in prison for participating in the Resistance. Later, my father was wanted by the Gestapo and had to go into hiding. Meanwhile, my mother was under surveillance and was constantly followed in the street. Life was hard. Did my mother's burning desire to tell us stories come from a desire to make us forget how hard the times were? Somehow, she always managed to stay calm and keep her sense of humor. When the Germans came and tried to arrest my father, she just kept to her knitting and mocked them as they ransacked our home from top to bottom. When they were done, she encouraged them to do it again. For several days, the Gestapo kept us trapped inside our house. We weren't allowed to go out or to have any contact with the outside world, and I was not permitted to attend school during this period. My mother was also involved in Resistance activities and distributed the underground newspaper, which she transported in the cart she used for shopping, with the issues hidden carefully beneath the lettuce, carrots, and leeks. This was really risky: She was helping to spread the forbidden word as widely as possible.

Gatherings around the Table

I was very young, but I can remember the time of the Exodus, when we welcomed people into our home. In May and June of 1940, my older brothers and sisters would go to the train station every evening to offer accommodations to those who didn't know where they were going to spend the night. I liked it when there were a lot of people around the table in the morning, having something to fortify themselves before they set off again. Some stayed longer. There was, for example, a Belgian couple who stayed with us for several months. We lived frugally during those difficult times, just like all the other French people who refused to buy on the black market. In addition, my father's salary had been suspended when he had to go into hiding. We were truly broke. But even though we were living on a shoestring, we were still generous. My mother offered hospitality to those who had even less and there were friends in the Resistance who helped on occasion.

I remember once asking my mother, "Are we going to win the war?"

"Of course," she said. "Because we're the ones who are right."

This was the answer I needed. That was how it was told in the storybooks, with justice, the generosity of the humblest, and the triumph of the truth.

We heard a lot of foreign names in our home. The name of a Czech woman, Eva Reiserova, sounded to my ears like a nursery rhyme or something from a distant land. This was also the case with a German philosopher, a friend of my parents who had fled Nazism, as well as a Polish Jew, a student my father had invited to live with us. "You will be a part of the family. You will be another son," he'd told him. I was four years old and I distinctly remember what it was like to have him around.

There was also an atmosphere of tragedy at school. I will never forget when the teacher announced, "Myriam and her daddy left in the night." It was February 1943, and the statement carried enormous weight, as if the teacher were fully aware of its devastating implications. Myriam had, in fact, worn a yellow star. Her father had been the rabbi of the Jewish community in Poitiers. Later, I learned that they died as soon as they reached Auschwitz. I was told that in the Drancy camp, Myriam had traded her doll for a book.

Everywhere, we were forced to show our veneration for Maréchal Pétain. One day, our teacher asked us to write a letter to him. I was six years old. I raised my hand to express my refusal. The teacher had me go up to her desk and then she took me affectionately onto her lap. This was how I learned that it can be good to not always follow the tide, that disobedience may be accepted, and that some adults appreciate it.

Rue des Carmes

All of this took place in my hometown, the fine city of Poitiers. For a long time, it had been considered the very symbol of provincial France, home to an old bourgeoisie that was relatively insular. I imagine that Balzac, writing *The Vicar of Tours*, was familiar with the alleys and cul-de-sacs near the cathedral where priests in cassocks and old women dressed in black would pass each other silently. We didn't live on the plateau, which was primarily inhabited by those who were well-to-do and "proper," but on a little street near the poor neighborhoods. It had a quiet charm that always appealed to me. Georges Simenon, one of our neighbor's friends, became attached to this street, the Rue des Carmes, and it provided him with inspiration for one of his detective novels, which even mentions my father.

Is Poitiers a dull and narrow-minded city? It certainly was at that time, but I still have heartfelt memories of some of our neighbors from the 1940s and 1950s. After the war, my parents told us about the bravery of one neighbor, a social worker who never mentioned her multiple acts of resistance. There was also a father, a great handyman, who created strange machines for himself and his children to enjoy. Sometimes I'd see him perched atop a strange vehicle, making his way noisily down the street. It was like a skeleton of a car, just a chassis with simple canoe seats to sit on. His youngest son was in the same class as one of my brothers, who liked to go over to his house. He'd tell me how much he enjoyed the rich conversations they had there.

When I was a little girl, I used to go to the local school by myself. I'd walk up the street and sometimes had to stop. There was a kind of German barracks there and when the watchmen were changing shifts, I had to wait. I'd watch the soldiers, dressed in green like grotesque puppets, goose-stepping across this unassuming street. Opposite, there lived an old woman who would throw open her window and yell at them in German. From the tone of her voice, I could tell that she was insulting them. Who was this woman with the beautiful white hair who took such liberties? She lived very modestly in a small house, surrounded by her cats, and gave a few piano lessons to support herself. Her name was Marie Delvard. She claimed to have met many major figures of the time, including Hitler, Pétain, the future Pope Pius XII when he'd been living in Munich, and many others, but nobody believed her. We knew about all these stories because she talked to the cobbler next door, who was the real gossip of the neighborhood. As children, we liked to linger in front of his shop. He'd tell us all manner of fascinating things as he fitted shoes with new soles.

Now, having consulted the Internet, I've discovered that Marie Delvard had been an exceptional singer, actress, and diva who had performed in avant-garde cabarets frequented by great minds. According to what I've read, she electrified audiences. Her fervent admirers included Guillaume Apollinaire, Oskar Kokoschka, and Bertolt Brecht. At the beginning of the century, this woman had been famous throughout the Germanic world and in Central Europe. In Poitiers, she was an unknown who lived in poverty and was often mocked. But her life ended like a fairy tale. Some of her previous admirers came looking for her so that she could spend her final days in Munich, supported and with the recognition she was due.

The New Classes

After finishing at the *école communale* where, like all the children back then, I'd learned to read and write very early on, I entered the *lycée de filles* in Poitiers, in the lower classes. I was not yet six years old. My secondary education, from the 6th to the 3rd class, was at the same *lycée* in what at the time were called "the new classes" ("les classes nouvelles"). These had been created at the time of the Liberation and were part of the Langevin-Wallon reform. There, the emphasis was on teamwork, self-discipline, and research around the city for "environmental studies." These pedagogical approaches were undoubtedly inspired by the Freinet Modern School Movement.[2] The teachers would work in teams as well—the drawing teacher sometimes joined the natural science teacher, with art and science thus combined into a common curriculum. The library, however, had not yet found its place there, and there were just some bookshelves in the classrooms.

A visit to the town newspaper's printing works made a strong impression on me. The noise and heat we encountered as we toured the

---

2. Célestin Freinet (1896-1966) was a teacher who created the pedagogical movement that bears his name. It is based primarily on children's free expression, networking between schools, investigation, printing, and a school newspaper.

facilities made me realize what harsh conditions the working class had to endure. Manual work also had its place at school and I remember the bookbinding workshop fondly. It was led by the artist Gilberte Weiller, who was known in the world of bookbinding as Gilberte Givel.[3] I loved the way she treated us. She was a wonderful woman and she gave her full attention to each student. It was as if we were apprentices, and she respected our work while also giving us advice.

By the time we reached the 2nd class, we had to fall in line to finish up our secondary education. Falling back in line really is the right expression: The students in the traditional classes and their teachers thought that it was our time to get to work, after having had our fun. As the ant says to the grasshopper in La Fontaine's famous fable: "What were you doing when the weather was warm? You were singing? Good for you. Well then, now's the time for you to dance!" In other words: "You had your fun. Now you're going to work and find out what it's like!" It's true that we didn't have a great reputation at the school. People were disturbed by how free we were. Since we didn't do what the others did, we were suspected of not working seriously.

Rue Boutebrie

I had a strong desire to become a teacher in a rural area. Every summer, our father would ask us to accompany him on his digs. This gave us the opportunity to experience the day-to-day life of a village, of a farm, and to get closer to its inhabitants. I wanted to get to know them better, to share their lives, and to find my place alongside them. I liked the school in the middle of the village, close to nature. It got me dreaming. I also liked the social dimension of being a schoolteacher.

A few years later, I discovered the librarian profession with great enthusiasm. I had just passed my baccalaureate exam. Thus liberated, I couldn't wait to discover the world in all its realities. This was to begin with Paris. A Chinese friend who spent all his vacations with us invited

---

3. Gilberte Givel, *Une relieuse du XXe siècle*, Éditions Manson, 2013.

me there. To celebrate the end of my high school years and the start of a new life, he offered to show me around the capital. It was his gift.

We left together on his scooter, first to take a three-day trip to the region of Touraine, where we visited some castles of the Loire Valley, and then to enjoy the charms and riches of Paris. Tzou Kuo-Hsien was a very young, particularly brilliant scholar who had come to France to work with the physicist Louis de Broglie. He was like an older brother to me.

He lived in a squalid hotel in the Latin Quarter on the Rue de la Parcheminerie, near the church of Saint-Séverin. It was thanks to this Chinese friend that, one winter evening, I discovered the library close by on the Rue Boutebrie. It was called L'Heure Joyeuse.

What I saw through the illuminated windows delighted me: children moving about freely in a world of books. Some seemed to be absorbed in their reading while others were consulting the card catalogs. I also noticed the unobtrusive, attentive presence of two women who would speak with the children, one on one. All this was so unusual to me that I was amazed.

The very next day, I met the librarians: Marguerite Gruny and Mathilde Leriche. They had a lot of questions for me and wanted to know everything about my reading and my tastes. I told them about the books that had left their mark on my childhood. I told them how much I had loved the books of the Père Castor series, including the works of Nathalie Parain such as *Let's Go to the Market* (*Faites votre marché*) along with "What the Old Man Does is Always Right," a tale by Andersen illustrated by Rojankovsky; and also *Froux the Hare* (*Froux le lièvre*) and the entire "Roman des bêtes" collection. I told them that I had read and re-read Marcel Aymé's *The Wonderful Farm* (*Les Contes du chat perché*), as well as Colette Vivier's *The House of Happiness* (*La Maison des petits bonheurs*), and I told them how I had been moved to tears while reading and re-reading Colin Shepherd's *We Need a Mother* (*On demande une maman*). I also told them how much I had appreciated the "Joie de connaître" collection published by Bourrelier. I mentioned reading and re-reading Charles Dickens and Hector Malot, plus the works of Christophe, which I'd made my way through a hundred times over.

The librarians at L'Heure Joyeuse were impressed that I'd avoided the *Prince Eric* series. They found it insidious and thought that during the time of the war, it had been tinged with Pétainism. I had in fact been influenced by my brothers, who'd kept track of what I was reading.

I'm certain that I told the librarians how much I'd enjoyed reading to the children around me. They concluded that I was up to the task of being a children's librarian, but they gave me some advice. I'd have to attend college first and get as far as I could in my library studies, because it was necessary for the importance of work with children to get its due recognition. It's true that the profession did not treat it with respect.

Becoming a Librarian

My decision was made: I would be a children's librarian. I proceeded to obtain a *licence* degree in German before training for an advanced degree as a librarian. Most of the courses took place on Rue de Richelieu, at the French National Library (Bibliothèque nationale de France, or BnF), and all the students were destined for the large study libraries or the classified municipal libraries, which held important conservation collections. I was the rare bird whose sights were set on children's libraries. What I enjoyed most about my schooling was the time I spent in the reserves department of the BnF. There, perceptive experts shared with us the art of the book in all its splendor across the centuries. I later experienced this same pleasure in the Rare Book Division of the New York Public Library, where I enjoyed the wonders of children's books collected by connoisseurs who had traveled the world in search of the most beautiful books. At L'Heure Joyeuse, at the New York Public Library, and later at the Bibliothèque des enfants in Clamart, children could have access to these treasures. I loved seeing how astonished they were when we'd carefully and respectfully remove such books from the display cases for the sole purpose of sharing these objects of art, which had delighted generations of children before, with them.

Other aspects of my studies had a profound impact on me. Julien Cain, a tutelary figure in French libraries, would ask the greatest names in various disciplines to tell us about their field of study and the bibliographic resources we needed to know. They were all very passionate, which made it exciting. We were spellbound as they opened up their favorite areas to us. I remember the lecture given by Jules Marouzeau, a distinguished Latinist and professor at the Sorbonne, and especially Henri Mazeaud, a professor of private law. I was seduced by these incursions into the heart of domains that seemed austere at first, but which were revealed to us in their dazzling splendor. This is what should be offered to all young people towards the end of their secondary education, at the time when they are considering their life choices.

Three Months at L'Heure Joyeuse

I was then trained at L'Heure Joyeuse, the first public library for children, and the original source of my commitment. A three-month practicum was decisive for me. I never stopped referring back to it throughout my career and I still do today. The fact is, I was trained by remarkable women.

The library had been created in the 1920s by the American Committee for Devastated Regions, but L'Heure Joyeuse had given it a French touch by proposing an original form of communal life.

Inspired by the new education movements that were flourishing in France at that time thanks to Célestin Freinet and Roger Cousinet, the librarians emphasized the children's responsible participation and initiative. The library thus became a place for learning how to coexist, to gather, and to develop projects with others, with every individual still free to act and make decisions autonomously; a place of socialization, in short, that differed from the kind found at school. What a privilege it was to have worked with those who were true trailblazers, to have been able to share their thoughts, and to have been close to such an inexhaustible wellspring! They were attentive to the children, dedicated to offering them the best and respectful of how they did things. These women were always ready to forge new paths.

There was a special ambiance at L'Heure Joyeuse. The space was simple, with just a single large room. Someone told me that it had been converted from what had once been an indoor recreation area. Unappealing? Not in the least. It was a space that had been lived in, and this was noticeable right away. Indeed, there were children who spent a good part of their childhood there. They didn't just come and borrow their books of choice and leave. They experienced connection. It was a world of relationships, and they entered into it directly and played an active part. They were welcomed by bouquets of fresh flowers on the tables. The walls were lined with shelves full of books. There was nothing about the furniture to remind them of school. Instead of desks, there were beautiful large oak tables that children could sit around, alongside one another. The furniture was reminiscent of what you'd find in the *Little House in the Big Woods*, the masterpiece written by Laura Ingalls Wilder and illustrated by Garth Williams. It also reminded me in some ways of the watercolors by the Swedish artist Carl Larsson, who so effectively depicted the quiet joys of domestic life at the beginning of the 20th century. A kind of lively tranquility reigned. There was no shouting. Children and librarians would speak softly, and interactions were calm. Everyone went about their own business, and everyone knew what they had to do. People would come and go quietly. There was no need for imposed discipline.

Boys and girls coexisted without difficulty. Back then, this "coed" arrangement was truly revolutionary. It had come to us from the very first American libraries. In France, it didn't exist in schools or in youth movements like the scouts. This did not fail to shock some teachers who, when the library opened, suggested putting a barrier in the center of the room to separate boys and girls.

Here, children of all ages were all mixed together, and this was one of the library's richest attributes. Everyone would go at their own pace and find their own way. We appreciated the uniqueness of every path, the different sensibilities and types of intelligence, and how valuable the interpersonal connections were.

Not all the children who used the library were avid readers. They weren't all looking to do research. But everyone could find a place of their own in this home where we learned to live together and where we felt good. Children who were sometimes not very interested in reading were happy to participate in their own way to help the library run smoothly. I remember seeing one of them, a regular, taking his time to carefully gather documentary images and files that would be made available to the children. He didn't seem to have much of a taste for reading, but he simply liked to be there among other children and in the presence of caring adults. And his contributions were valuable.

For many, the library was like a second home. It was with infinite sadness that I would think of the children with yellow stars who, in the 1940s, had had to remain at the door, banned from the library. It seemed that the librarians who had experienced this horror without being able to do anything about it still lived with it every day, like an incurable wound.

In its early years, this library was really a source of amazement. It was meant for schoolchildren, but it was so different from school! People came from all over France to see this place where children could freely and confidently take part in the joys of reading, experience the pleasure of listening to stories, and partake in an original form of community life. Decades later, the Bibliothèque des Enfants in Clamart would again arouse the same curiosity among the general French and foreign public. People came from everywhere to see how children could behave in such a setting and how, far from being simple consumers of cultural goods, they voluntarily contributed to the richness of the place, all the while respecting the rules required to coexist with others.

Everyone Welcomed as an Individual

The children appreciated the freedom and the attention they were given. They were there because they wanted to be, of their own accord. I noticed that they submitted to the rules of the house without complaint. Back then, the rules were very strict, but the children didn't seem to have any problems with them. They were taught to respect books. Their hands had to be clean, and they had to turn the pages carefully. They were even asked to grasp the page by its top corner in order to turn it.

The situation was surely quite different at home, but in the library, it was important to behave properly. Freedom has its limits and its requirements—those of coexistence, mutual respect, and the common good.

For the children, perhaps these proposed rules seemed like rites that gave them a sense of belonging. They were likely aware that what was offered to them in this place was both unusual and precious. Everyone was welcomed as a person and not as the member of a group. Each individual, depending on their tastes and desires, could make their own way, and there was no need to stop when the schoolyear came to an end. They learned autonomy while still getting support, if they so chose. At the time of my internship in the late 1950s and later in Clamart, children's libraries barely existed in France, even though they had long since spread throughout Anglo-American countries. The readers were aware that they were lucky.

At L'Heure Joyeuse, I was surprised by some of the rules and obligations regarding the lending of books. For example, it was permitted to borrow two novels provided that one non-fiction book was taken out, too. But why? In our libraries today, non-fiction books are appreciated by everyone. It must be said that there has been great progress in terms of how they look. They can be read in countless ways, and their presentation attracts the most hesitant of readers. The illustrations are clear enough that it is enjoyable just to leaf through them. But back then, works of non-fiction tended to look more austere. I remember, however, having been fascinated by some of them as a child—specifically, those written by scholars and published by Michel Bourrelier. They read like novels and would take me to worlds both near and far. With the astronomer Paul Couder, I could walk among the stars; with the linguist Albert Dauzat, I explored words. With the geographer René Clozier, I discovered how houses were built throughout the world, and paleontologist Leroi-Gourhan brought me into the company of prehistoric hunters. I was captivated. I also read and re-read many times over the astonishing account of René Caillié's trip to Timbuktu. This young boy, the son of a penniless baker in my native Poitou region, would look at the mysterious names written on the maps of Africa and get to dreaming. He left to discover unknown regions, making his way to the Tuaregs. How could I have remained unmoved by these works of non-fiction? Is this how my taste for distant worlds was born?

Strict Literary Criteria

There were no comic books at L'Heure Joyeuse. Such a shame! I had so enjoyed reading *Bicot* and *Bibi Fricotin,* which I'd borrowed from my brothers. There was, however, one exception: Christophe's picture books had found favor with these demanding librarians. But could these picture books made up of vignettes really be considered comics? In addition, Töpffer's *Zig Zag Journeys* had a place in the collection of old books that the library made available to the neighborhood children on certain days. I wondered if this wariness of comic books reflected a misunderstanding of their particular language. No doubt there was, among the educators of the time, some resistance with regard to a certain kind of American culture.

When I was an intern at L'Heure Joyeuse, it was the golden age of the works by Enid Blyton, of *Caroline* by Pierre Probst, and of *Alice* by Caroline Quine. But at this library, there was no question of making these series available to children. Was it because they were series that they were forbidden? Certainly not. *Babar* by Jean de Brunhoff and *The Borrowers* by Mary Norton had a special place there. What was important was the literary and artistic quality of the works. We wanted to introduce children to characters portrayed with subtlety, not stereotypical ones.

I remember how the librarians at L'Heure Joyeuse reacted when *The Adventures of Petit Nicolas*—the first of a series—was published. They howled with laughter as they read this masterpiece of childhood, but they wondered if children would be able to enjoy it like they did. Wasn't it necessary to be a certain age, with a certain distance, to appreciate the humor? It didn't matter. They'd have to try. They left the book on the big table and watched. The children snatched it up eagerly, and they fought over who would get to read it. The evidence was clear: These books were for everyone, with no age limits. Later, in Clamart, I often saw that these books would invariably bring joy to the hearts of the children who were the most indifferent to the pleasures of reading.

Offering the Best of the Best

These librarians were, in fact, quite exacting. They wanted to make sure that all children, without exception, had access to the finest publications. That's why they felt it was so important to select and showcase the best books.

But it was up to the children to decide if they were interested, and they knew how to fend for themselves. I delight in the words of the author Claude Roy who, recalling these moments of personal guidance, wrote: "The first time, the librarian suggested I read Dickens or a 'lovely' children's book. I remember having preferred the less 'respectable' *Piccolo Circus* (*Cirque Piccolo*) by Madeleine de Ginestoux, which I had started reading at a friend's house and then finished thanks to L'Heure Joyeuse. I've never forgotten it since. Is it a masterpiece? For me it is. I made a marvelous book of it in my ten-year-old head, where I played all the roles of these children who go on the road with the travelling circus they created in the absence of their parents." He continues, "It is not just the writers who bring L'Heure Joyeuse to life. The readers have also got to have talent, and bringing the library to life is the fine work of those who create a thousand 'heures joyeuses.'"[4]

These are the perennial questions that beleaguer the public libraries: Offer a real selection or just accept everything? Emphasize quality or put excellence and mediocrity on an equal footing? How to recognize children's demands and satisfy them? L'Heure Joyeuse chose a side and distinguished itself in this way, deliberately positioning itself as an educational institution. Paul Hazard, a professor at the Collège de France and a specialist in comparative literature, reminded us that all children

---

4. Claude Roy, *L'Heure joyeuse. Soixante-dix ans de jeunesse. 1924-1994*, Agence culturelle de Paris, 1994.

deserve respect, and this is why the librarians passed over what they deemed unworthy.

Before starting my internship at L'Heure Joyeuse, I went around Paris to visit the libraries open to children, just as a French artisan makes a tour of the country. They were few and far between, and for the most part, disappointing. The librarians passively acquired all the books listed in the children's book section of "La Bibliographie de la France"[5] without taking the time to familiarize themselves with them. They had no personal connection with the children and didn't talk with them, listen to them, or help them make their choices. The library was limited to a distribution role. Curiously, these libraries were favored by the Parisian administration, which was tough on L'Heure Joyeuse even though it enjoyed—as I was to see while I was working in New York—an excellent reputation abroad. Why was there this obliviousness? It seemed as if it these officials had a really hard time admitting to the quality of something that came from elsewhere, especially from American public libraries. It was also certainly challenging to allow for differences within a network. Everything had to be the same. Creativity was reproached for giving rise to something different.

At that time there were, throughout France, happy exceptions, and the librarians of L'Heure Joyeuse acknowledged them. The library on the little Rue Boutebrie granted the "Heure Joyeuse" label to certain libraries that met its requirements. Its same spirit was to be found in Versailles, Toulouse, Troyes, and a few other cities, in libraries where the quality of the books was ensured, efforts were made to introduce the books to novice readers, and the sacrosanct "storytime" was celebrated.

The Art of Storytelling

At the time of my internship, the "lady librarians" of L'Heure Joyeuse had been in the profession for almost forty years. I was impressed

---

5. Since 1979, this publication has been included in *Livres-Hebdo*.

that they appeared to have kept the same high standards and the same enthusiasm they must have had in the 1920s when they were starting out. They had always remained close to the children. Every day, they would listen to every one of them attentively and with interest. This is what had kept L'Heure Joyeuse lively.

On Mondays when the library was closed, Marguerite Gruny, who was in charge of our training, invited us to her home, where we would speak by the fire at our leisure. She would talk about some of the great works and share important elements of her library's history with us. In addition, she taught us the art of storytelling.

Inspired by the first Anglo-American children's librarians, the ladies of L'Heure Joyeuse were really offering the children something completely new, and certain good souls were absolutely opposed to it. How audacious it was for an institution that claimed to be educational—and secular—to offer tales that warped minds and got children to live in a bygone world of palaces, kings, and queens! When the children's library of Clamart followed suit forty years later, there was a similar response. Opponents seemed to think that these kinds of materials were deeply backward. It wasn't until the publication in 1976 of Bruno Bettelheim's *The Uses of Enchantment: The Meaning and Importance of Fairy Tales* that educators started to look at fairy tales and children in a different light.

I still get emotional when I revisit the lovely words that Paul Hazard, in his praise of children's libraries and of L'Heure Joyeuse in particular, wrote about this approach. He admired the reading choices that were available and appreciated these tales, which he calls "beautiful mirrors of water, so limpid and so deep." He goes on, "In these tales, which so many people find to be simplistic, one encounters [...] a whole poetic mythology and the reflections of the first dawn of the human imagination." He likes to see "each child repeating the history of our species through the stories and joining the course of our spirit at its very beginnings."[6]

---

6. Paul Hazard, *Les livres, enfants et les hommes*, Flammarion, 1934; published in English as *Books, Children and Men*.

For the librarians of L'Heure Joyeuse, telling stories to children had been an integral part of their mission. As early as 1924, they'd brazenly leave the library to tell stories outside at the Parc Montsouris or at the bandstand of the Vaugirard square. The audacity—these respectable young women performing in the street, in an era when women would never even leave the house without a hat! They were most decidedly a far cry from the traditional image of the librarian trapped behind her desk. When it came to storytelling, nothing stopped them. No story room on the Rue Boutebrie? No problem! They would go down into the basement to tell stories. It probably wasn't very comfortable, but the atmosphere was right, and the audience willing.

The libraries of today often have a special room for storytime, but this has not always been the case. Back then we had to find makeshift solutions, and sometimes these were quite unusual. I remember some of the story hours held in New York City at the imposing 42nd Street library, which has the look of a national library. When I worked there in the 1960s, it housed the Central Children's Room, which didn't have a special area for storytime. But the librarian-storyteller would lead the children through the impressive corridors of the large, austere building in search of a quiet space, inspiring a sense of mystery and offering a change of scenery that helped prepare the children to listen.

I was very interested in Janet Hill's book, *Children are People*, which recounts her experience in the 1970s as an activist librarian in a working-class suburb of London. Eager to connect with people from countries where reading and the written word did not have so prominent a status, she boldly brought certain practices into question. By choosing to tell stories outside, she was joining in with what the ladies of L'Heure Joyeuse had practiced in Paris in the 1920s. Hill vehemently rejected the idea of having a room for storytime and the traditional way of bringing children together in a kind of hushed intimacy so they could listen quietly and attentively. Why isolate storytelling from the rest of the library? Why lock it up in a room? Why just have it for children? Didn't this violate the age-old tradition of storytelling, which had always been practiced where people lived and spontaneously gathered? In Lambeth, librarians would tell stories everywhere, mostly outside in public parks. There was no fixed place for this event. Hill asked: Do we see the ice cream man waiting inside his store for customers? No, of course not. He takes his little truck from one place to another, where he is sure to catch the children's attention.

Individual Ways of Telling Stories

Our Parisian librarians may very well have told the same tale a hundred times, but they spared no effort in preparing to tell it yet again. I'd see these *conteuses* carefully arranging their chignons and applying a little powder to their faces before introducing themselves to their young audiences. Storytime had to be a quality event.

 I loved listening to Mathilde. She had more or less memorized some of the most moving episodes from Selma Lagerlöf's *The Wonderful Adventures of Nils*. Yet I would see her preparing to read them aloud again, just like in the early days. She would share an excerpt from this long novel, a story within a story that resonated with her personally. She knew how to communicate her own emotion to her young listeners without being overly dramatic. I would leave my work to draw closer and listen to the beautiful story of Asa the goose girl and little Mats. Eventually, I had a lot of fun reading it for myself and for the children around me. "In the year when Nils Holgersson traveled with the wild geese, there was a lot of talk about two children, a boy and a girl, who were crossing the country on foot." Brave little Mats dies from tuberculosis and his sister Asa decides that little Mats should be buried "with as much dignity as a grown-up." She wants to give him "the grandest funeral ever." For this, she needs everyone's help. But how can she get anyone to listen to her, given that she's just a child?

 Marguerite Gruny was also a great storyteller and loved to tell the amazing tale of the ghost ship. The children were enthralled as she'd recount the tribulations of the cursed Dutchman who, having defied

God, was condemned to wander the oceans forever. The tale even gave them shivers.

Every storyteller had her own repertoire of stories shaped by her personality and taste. Meanwhile, the children would encounter several adults on a given day, in contrast to what they'd experienced in the classroom, and they were even free to choose which one they'd speak to, depending on their affinities, tastes, and expectations.

Marguerite and Mathilde were very different from one other, and each had her own style of interacting with young readers. Marguerite was very serious. She tended to speak to the older children, whom she presented with more literary works. Mathilde, on the other hand, was rather mischievous. How she liked to laugh! Sitting behind the loan desk, she would take a child affectionately onto her lap and read a book or a passage aloud. Her excitement was contagious, and the both of them would delight in such moments. I can still hear her tinkling laughter as she'd share some stories from her dear Comtesse de Ségur or from *Winnie the Pooh* by Alan Alexander Milne, reading from the beautiful old version translated by the poet Jacques Papy. She was very fond of the clumsy and greedy Pooh-bear. She'd laugh while describing how one day after visiting Rabbit in his burrow, Pooh got stuck in the hole on the way out because Rabbit had given him too much honey and condensed milk. In order to break free, he'd have to lose weight. This was going to take some time, and he'd have to be patient. Rabbit offered to read to him. Rabbit, who also had a sense of practicality, asked Pooh, "Do you mind if I use your back legs as a towel-horse? Because, I mean, there they are—doing nothing—and it would be very convenient just to hang the towels on them."

Stories Up One's Sleeve

Those of us who were in training also had to develop our own repertoire, and we often had to read to the children and tell them stories. There was a lot of pressure when one of these great storytellers was in the audience, too, but this is what it took to learn.

So I started telling stories, too. This was a pleasure I had experienced in my early childhood with my family. During my internship, I would spontaneously suggest to a child that I sit next to them and that we read a story together. Others would quickly join us. I had already experienced such moments of grace with the children in my life, especially with my many nieces and nephews. At the library, these moments were characterized by the same naturally affectionate simplicity.

I told stories everywhere, and at every opportunity—even at the Broussais Hospital in Paris, where I was admitted before I left for New York. At that time, in the early 1960s, a state-of-the-art surgery department there performed major heart operations on children from all over the world. These children, called the "enfants bleus," would stay there for a long time. Many of them liked to gather around my bed. They knew that I always had stories up my sleeve and in my head, as they liked to say. It was in this way that I created cozy, happy encounters in this public, often impersonal, place where people were worried and bored. We had a lot of fun together.

My Experience in Munich

I was about to finish my internship at L'Heure Joyeuse when the library received a visit from Walter Scherf, the director of the International Youth Library in Munich. Right away, he offered me a scholarship to work there. Since I was a Germanist by training, I accepted immediately. I was to stay there for five months during the 1959-1960 schoolyear.

The war had ended less than twenty years before, and Munich was still largely destroyed. To get to the library, I had to take one of its major thoroughfares, Ludwigstrasse, which was lined with mountains of rubble. I would walk past the university buildings and cross the square named for the illustrious Hans and Sophie Scholl, student martyrs of the White Rose resistance movement. The International Youth Library was on a quiet street, Kaulbachstrasse, a short distance from the English Garden.

It was located in a middle-class home that suggested a kind of affluence and that appeared to have escaped the worst of the destruction. It was quite a change from the run-down, dusty, and sad premises where we future curators had received our training—a building on the Rue de Richelieu that was later torn down. In all honesty, the dilapidation of this building had given a decidedly poor impression of the profession.

In the heart of Munich, which was still deeply scarred by war, was the library: a bright house that represented the hope for a new world, a world of peace. It was the brainchild of Jella Lepman, a German Jew who had emigrated to Great Britain during the Nazi era. She had returned to her home country at the end of the war and in 1949, she created the International Youth Library, which was to become the largest children's library in the world. *International understanding through children's books*—this was her project, her utopia. It was a testament to the faith she had in children. It was up to them to build a better world. For this to happen, they had to be open to the rest of the world from the earliest possible age, to understand the "other" and everything that makes the world more humane. She believed that books were the ideal way to foster such attitudes. The International Youth Library collected books from around the world and granted scholarships to researchers, and still does to this day. Although I was a novice in this field, I was invited to study the French collection and bring it up to date. I also organized an exhibition open to professionals and lovers of children's books. I was the first French woman to have received a fellowship to work there.

I followed developments in German publishing with great interest. At the time, the two Germanies were experiencing a kind of revival in literature for children. Curiously, French publishers seemed to have little interest in it, whereas there were real masterpieces in German that children would just gobble right up. I'm thinking in particular of the works of Otfried Preussler (now available in French translation), such as *The Robber Hotzenplotz* for the youngest readers, and *Krabat*, a mesmerizing novel for readers of all ages.

While I was in Munich, I had the opportunity to speak with specialists from all over the world. Some had come with the desire to foster high-quality literature in their country. This was the case for a young woman from Sri Lanka whom I befriended. Communist countries were also well-represented. I admired how important children's publishing was in those countries, even though at that time France did not pay much attention to it. The state-produced editions included illustrations by great artists, some of whom were venerated as national heroes. The aim was to educate future Soviet citizens while showing the world how rich art for children could be. I remember visiting the illustrator Albin Brunovsky at his home in Slovakia. In fact, he lived in his own personal museum, where he would constantly exhibit his illustrated books for visitors. What a testament to the man and his work!

I later had the opportunity to meet other Soviet artists. I was invited to attend Sergey Mikhalkov's 60th birthday party at the Bolshoi Theatre in Moscow, capital of what was then the USSR. This was a national event. Forty years later, UNESCO celebrated the centenary of this children's poet, who had passed away just a few years before. I also received an invitation to this celebration, where I learned that more than 500 million copies of his books had been printed and that his works had been translated into 286 languages. I also found out that a minor planet had been named after him in 1999. What an honor for an author of children's books!

The Cautious French Publishing Revival

All these imaginative books that I discovered at the youth library in Munich, and then later at the New York Public Library, were quite different from what I knew of French post-war publishing. The latter seemed, with a few exceptions, very dull in comparison. Fortunately, in the 1950s the brilliant publisher Robert Delpire started giving great artists (including Alain Le Foll, Jacques Prévert, André Francois, and Claude Roy) the opportunity to participate in the creation of masterpieces for children. There were also remarkable translations of books by authors such as Hans Fischer from Switzerland and Reiner Zimnik from West Germany. For Delpire, these were always personal choices. Later, he published a French translation, *Max et les Maximonstres*, of *Where the Wild Things Are* by Maurice Sendak, which the publisher L'École des Loisirs was quick to pick up. Delpire had an appreciation for the art of the book and always gave pride of place to the story—to the words, to the text—so that children could easily enter into these works of art that these picture books, each one with their own personality, can be. Going against the grain of French publishing and the paperbacks that were all forced onto a Procrustean bed of standard dimensions, Delpire made each book unique in size. *Houpi the Kind Kangeroo* (*Houpi le gentil Kangourou*), dreamed up by the poet Claude Roy, longs to see the Eiffel Tower—but how could that be fit into a book? It was no easy matter, even if the book itself was large. The ingenious illustrator Jacqueline Duhême found a solution. The tower was too tall, so it was to be put on its side, with the top floors folding out. In another picture book, André François' famous *Crocodile Tears*, the crocodile on the cover fits easily in a full-length box disguised a simple postal package.

There was also a dynamic communist publisher called La Farandole. The director was a woman of refined taste, Madeleine Gilard, and they made excellent novels and picture books from the Soviet Union, along with lovely works from the United States, available to the children of France.

Setting Out for the Land of Public Libraries

My stay in Munich was over, and the time had come for me to return to France. People at the International Library were surprised by this. "Is there a future for children's libraries in France, apart from L'Heure Joyeuse in Paris? Why don't you go to the United States where libraries and children's literature are flourishing?" It was a tough decision. At that time, New York was a distant city. Getting there wasn't just a matter of hours, and the trip was a real adventure. I had no problem spending five months in Munich, but Germany was nearby, and I was a Germanist. But

I finally allowed myself to be convinced. By chance, I met a particularly open-minded American couple, the Bergners, in Poitiers.

They were New Yorkers. Larry, a doctor, was performing his military service at the American base there that had been set up by NATO. Unlike the other Americans in Poitiers who lived cut off from the rest of the city in the barracks or in housing estates designated for them—consuming only imported American products, much to the displeasure of the Poitiers merchants—they resided in the heart of Poitiers and lived in the French way. They showed me the positive side of the American people. Their view of French life was both sympathetic and critical, and it changed my perspective on the reality of my own country. As was the case for the American anthropologist Laurence Wylie, who published *Village in the Vaucluse* at around the same time, they were surprised by certain aspects of French child-rearing. For example, they were astonished to hear parents in the park shouting to their little ones, "Don't run, you'll fall!" American-style education was apparently quite different.

I got a great deal of help from my American friends as I organized my trip. I had to find a library to host me and also obtain a scholarship, so I approached Mildred Batchelder, president of the Children's Library Association within the American Library Association. She was an exceptional woman. The Batchelder Award, which supports the publication in the United States of high-quality books from abroad, was named after her in 1966. It's a wonderful initiative! For, as I was to notice during my stay at the New York Public Library, in the United States there were very few foreign works for children available in translation.

Those were happy times, with no shortage of job opportunities. I got dozens of offers. Sometimes they were from remarkable libraries, like the Enoch Pratt Free Library in Baltimore. My friends helped me make my decision. They advised me to accept the invitation from the famous New York Public Library. Since the beginning of the 20th century, it had occupied an exceptional place in the history of children's services and public libraries in general. For me, this would be like returning to the very source of L'Heure Joyeuse. I applied for and received a Fulbright scholarship, which was granted for two years. I left in September 1961—a particularly turbulent period. It was the time of the Algerian War, the Cuban Revolution, and the Bay of Pigs incident. There was also the looming threat of nuclear war. I left France with strong concerns about the future of the world. What state would my country be in when I returned? Would I even see it again?

Like other Fulbright scholars, I embarked on the Queen Mary for a trip that lasted one short week. These were carefree days that I spent in the company of students and scholars. Since the schoolyear was about to start back up again, there were a lot of students aboard the ship. A number of them had scholarships from universities or other research centers. Some had made the trip before, and they were happy to give me advice.

My Discovery of the New World

I was the only librarian to have received a Fulbright scholarship. I had brought a trunk full of books with me, and this worried the customs officers. They inspected the books one by one. What were they looking for? *Tropic of Cancer*, by Henry Miller! This book had been banned in the United States. Surprise number one… how could it be that this country praised for its democratic spirit could prohibit access to works of literature? I started working at the 96th Street library a few days later, and the ban had just been lifted. Many readers rushed in to reserve this book now that it had finally been made available. But they'd have to be patient, since the waiting list was long. Who could have asked for better publicity? Meanwhile, at this time France was in the midst of the Algerian War and there was also censorship, but for different reasons.

I was going to have to adapt to a country that I knew only from movies and from the GIs' presence in France. Right after I arrived, I found myself on 5th Avenue amidst the famous yellow checker cabs. A major fire had broken out in the city and there was a long, slow procession of fire engines making their way up the street. The horns were playing the music of the Christian hymn: "Nearer My God, To Thee." I had only just gotten off the ship and had already entered another civilization.

It was lunchtime, and everyone on the sidewalks appeared to be in a hurry. The men, wearing hats and dressed in gray, seemed immense to me, and the old ladies dressed in pink or baby blue were heavily made-up. From time to time, I heard the plaintive and distressing sirens of the police cars.

In general, I was to enjoy a fascinating sense of culture shock in the United States. Would this even be a possibility today? At that time, the differences between the North American and the European worlds were significant. Clothing and hairstyles were distinctive on this side of the Atlantic, as I had already noticed back in France while leafing through American magazines. These days, even when we're far from home, we don't really leave our own world. With Skype and the Internet, you can travel back home to the family and friends you've left behind.

My mother and I used to write to each other regularly when I was away on my distant travels, and I still treasure these letters. My mother had a great gift for writing, and every last detail was suffused with her style. I, in turn, would describe my discoveries, my surprises, and my joys. My letters were like travel diaries.

Throwing the Door Wide Open

As soon as I arrived in New York, I got down to work. Though my command of the English language was very poor, people trusted me immediately. I had a hand in just about everything, as if I'd been there forever. I immediately found myself behind the information desk in the library's main section, with the responsibility for answering adults' questions. I'd have to figure it out on my own, so I learned how to do my job and speak the language. It was, however, challenging to answer the readers' questions over the phone. I only knew the names of a few great American authors. But what about the rest? I'd ask how their names were spelled. Because of the vowels, this just made things worse.

Since the French letter *i* is pronounced like the English "e" and the *é* is pronounced like the "a," it's difficult to keep everything straight.

The families of my American friends in Poitiers were wonderful hosts. They took me in as soon as I arrived and were generous as well as patient, given my linguistic limitations. But we managed to understand each other through a combination of German and the Yiddish that the older members of the family still spoke. Are Americans so welcoming because immigration has made such valuable contributions? Library patrons would generously extend invitations to have dinner, to celebrate traditional holidays, or to explore the natural and artistic beauties that were such sources of pride for them.

Because of this, I was able to explore the cultures, relatively little-known in my home country, of Black Americans. I explored the world of Harlem together with my Black friends. From them, I learned about the suffering of those who are excluded and scorned. I was shocked to discover that the grandfather of one of my friends had been a slave. In the early 1960s, as I saw, racial discrimination had left deep scars. The magnificent novel by Richard Powers, *The Time of Our Singing*, eloquently describes this pain constantly inflicted on the "wretched of the earth." This was not the case at the New York library, but on the street, passersby were sometimes surprised to see a white woman rubbing shoulders with people of color and would turn around to stare as we passed.

A Flower Amidst the Garbage

In 1961, while I was working at the New York Public Library, I could still feel the spirit of the trailblazers. Anne Carroll Moore, born in 1871, had just died. In 1896 she'd been at the forefront of the first children's libraries, and from 1906 onwards, she'd directed the one at the New York Public Library with great authority. She closely monitored the library's growth until her death. All the children's libraries in the world were inspired by the American model she'd helped to establish at the beginning of the century. What I discovered reminded me in many ways of L'Heure Joyeuse: There was the same attention given to making quality works available to children and advising them if they wanted it. Storytime had a central place there, as Moore had wished.

For a long time, I worked at a branch of the New York Public Library located in what was a very poor neighborhood back then: the Bowery, on the Lower East Side. There was a significant Puerto Rican population as well as recent Jewish immigrants with limited resources. There were also a lot of homeless people. The brand-new library, simple and beautiful, had been built amidst the slums. From the street, it was possible to look through the thin curtains and see a place that was comfortable and, in a way, homey. I liked to work there at sundown when many adults who appeared to be vagrants would come in after they'd eaten dinner. They'd dive into newspapers, books, and magazines that would keep them in touch with their home countries. They felt good there and we enjoyed talking with one other. Often, I was impressed by their culture. One of them, for example, introduced me to the work of Erik Satie. I could tell that they'd known other lives and that bad luck had brought them to where they were. The big city had crushed them. They were people with no money who lived mostly on the street, but they were proud of their library. They liked to tell me, a foreigner who was just passing through, that it was "a flower amidst the garbage."

How Beautiful!

The children's section of the library where I worked was very busy. Hordes of children would descend on the library at the end of the school day, and librarians from the main section would lend a hand. Most of the children had come there to do research for class, and the librarians would help them to quickly find the right book, and even the right passage. The children would then dutifully copy the paragraph that seemed to answer the question they'd been asked.

"What should I copy?" they'd ask. This puzzled and disappointed me. At L'Heure Joyeuse, I'd learned different approaches. Wasn't the purpose of such exercises to learn how to learn, to know how to conduct research? I was always happy when some were there simply because they wanted to read.

I remember a child who came running to the library at closing time one evening. He waved at me impatiently and shook the door, so I had to open it for him. "I've got an emergency," he explained. His hamster had just given birth and he didn't know what he should do. He came in and we searched together. He wasn't just going to take the first book that came along and doggedly persisted until he'd found the right information. Today, of course, it's just a matter of consulting the Internet, but this was different. In the library, there's a personal interaction. Somebody listens to you and you feel important.

In this neighborhood where families faced many challenges, I enjoyed being among the children. They would play in the street all day long but came to visit me from time to time. What I offered them is similar to what I often practiced in my later years, but it was unusual there. I would sit down at a table and start reading a book to a child. Others would come closer to listen and look at the pictures. We'd take our time. We'd talk to each other. The children always wanted more. When I was working in the main section, they would come and gather around me, then follow me around as if I were the Pied Piper of Hamelin. They weren't allowed to enter the main section for adults, however, and they'd have to go back to the children's side.

Long afterwards, when I had to leave this library to work in another neighborhood, they would send me drawings and leaves they'd found. They'd give them to sympathetic librarians who'd slip them into kraft envelopes usually reserved for administrative mail sent from one library to the next. The simple act of reading books with them had won them over. In these moments that we spent reading together, they felt acknowledged and really happy. They would follow along, page after page, as I read the books aloud, exclaiming, "How beautiful! How beautiful!" They also knew how much I enjoyed being with them.

My approach was completely informal compared to storytime, which was sacrosanct, a true ceremony with its own rituals. It had to be absolutely quiet, of course, and a candle was lit for the duration of the story.

When the story was over, a child would blow it out and everyone was asked to silently make a wish. Undoubtedly, in these large cities where immigration was particularly heterogeneous, ritual had the power to bring the children together in a kind of solemnity. Certainly, there was a desire to provide storytime with something of the poignant magic of an ancient tradition.

The Library as a Haven

Miss Finkel, the director of the library in the Bowery, was particularly welcoming. She told me about what it was like when she had come to the United States, how strong her desire to integrate had been, and how the library had immediately offered her hope: the hope of finding her place in the country where she was going to live, and the hope of discovering a new culture and a new way of life. She felt welcomed, recognized. The public library in her neighborhood, she told me, had immediately become her second home.

Years later, I visited Ellis Island. Most immigrants arriving in the United States had to rebuild their lives in their new country from scratch. I can imagine how confusing it must have been for these anonymous masses who had left everything—their homes, their parents, their friends—and had lost all their familiar points of reference. I imagined what the library could provide for them. The doors of the library had always been wide open to them. The librarian was there to welcome them personally, to listen to them, to answer all their various questions, and to guide them. The library was like a haven and was further enriched by the presence of newcomers, with their hopes and their cultures. I was moved by this unique form of welcoming those who had come to the United States and appreciated the quality and discretion of what the library offered. There, people with foreign backgrounds were, first and foremost, people. This was the true wealth of this institution, which remained open to all forms of culture and thought.

At the New York Public Library, I immersed myself in books and activity reports, read all kinds of writing, and discovered how much, especially in big cities, attention to newcomers helped to shape the face of public libraries that we see today. Based on the diversity of languages and literatures represented in the collections at the branches of this network where I worked, I could easily guess at the diversity of the neighborhood populations.

Recognizing Cultures and Traditions from Elsewhere

By encouraging the positive recognition of cultures and traditions from elsewhere, librarians foster in newcomers a desire to belong to the country they are discovering and where they've come to live. The library is thus enriched by the uniqueness of individuals and of books.

The objectives underlying each of the policies in the United States, a country of immigrants, responded to social and cultural needs that were not so far removed from those we see in France today. But in the early 1960s, all of this was new to me. In France, what were public libraries doing to open up to immigrant populations at that time? To what extent, in their collections and programs, did librarians take into consideration the newcomers from Italy, Spain, Poland, or Armenia? Today, fortunately, France is more welcoming, especially in the libraries located in the *banlieues*, or suburbs.

The first public libraries were established in the United States at the end of the 19th century. This was the great era of railroad construction, of the important migratory flows that it enabled, and of the rural exodus to the cities, where the number of impoverished inhabitants was growing at a dizzying pace. The figures on the Internet are staggering: in 1833, the city of Chicago had only 350 inhabitants. In 1900, the population was approximately 1,700,000. Children were easily overlooked in these cities that grew too quickly.

At the turn of the century, the country experienced waves of immigration that differed from the previous ones. It was no longer mainly Anglo-Saxons, Germans, and Scandinavians who settled in the rural areas, but families from Central, Eastern, and Southern Europe who were moving to the cities to work in factories. Cultural and religious traditions, as well as the diversity of languages, made it far more challenging for these newcomers to integrate into this predominantly Anglo-Saxon society. The difficulties of learning the English language encouraged immigrants to group themselves according to their native languages. Longer-established Americans had trouble accepting the presence of new arrivals who spoke foreign languages and behaved differently than they did.

The various communities tended to live in isolation. Family tensions were strong and painful: The parents had left their country of origin and had, in a way, been robbed of their past. The future was in their children. The children, however, quickly adopted the habits and customs of their new country and became like strangers to them. Children and parents alike suffered from the tensions created by the differences between the patriarchal family lifestyle of their country of origin and the children's American education, which gave them another status that was immediately more attractive to them. The children were torn between two cultures: they were not entirely accepted by their new compatriots, who often treated them with contempt, whereas at home they were criticized for being too American.

Attention to the Displaced

The first public libraries in the big cities showed great humanitarian concern for these children and their families who, as victims of the troubles brought about by industrialization, experienced such great destitution—destitution likely to encourage delinquency. In the 19th century, the prestigious Boston Public Library focused on providing a place for children. These places had to be more welcoming if any of these children roaming the streets were going to make their way into these impressive monuments. The director of the Boston library had the idea of introducing storytime to attract them, and he invited storytellers, notably the American Sara Cone Bryant, whose collections are still well-known today in France. At the beginning of the 20th century, children of immigrants started to fill up the children's sections of libraries. The first public libraries that were open to children responded to the violent displacement of these families that had been uprooted and torn apart, to the loneliness that it entailed, by offering cultural activities that fostered human connections. This attention given to the "victims" of immigration was to determine many ways of doing things for the greatest benefit to all, whatever their social origin.

Ruth Sawyer, the great American storyteller who learned so much from her Irish nanny as a child, explained that she would encourage children who were new to the United States to tell stories about home.[7] This was a way for her to enrich her repertoire; at the same time, entrusting children with the responsibility of transmission helped them to appreciate aspects of their family culture that were too often depreciated and get them to share it proudly with their peers. This idea that Sawyer had of sharing the storyteller role with the child was a wonderful one! There was, for example, one child with a Russian background who regularly asked his father to tell him a story that he could then share at the library every Saturday. Some of the young listeners would transcribe the stories faithfully, then add them to a whole collection that later took its place alongside the storybooks.

A Lovely Place for Great Books

What were the stories told in the first American libraries? The fairy tales of the Grimms and Andersen, of course. Folk tales also featured prominently, as well as stories from the indigenous tribes or the planters in the South. The librarians weren't shy about introducing children to the great classics, myths, biblical stories, the *Iliad* and the *Odyssey*, the beautiful Nordic sagas, and even tales from Shakespeare. The decision to share these great texts had been inspired in part by the desire to enrich the culture of those children who'd had little schooling. In 1914,

---

7. See Ruth Sawyer, *The Way of the Storyteller*, Penguin Books, 1977.

even though school had become compulsory, 93% of children did not advance beyond elementary school. Storytime, where children could be avid listeners, was intended to somewhat compensate for this lack of education. Today, I think of children who have great difficulty reading and who risk missing out on marvelous works if the stories are not read aloud or told to them.

It was in this way that children were encouraged to get swept up by these vast and timeless currents, these universal streams of a common culture that brings us together across time and space. There was one young listener who confided to a storyteller: "Every time I go into the subway, I think of Proserpina descending into Pluto's kingdom." Storytellers had a recognized place in the neighborhood. I think of the child, a newspaper vendor, who stopped the same storyteller in the street and asked him worriedly if "Leonidas and all those brave Greeks perished in the end."[8]

Where would stories be told? Some libraries did have story rooms but, in fact, early librarians like Janet Hill would tell stories anywhere. Stories were the best way for the library to reach out to children and build positive relationships with them. They would tell stories in playgrounds, houses around the neighborhood, orphanages, hospitals, and museums. As such, in turn-of-the-century Boston, children from the streets and the slums would fill up the museums every Sunday, and the tales the storytellers shared would give new life to the works on display while inspiring the children to further explore. The library's reports tell of how happy it made the guides at the Museum of Fine Arts to see the children's curiosity stimulated in this way. The storytellers' considerable repertoire always made it possible for them to share something related to the items on exhibit. Thus, before a magnificent German earthenware stove, children sitting on the floor listened attentively to *The Nuremberg Stove*. The curator took a finely embroidered vest out of his reserves as an accompaniment to *The Tailor of Gloucester*.

---

8. Story recounted by Jane M. Filstrup, "The Enchanted Cradle: Early Storytelling in Boston," cited in *The Horn Book Magazine*, December 1976.

One of these passionate volunteer storytellers was Mr. Gronan, an accountant by profession. On sunny days, he chose to tell stories on the library's roof terrace because, he said: "What could be more beautiful for these young people, whose lives are so serious and matter-of-fact, than listening to a man tell stories under a summer's sky filled with stars?"

At the beginning of the century, some storytellers chose careers as librarians because it afforded ample opportunities to tell stories. In the library, stories were told all year long, but they were especially important for the traditional celebrations of the neighborhood's folk and religious cultures. The practice of storytelling creates a festive atmosphere and provides an opportunity for collective rejoicing. In New York, I saw how the American holidays of St. Nicholas Day and Thanksgiving, as well as certain Puerto Rican and Haitian holidays, marked life at the library.

In the Heart of Manhattan, the Central Library for Children

I worked in the Central Children's Room for several months. At the time, it occupied two large rooms on the first floor of the imposing and remarkable library, guarded by two stone lions, located in the heart of Manhattan at the corner of 5th Avenue and 42nd Street. It had an old-fashioned, respectable air about it and was frequented by children as well as artists, publishers, and lovers of children's books. I remember meeting the young Tomi Ungerer, who seemed particularly interested in the foreign book collections, when I was there. Paul Galdone, who illustrated *The Little Red Hen* and whose work is so beloved in France, was a regular. So was Marcia Brown, also a great children's book artist, and Remy Charlip. The pages from one of Charlip's storybooks were displayed like a fresco on a wall of the children's room.

The librarians at the Central Children's Room had a lively interest in graphic design, and I knew they were in regular contact with the American Institute of Graphic Arts. They admired the work of French illustrators such as Edy-Legrand, who had been a source of inspiration for some American artists. Curiously, at that time, Edy-Legrand was completely unknown in the French publishing world, though he enjoyed a prestigious reputation across the Atlantic. The same was true of the Babar books. Jean de Brunhoff was appreciated in the United States, whereas his French publisher Hachette had stopped publishing him, deciding that the elephant Babar had had his day and opting instead for the *Caroline* books by Pierre Probst.

Generally speaking, storytime was the essential, if not the only, form of entertainment in the children's sections of New York's libraries as I knew them in the early 1960s. Children would come to listen, to watch a performance. I could see that they didn't take part in the life of the library. They didn't really have the kinds of shared experiences that I had so enjoyed at L'Heure Joyeuse during my internship there, and that today are such vital resources for our library in Clamart.

For Young Adults, a Library Open to All

At the New York Public Library, I sometimes felt that, in the children's sections, the respect for the traditions the librarians were so proud of could be a little stifling. Since Anne Carroll Moore had passed away recently, she was veritably revered, and her picture was on display at training sessions and conferences. In many different ways, her vision had made a lasting impression.

On the other hand, librarians who worked with teens were not restricted in this way. They had no weight of tradition nor model to burden them and therefore had to make everything up themselves. I was therefore especially interested in what was happening in libraries with young adults. It was very new for me. In France, such services did not exist at that time, whereas in the United States, even as early as 1919, interest had been focused on teenagers. In the Lower East Side library where I worked, there was, as in other neighborhoods, a staff member responsible for greeting and orienting them, listening to their requests and suggestions, and drawing their attention to the books and documents that might be of special interest to them. There was no section specifically for teenagers; there, they were called "young adults," and the librarians welcomed them in the main section. Being considered a young adult is far more empowering than being labelled a teenager!

I was struck by how open-minded Emma Cohn was. She was the librarian responsible for young adults at a library in the Bronx. Thanks to her, the library was open to the winds: the winds of curiosity, questioning, and passion. What Emma offered was both simple and rich at the same time.

Emma was always attentive to what was likely to get young people excited and would organize events around a great diversity of topics. She was deeply interested in the people she met; they appreciated her openness and liked to be close to her. At the library, she told us, she spent a lot of time talking with the members of her community. She learned a lot about them and, more broadly, what interesting things were going on in the neighborhood. She'd find out who had a special place in the discussions and lives of young people. This is how, for example, she came to invite a hairdresser who worked at a place called "The Electric Hair Company" and who was very popular with the neighborhood teens to the library. People talk a lot when they're at the hairdresser!

She had a leaflet created and distributed: the theme was "hair as a symbol of social status." There were also plans to discuss and provide information about the importance of a hairstyle, a good haircut, and hair care. The event was a great success, probably because the young people discovered that their seemingly trivial questions were not at all pointless and that they could lead to unexpected lines of inquiry. With the library being right in the middle of New York City, it was easy for them to see how, in a few short years, hair styles had evolved from straightened hair to the Afro. There was a whole concept of Black identity that was expressed in this way. We also came to talk about what it meant to "belong to a group," to be admitted into it, and then about the actual rites of initiation in Western society. Starting with one small question and with one topic leading to another, we were able to describe what ethnology was and mention the names of some great ethnologists likely to be of interest the young people in attendance. For these teenagers, the notion of belonging to a group took on greater meaning when it was part of a universal framework. Recognizing the value of an apparently trivial question could, we saw, open up a whole new array of knowledge.

Librarians know that any question an individual might have can stimulate curiosity, provided there's someone to listen and try to answer it. This is how librarians help patrons move freely from a question to an answer and then another question, knowing that they are guiding without taking over. Emma would bring in close friends and personalities of all types based on the young people's interests and, in so doing, proposed a notion of culture that was not, as is too frequently the case, limited to certain artistic or literary forms. She recognized that young people's interests lay beyond the academic subjects that are generally valued. She also acknowledged the adults in their lives. I introduced Emma to some particularly dynamic French librarians, and she was surprised by their emphasis on elaborate activities. It could all be so much simpler. Listening, guiding, connecting, and bringing people together—these were all things that Emma did naturally. She was able to forge surprising partnerships and unusual relationships with people who could engage children and adolescents. The Bronx Library also offered poetry workshops, sponsored by the poetry academy, for young people. The academy had attempted to hold these in the schools, but the young people had found the framework too rigid. They felt freer at the library. It wasn't really a program. Each participant came with a poem to discuss with the poet who was there that day. Emma noted that many young adults in the Bronx were particularly responsive to the rhythms and emotions of poetry.

This was in the 1960s. At that time, there was not a separate concept of the "media library," but there was a strong audiovisual presence at the Bronx Library nonetheless. Emma was an avid film buff and liked to share her enthusiasm. She borrowed an amazing variety of films, both fiction and documentary, American and international, from the NYPL's film library. She had a penchant for French cinema and liked to introduce young people to films by Marcel Carné, René Clair, or the lesser-known French ethnologist Jean Rouch. At that time, there were not many librarians who brought the world of cinema into their libraries. Film librarians like Emma knew how to give the art of cinema its rightful place. Books aren't capable of satisfying certain questions, certain expectations. It's a mistake to always look to books for all the answers, and it's important to offer other resources for answers. This was Emma's conviction, and she knew that making use of other media and events, when necessary, made it possible for books to assume their full importance. Expecting that books can provide an answer to every question means that in some cases they will disappoint.

Back in France

Before long, I was offered a permanent position as a children's librarian at the New York Public Library. I was told that I would have a great future there and assured that, with the institution's support, I would have no problem obtaining American citizenship. However, I decided to return to France. I dreamed of working in Paris, the city of L'Heure Joyeuse, because I admired their way of making children feel welcome.

Back in France, while preparing for the competitive examination for library curators, I decided to deepen my knowledge of the children's sections in the Parisian libraries. I was, to tell the truth, quite disappointed. For the most part, libraries at that time were confined to a simple distribution role, with the librarians remaining in their offices. The employees behind the checkout desk would process the loans rather apathetically. The children couldn't expect to get any help finding reading material suitable to their tastes and needs and, apart from exceptional cases, there was no storytime.

L'Heure Joyeuse was something else entirely, though the city authorities held it in very low regard. As soon as I came back from New York, the librarians of Rue Boutebrie encouraged me to prepare for the exam. They were just a few years from retiring, and I later learned that they'd wanted me to take over the direction of their library. Having passed the competitive examination, I had first pick of where to work and I immediately communicated my wishes to the Paris library administration. The response? "Impossible. You were trained at L'Heure Joyeuse. It's high time for the mentality of this library to become a thing of the past. We're saving you for something much better." Decades later, the Clamart library nearly suffered the same fate: "Is there really a need for such a library?" I wondered if the administration was afraid of what was emerging. Was it difficult for it to accept innovation when it came from the outside?

La Joie par les Livres

Just before starting to prepare for the library curator examination, I was very surprised to receive a letter from an association called La Joie par les Livres. Its goal was to create a pilot library for children in the suburbs of Paris. Would I have any interest in participating in this project? I didn't pay much attention to this letter, as I wasn't familiar with the suburbs. And working in a library run by an association? This didn't appeal to me, at first glance. At L'Heure Joyeuse, I had appreciated a kind of open secularism that was very respectful of differences. And in terms of the book collections, the librarians felt strongly about giving equal space to different schools of thought as long as they were honestly represented. At that time in France, the libraries run by associations (bibliothèques associatives) were essentially denominational or had strong political orientations. I was hesitant, therefore, to accept the invitation from La Joie par les Livres. For me, the name of this association sounded like something dreamed up by some well-intentioned ladies. Nonetheless, I decided to go, certain that I would end up turning them down.

Their little office was near the Montparnasse train station. Right away, I informed the head of the association, Anne Schlumberger, that I wasn't interested. I told her I was preparing for the competitive examination to work as a curator for the city of Paris and that I'd be taking the test in six to eight months. She offered to hire me for this period: "You can decide then if you'll want to leave…" And she invited me to develop the collection of storybooks from abroad.

Opening up to the World

I've always been interested in what goes on outside of France. Thanks to my mother, our home was a hospitable one. My older sister, Colette, was herself drawn to discover what life was like beyond our borders, especially in Britain. She had lived for a while at the Cité Universitaire in Paris and had made friends with students from Africa and Asia, and also from the Netherlands, Denmark, and Sweden. She decided to learn Chinese, which was very unusual in the 1950s. At Langues O, what is today called Inalco, there were no more than two or three students studying the Chinese language and culture. They were practically private lessons. She readily gave out our family's address to people she met on her travels, so we would have surprise visits at our house from friends from all over the world! It was so interesting to listen to them, and I was touched by their personal stories. I remember large family gatherings with friends from Africa, Asia, and various European countries happy to have found their niche. I was captivated. They had a new and curious perspective on our forms of culture and our ways of living in France. This sharpened my focus on what to my eyes had been self-evident. In the city of Poitiers, it was quite unusual to meet somebody from China. There was a Chinese man who sold lingerie at the market, but he had completely forgotten his native language. There was also an African: just one. I believe that Taza was from Togo. He was often on the street, surrounded by children. We liked to run into him because he was always happy to talk to us.

Anne could tell how interested I was in the rest of the world. I had, after all, chosen to work in Munich and the then the US. She wanted to open the library to the best of what was being produced internationally, so she gave me carte blanche to create a collection of foreign storybooks. If I wanted to, I could travel, look around, meet people, and find the most beautiful books. Indeed, she wanted the neighborhood children to be exposed to the best—to the most beautiful, the most interesting. It was also a question of communicating with the creators and publishers of masterpieces from all over the world that were most likely to interest the children here. In the United States, it was the golden age of children's books—those of Sendak, Lobel, Ungerer, Charlip, Lionni, and Spier. In other parts of the world, Bruno Munari, Anno Mitsumasa, and Jiří Trnka were revealing new ways to connect with children.

How was I going to develop this international collection? Would I be satisfied with publishers' catalogs or with a few visits to book fairs in Frankfurt and Leipzig? I tried this and just felt lost. How was I to assess the quality of the books? Just a cursory glance wasn't enough. The Bologna Children's Book Fair had just come into being and many publishers chose to ignore it, preferring the Frankfurt Book Fair instead. My visits left me dissatisfied. I was most interested in how children responded to high-quality books, so I needed the expert advice of librarians from Japan, Sweden, Italy, Czechoslovakia, England, and many other countries. I was able to call on them thanks to the help of the librarians at L'Heure Joyeuse who had frequent visits from foreign colleagues they could put me in touch with. They often had daily contact with children and were true connoisseurs of the art of the book. I asked each of them to tell me about the ten best books from their country, classic or new, that were also very popular with children. The idea was to present the children with some of these books and stories that had marked the lives of families beyond our borders.

This was my first task, and it gave me time to become better acquainted with La Joie par les Livres, a very new association. Lise was the sole librarian back then, and all of her time was spent acquiring and preparing books. I joined in and together, we took the time to get to know these books. For each one, we'd write a card with a brief introduction to the content. Our goal was to teach students how to use the catalog thoughtfully so they could do their own research independently. I remember how astonished the university professors were as they saw the children navigating the catalogs with ease. They would tell me they wished their students had the same research skills.

I liked to mull things over with Lise, who had already worked there for several months. If she hadn't been there, would I have agreed to sign up for the Joie par les Livres adventure? We really were on the same wavelength. Together, we thought about the library's pedagogy. This was an establishment built on enthusiasm, but it was not free of doubts. I had great confidence in Lise and felt the need to constantly talk things over with her. I also liked the tenacity of our patron, how forthrightly demanding this sensitive and quiet woman behind the project was. As a result, I decided to give up my career as a civil servant and accepted the offer I was given: I would work at La Joie par les Livres. We were soon joined by a third person who had just finished her librarian studies: Christine Chatain, who was also seduced by the project's overall quest for beauty. With her arrival, the library's small team was complete.

Anne Schlumberger

Who was the generous woman who made this adventure possible? Anne came from a family of Alsatian Protestants. They were major industrialists, but also brilliant innovators and lovers of literature. Her family was well-known throughout the world for their exceptional and intelligent patronage, both of the arts and society. However, her desire to provide children and families with an exceptional library was met with strong reservations in the French world of libraries. It seemed that at that time, France was not ready to accept the generosity of patrons, and even seemed to distrust it.

For Anne, however, this had been no whim. It was a decision that had been germinating for a long time. I found journals in her archives that dated from the 1930s, including Roger Cousinet's *La Nouvelle Éducation*. Some passages were underlined and there were notes in the margins. From very early on, she had been deeply interested in new educational movements that were gaining traction in France and that had a lasting impact on L'Heure Joyeuse. She had also traveled all over the world and spent a long time living in the United States, where she admired the role that public libraries played in the daily lives of children and their families. She was well aware that there were hardly any children's libraries in France, despite remarkable initiatives that had started forty years earlier. She decided, therefore, to instigate a new movement by creating a library. She was passionate about architecture and knew how important it was to have a beautiful and welcoming place that was open to all. Anne had spent long hours at L'Heure Joyeuse in Paris and had taken short trips to the International Youth Library in Munich. She'd created a library for a summer camp in Quiberon, on the west coast of France. These were all ways that allowed her to get a concrete sense of what reading outside the context of school meant for children. Julien Cain, who at that time was the emeritus director of French libraries, was impressed by the seriousness of her undertaking and agreed to sponsor her; he became the honorary president of La Joie par les Livres.

Anne had fought against all odds to find a municipality that would agree to make a site available so she could build her library. She knocked on a lot of doors, offering an exceptional gift: She'd build a reading library specially designed for children and take full responsibility for running it over the course of eighteen years. After that, the municipality would have to take over. But there weren't many people who believed in her project. Why offer a library to children? Had this rich lady lost all touch with reality? Did she really believe that, in the age of television, children would still be interested in reading? It was necessary for the Schlumberger company, located in Clamart, to back the proposal in order for it to be accepted in the same municipality. When the city voted to make a plot of land available, some councilors objected that this would decrease the number of parking spaces, but the project was finally accepted. The library would be located in the heart of the *cité* of La Plaine, a low-income housing development later designated as a "priority education zone" (zone d'éducation prioritaire, or ZEP), which had a transitional *cité* (cité de transit) as it was called at the time—the Bourgogne development, where there was a significant foreign population. Anne, attuned to social issues, was delighted with this location. It would only make the experiment all the more significant and vital. By chance, the La Plaine housing development where the library was to be built had been the subject of an in-depth study.

Setting Up a Library in a Cité

Researchers had studied the housing development in the late 1950s. The aims had been to understand how social relations evolved within these large architectural complexes that were popping up all over the French suburbs, on the one hand, and to make proposals for these areas' specific needs, on the other. They published their results in 1960. What a disappointment! In their proposals, there was no mention of a library! Unlike their Anglo-American counterparts, these researchers were part of the dominant French culture that at the time ignored the public library, which had not yet become part of everyday life in France. In the center of Clamart, the more well-to-do part, there was indeed a library hidden behind the town hall. It wasn't very easy to find, and it was a sad place. There was a box on top of the lending desk for collecting dues and fines. At the entrance, there was a big machine that looked like a commercial-sized refrigerator and was used to disinfect the books after they were returned. Since these books passed through many hands, were they really sanitary? Truth be told, we never asked ourselves that question in regard to banknotes. I remember the child in Clamart whose grandmother had forbidden him from visiting our library for this very reason. His desire was strong, however, and he ultimately circumvented this prohibition. He was to become a pillar of our theater workshop.

The children's library (Bibliothèque des enfants) of Clamart really broke new ground. In the large housing estates that were being built in the outskirts of French cities, there were no viable public libraries.

Beautiful and Daring Architecture

For the project, Anne had called on the Atelier de Montrouge, an association of four young architects. In 1962, when they started to think about the Clamart library, they had already designed buildings with Le Corbusier in France as well as in other countries such as India. They had travelled the world, including Africa and the Middle East, and they were remarkably open-minded and innovative. The studio was a place of rigorous deliberation, of a quest for beauty that accounted for their clients' individual ambitions. The architect Louis Arretche, who had been their teacher at the École des Beaux-Arts and liked to visit them in Montrouge, said they were true monks. They worked as a team, but it was Gerard Thurnauer who was in charge of implementing the library's construction.

Significant progress on the building site had already been made when, inevitably, Anne had her doubts. She felt the need to send the plans to Marcel Breuer, a great name in architecture associated with Bauhaus and the modernist movements that followed. He admired the project: "It will be very good." This completely reassured her.

Like Anne, Gerard spent a lot of time at L'Heure Joyeuse before setting to work. Later, many of the great architects who came to visit the Bibliothèque de Clamart expressed their admiration for this exceptional achievement. I remember the enthusiasm of Richard Neutra, the great architect who had done such prominent work in California. Many architects and architecture students still visit the library today. Directors of architecture schools have approached me over the years. Their interest in this masterpiece has never waned, and they appreciate hearing the perspectives of those who call it home.

The library has even inspired architectural imitations. I was visited by the first counselor and close friend of Farah Diba, the wife of the Shah of Iran, and I was surprised to learn later that she'd had a similar library built in Tehran. It was called the Institute for the Intellectual Development of Children and Young Adults, and it was a place where storybooks were designed and produced in accordance with the artistic traditions of the Persian world. It still exists, though today it is quite different. Some of its officials paid me a visit in the 1990s.

Anne knew that in order to innovate, it was necessary to draw on multiple models. She ensured that the very first librarians, whom she hired personally, had the usual diplomas and had also visited the most dynamic libraries—not just those in France, but also those abroad. She sent Lise to complete her training at the New York Public Library. She asked me to join her project because I had already worked in foreign libraries, first in Munich and then in New York. It was indeed important to know what the most remarkable institutions were and, better yet, to have already worked in them.

Against All Odds

Launching such a project in France was not easy. Who would agree to go along with Anne's crazy idea? Librarians with diplomas recognized by the public administration probably wouldn't want to venture into work at the community level, so her search took a long time.

Anne had consistently asked the founders of L'Heure Joyeuse for help. Their reply had been ruthless: "We have someone to suggest, but we won't tell you who it is." I later learned that they had responded in this way because of the fact that they wanted to put me in charge of their library when they retired. But Anne had been undeterred. Since she was eager for the little library in Clamart to be international in scope, she continued traveling abroad. In Vienna, she'd visited Richard Bamberger, the president of the IBBY—the International Board on Books for Young People. She'd also met Walter Scherf in Munich, who gave her my name. This made a lot of sense, given that I had been the only French woman to have worked there. And it was then that she'd gotten in touch with me, shortly after my return from the United States.

The first contact we had with the *cité* was not very encouraging. The parent volunteers working in the neighborhood predicted the worst "Ah, you'll see what it's like in our suburbs. There will be ongoing destruction, theft, and aggression. Are you coming in from the city? You should know that every day, the tires of your cars will be slashed."

As soon as the library opened, there were some parents who tried to find out what propaganda there was lurking behind this apparent generosity. They sent their children to borrow books on certain subjects, hoping these could shed some light on the matter. They were immediately reassured and later became some of our most loyal allies.

More generally, the activists in France who championed reading and books for children were wary. What were these young librarians doing on their turf? Where did they come from? Who was behind this project? Was there secret financing? The rumors were flying. Was the CIA involved? Didn't the librarians go to the United States to complete their training? Or else there was a powerful publisher behind this initiative to bombard France with its mediocre and/or manipulative publications. Admittedly, Anne had always been remarkably discreet, refusing to associate her name with this generous enterprise.

The Power of Conviction

Had it taken unflinching bravery to embark on the Clamart adventure— or just incredible naïveté? We could tell that what Anne was offering us was unique: the trust and the freedom to innovate and strive for excellence. For me, having just returned from the United States, it was an opportunity to build on what I had appreciated so much at the New York Public Library and what I had learned at L'Heure Joyeuse. From the outset, I loved our small team's enthusiasm and high standards. We were bound by a common conviction and enjoyed working together.

This children's library was Anne's project, and she provided the overall guidelines. The three young librarians—Lise Vuilleumier-Encrevé, Christine Chatain, and myself—adhered to them fully. We never had to comply with any statistical criteria, quantifiable profitability requirements, or ideology. This was Anne's gift to us: in all confidence, she gave us the opportunity to invent, with due regard for the people and the realities of the neighborhood. It was an invaluable gift for the architects and the librarians alike. This trust encouraged us to live up to the challenges of her project. We were guided by the sole desire to offer the children of this low-income housing project a library that would delight them, arouse their curiosity, help them to live their childhoods to the fullest, and open them up to the world.

Anne gave us complete freedom to implement a project that could thus develop in a natural, coherent, and robust way. The last thing we wanted was to create a fixed project determined in every detail and outcome, a program drawn up in advance by erudite experts. No—we let ourselves be guided by the reality of the needs as they appeared over the course of our actions in the field. By taking these into account, we were able to adopt a simple strategy that valued what was essential without ever losing sight of the children.

What we wanted was clear: to show children that a library designed just for them could give them a place where they could experience the joy of reading and spend a part of their childhood, a place where they played an active part. This would all take place within the context of simple, natural relationships with their peers and adults. We were eager to offer them the best in publishing while helping them to experience reading on a personal level by way of meaningful interactions to spark their curiosity, open them up to the world, and nurture their inner lives, their awareness, and their imaginations. Human mediation thus played a central role.

Allies from Day One

Several individuals and institutions supported our project from the beginning. This included François Clément, who was responsible for public relations at the Syndicat National de l'Édition. He sensed what an important role public libraries played in the evolution of publishing and, more broadly, of reading. I appreciated how open he was, along with his honest approach to envisioning how publishers and librarians could collaborate. François fully respected our freedom and never interfered in our decisions. He was simply committed to providing greater visibility to our profession and its achievements, and he was among the first to support the actions of the Clamart library, even before it had opened. He offered us a space at the Paris Fair (Foire de Paris) where we could present a small collection of children's books. What a welcome and unusual suggestion it was to display books to the general public rather than being limited to specialized fairs and shows! Clément always tried to get the people and institutions responsible for selecting books to work together. This was a difficult task in a country like France, where the weight of ideology could sometimes be a burden on children's books.

Jean Hassenforder was another early supporter. I remember the first time we met: He had invited us to attend a meeting of a small group he'd created within the Association of French Librarians (Association des bibliothécaires français) that was called the Division of Small and Medium-Sized Libraries (Section des petites et moyennes bibliothèques). These activists came from a variety of backgrounds: hospital libraries, corporate libraries, libraries at educational institutions, and suburban libraries. Jean was a researcher at the National Institute for Pedagogical Research (Institut national de la recherche pédagogique), which is where the meeting was held, in a sinister, prefabricated building at the end of a courtyard on the Rue d'Ulm. There was no room available for this meeting, and we had to set up metal chairs in a hallway. In contrast to these meager resources, the determination of the few participants in attendance was powerful.

I was especially impressed by the welcome Jean gave us, and the trust and deep interest he had in our work from the outset. I had heard of him before, as he had published a number of articles I'd read while studying to be a librarian in the late 1950s. Even today, he continues to closely follow the developments—especially digital ones—at the children's library in Clamart, which is now called La Petite Bibliothèque Ronde. He was well-acquainted with the Anglo-American world as well as public libraries, and was aware of the role that foundations had played in the development of such libraries, particularly in the United States. For all these reasons, our project interested him. He was impressed by my training abroad, especially my work in the United States. He would later tell me that from the first time we'd met, he'd sensed that our library would play a decisive role in terms of innovation. His own project was clear, simple, and ambitious. It was to create a full-fledged movement within the profession and to draw the attention of public authorities and book professionals to how crucial the development of public libraries in France was. In this respect, our country really was behind. His activism was strongly criticized and troubled the ruling authorities, from the ministry to the leaders of professional associations.

I had always admired his generous courage, his lucidity, and his determination. I was struck by his extraordinary erudition, his ability to negotiate politics while always being respectful of others, and the clear vision he had of the transformations that public libraries could provide when truly at the service of all, without exception. He believed that such libraries should find their rightful place within a civilization of leisure, as explored by Joffre Dumazedier and the popular education movements. He admired the association called Peuple et Culture, which at the end of the war had initiated a struggle with the aim of fighting "against cultural inequalities and for the lifelong right to knowledge."

Launching a Major Movement

When I joined La Joie par les Livres in March 1964, I had no idea that I was going to be participating in a vast movement in support of children's libraries. It was necessary to invent just about everything. First of all, there was the matter of preparing the book collections. Lise and I spent a lot of time reading, comparing, and deciding. It wasn't long before Christine joined us. We'd visit some of the large Parisian bookstores, notebooks in hand. At the time, there was nowhere we could go in order to research and read new publications. Fortunately, to create the initial collection we were able to refer to the choices made by the librarians at L'Heure Joyeuse. They'd had the good idea of publishing a small but useful book on the subject: *Beautiful Books, Beautiful Stories (Beaux livres, belles histoires)*. But that wasn't enough.

We needed to know about the latest releases, too, which meant we had to read a lot, discuss, analyze, and write. We also had to put our choices to the test. Well before the library had opened, Lise would go to Clamart every week to meet with students at the girls' school. We'd gotten permission from the director, Madame Delpoux, who was generous and trusting. At the back of a classroom, there were a few shelves of books available to the students. This made it possible for us to get to know them and engage with them.

In the mid-1960s, the annual editorial production was nothing like it is today: it consisted of just a few hundred works. We were able to easily decide what was worthy of our attention. Soon, however, we felt the need to work with other librarians.

Before the library had even opened, I sent out a broad call to librarians in France and abroad: "Come work with us. We'll examine new publications together. We need to pool our experiences and think together about the delicate matter of choosing books." Only a few dozen responded. This came as no surprise, given that children didn't have much of a place in libraries at the time. These librarians come from all over France. They worked in municipal libraries of various sizes or else in educational institutions. All were quite motivated and agreed to meet with us in our Paris office every month. All of them, without exception, were in constant contact with children. This is what was important to me. Each of them could refer to their own experience as an intermediary. Unlike many librarians, they weren't satisfied with just indiscriminately purchasing the books—one copy of each—listed in the children's book section of the Bibliographie de la France. They wanted to make a real selection that took the children and the quality of the books into consideration.

We were able to easily obtain free works as "review copies." I'd gotten help from Myriem Foncin, the chief curator of the Maps and Plans Department (Département des cartes et plans) of the BnF. She was the first woman to have such a high level of responsibility at this venerable institution. She oversaw a modest bibliographic newsletter produced for small libraries and offered to give us with the children's books she received from publishers. She was interested in the social role played by small libraries and in how their staffs were trained and informed. This is why she immediately showed support for La Joie par les Livres. Unlike most of her colleagues at large libraries, she had traveled extensively and had spent a lot of time in the United States. This was a rarity among library curators, who didn't travel much.

We set to work with enthusiasm. Myriem would sometimes participate in our meetings, where we would analyze and compare new works. It was really enriching and everyone left even more motivated to be attentive, in our daily work of recommending works, to how the children reacted.

An Original Publication

We were at the start of our reflection and writing phase and were well aware of our shortcomings. Nonetheless, we decided to publish a bulletin of our analyses of children's books (*Bulletin d'analyses de livres pour enfants*), which came out the day before the Clamart library opened. These two actions were therefore closely linked. As soon as the bulletin was released, I got a call from a particularly discerning editor, Tatiana Rageot, who had created and directed, together with her husband, the excellent collection "Les Heures joyeuses." She called to tell me how much she appreciated knowing how the books she had published were doing and that children tended to enjoy them. What encouragement for our humble work!

In the mid-1960s, we had just one office in the Montparnasse district. For this reason, we prepared the first issues of our publication in Clamart. Later, whoever was in charge of our publication would set up shop in a small Parisian apartment. At first, this was Geneviève Le Cacheux and later it was Simone Lamblin. Little by little, issue by issue, the modest bulletin became what was known as *The Revue of Books for Children* (*La Revue des livres pour enfants*), which is published today by the BnF. Our publication soon had an audience that did not just include professionals and researchers who specialized in books and reading. It also reached many parents, educators, journalists, and doctors.

We had not yet moved to Clamart when I received a long letter from Geneviève Le Cacheux, a librarian in Caen. She had heard about our project and wanted to meet me. I was surprised to learn that Geneviève and I had, without knowing each other, followed a similar trajectory. We had both chosen to be children's librarians. We had undergone the senior librarian training for future curators of large libraries. We had both worked in the United States—she for a brief time in Cleveland, and I for a longer time in New York. We also shared a personality trait: stubbornness. This was how an inspector general of libraries had characterized us. Since we both had advanced degrees as librarians and were also qualified as curators, he had tried everything he could to get us involved in what he considered more prestigious career paths, such as in university libraries or large classified libraries, but we had both remained deaf to his proposals. One day, exasperated, he finally told Geneviève Le Cacheux, "You are as stubborn as Geneviève Patte." This is why she wanted to meet me. Later, she joined our small team and directed our publications but unfortunately, it was for too short a time. For family reasons she returned to her hometown, where she took leadership of the remarkable Caen Municipal Library. At the time it was a very exceptional library and gave unusual attention to children. For a long time, we were the only children's librarians to hold positions as library directors. It is still quite rare, even in present-day France, to see curators who primarily focus on children's books working at the head of municipal networks.

Required Reading about Children's Literature

Publishing analyses and advising librarians about their selection processes was a great responsibility, and we were well aware of this. As novice analysts, we soon felt the need for more training, so we organized meetings in the cramped quarters of our Parisian office and asked Isabelle Jan, a great connoisseur of children's literature, to hold informal discussions with us. She began with Andersen—what a great start. Later, in the 1970s, Isabelle worried about how little value was placed on children's literature. She recalled that "someone reading *Babar* for the first time has an experience just as enthralling and unique as someone reading *The Brothers Karamazov* for the first time. With children's literature, it's important not to focus on whether it's literature or not, but the fact that it's children's literature; it is this specific character that makes it interesting and gives it its dignity."⁹ Later on, we would have to find large spaces to host lecture series, which all kinds of people would attend. Series editors, booksellers, journalists, parents, and teachers all showed interest. For years, the Bibliothèque Forney in the Marais district hosted us and we always had a full house.

From the Bathtub to the BnF

From the very inception of our little publication, I'd had plans to develop documentation resources and make them widely accessible to all who had an interest in children's books. Widely—that seemed pretty ambitious! Our space was small—just a one-bedroom apartment with the books piling up on a few shelves and even in the bathtub. This is how it all began. What started in a bathroom is now an extensive documentation center at the Bibliothèque nationale de France with the proud title, "National Center for Children's Literature" ("Centre national de littérature pour jeunesse"). To tell the truth, I had to come up with this name years ago at the last minute. It was a matter of being recognized by the City of Science and Industry (Cité des sciences et de l'industrie) in the Parc de la Villette. The name "La Joie par les Livres" didn't sound serious enough. But with its new name, our institution was taken into consideration. La Villette then asked us to take charge of the creation of the children's section in its media library.

Organization was required to choose books, to compare and contrast different points of view. It was necessary to get to know the books, to leaf through them to our hearts' content. Lise and I had experienced the irritation—entirely justified—of certain booksellers in the Latin Quarter when we lingered for hours, handling the books and taking notes for possible orders. All of this was not very comfortable and our approach remained superficial. We had to organize ourselves, therefore, to make the books we received available to all, together with the analyses, which were made primarily by the librarians who worked closely with children.

---

9. Isabelle Jan, *La Littérature enfantine*, Éditions de l'Atelier, 1985.

It was up to each of our visitors to then decide what was best suited to their library and their readers.

Our preliminary documentation library in the Montparnasse district remained modest, but the first seeds had been sown. I will always regret that, due to the lack of land to build on, it was not possible for us to house it close to the Clamart library. This would have been a wonderful site for investigation and daily observation, of interest to researchers and educators.

In fact, I did not want to limit myself to assessing books. I also wanted to see how children experienced the reading material and what relationships it could produce: relationships between the young readers and books, people, and the world. In this respect, the observations made by the facilitators who worked closely with the children were invaluable.

October 1, 1965

Let's return to the Clamart library. It was built in the heart of the *cité* of La Plaine on the Petit-Clamart plateau. It was a charming district. There was nothing dull about the brick buildings situated amidst green spaces with gracefully curved paths winding through them. There were no big towers at that time, but there weren't any community facilities either. For months, idle children followed the progress at the construction site. Truth be told, there wasn't a lot going on in this *cité*. There was nothing to encourage children's recreational activities other than the Catholic parish youth club. Otherwise, apart from the school, there was no place to meet. The case was the same for the adult population: there wasn't even a café. Just one noisy, sad shopping center. The shopkeepers didn't like the children and teens coming there to hang out. "They're always up to no good." The *cité* of La Plaine was working-class, with a large foreign-born population. At that time, there were also a few housing units for the employees of nearby companies. A few steps away was the "Million" *cité*, which was presented to us as "a development for welfare cases." We were told that families in great difficulty were grouped together there. This *cité* had been built on a low budget after the war to accommodate inhabitants who had come from the slums.[10]

Where to go to find something to read? There was only one news kiosk in the shopping center. It had newspapers, magazines, and just a few books—far fewer than in a train station bookshop. I went to meet the man in charge of it, and he didn't hide his irritation. We were stepping on his toes, after all, since what he was selling would be free at the library! But later, he would pay us a visit to let us know that ever since the library opened, he'd never had so many patrons.

"What are they making for us here?" asked the children who were following the construction. "A swimming pool?" We answered that no, it would be a library. "What's a library?" The word evoked at best a few shelves of books in the back of a classroom at the girls' school. "Do we need a whole building for that?" When we tried to explain to the children what they would find there, one child asked hopefully, "So Zorro will be there?" In the front window of the bakery, there were some books and posters to give them more precise information. The big day—October 1, 1965—was fast approaching.

On the eve of the opening, at nightfall, a bunch of serious people who seemed authorized to enter the library appeared. Who were they? We had just enough time to hide the brooms and rags so as to give them a proper welcome. They were journalists. Without skipping a beat, Anne asked me to tell them about the library and our projects. I was taken by surprise. "It's a press conference," she explained. This was intimidating. All lit up, the library certainly was gorgeous. Of course, I have no recollection of my impromptu remarks. I only remember insisting that we wanted to include books that would speak to children in all ways—to their interests, their curiosities, and their desires. There would be books on all subjects, I said, and workshops as well. I referred to our cookbooks by way of example. They could test them out in our kitchen. This was a unique vision for a library and the journalists were impressed by their visit. It was surprising to find such an original and beautiful

---

10. This *cité* was torn down in the early 2000s due to unsafe living conditions.

place in a neglected suburban development and the national press was buzzing about it the following day. Soon after, there was coverage from the international press as well. *Life* magazine put us on its cover to go along with a remarkable photo reportage by Martine Franck. One of her photos made its way around the world and is still famous. It has symbolic value, showing the perfect, clean spiral of the staircase with children's faces. I still remember their names. The staircase was worthy of *Alice in Wonderland* and did in fact lead to a locked door. Beyond the glazed pane was the terrace with its beautiful gray pebbles. It was like the beach there up on the roof, like being on vacation! The architects had decided to do this so that the neighbors who had a view of the library from their windows would be able to see it. It was in the center of the city, amidst the red of the buildings and beneath the blue of the sky, and surrounded by the green of the grass and trees.

I remember what it was like when Martine was there. She stayed with us for a few days, shortly after the opening of the library. She was preparing what was to be her first photo reportage. I can picture her long silhouette. Like the children, she was in her socks. As she moved discreetly from room to room, she was dignified and silent. Like many of our visitors, she respected the quiet atmosphere. I likewise remember the silent presence of Édouard Boubat, who also produced a beautiful photographic essay.

The UNESCO Bulletin featured the library on its cover and also dedicated longer articles to it. Later it was *Reader's Digest*, whose journalists impressed me with their professionalism. There were no rushed reports that only covered what could be sensationalized. The reporter stayed for days and days to observe and ask questions of each member of the team as well as some children. He participated in our lives, as did the filmmaker Marc Allégret. The television crews were constantly asking us for information. Word traveled all over the world. Shortly after the opening, I met a Peruvian student who was passing through Paris. To my great astonishment, he already knew about the library. In Lima, he had seen the film about Clamart, widely distributed in the French cultural centers.

Authorities in the French library world were offended by the amount of press that the children's library received. Wasn't it shocking that such an institution, which had emerged outside the system of traditional public libraries, got so much media attention? In their eyes, it was simply outrageous.

A Crowd of Children in Socks

The library opened its doors on the first Thursday of October 1965. A crowd of children waited, desperate to finally discover what had been hidden behind fencing for so long. The area around the building was not finished. It had rained a lot the day before, and the ground around it was really muddy. So, could we let the children in? "No," the architect said firmly. It would be too hard on the beautiful cork floors.

"Yes," we said. "But in socks."

"No problem," said the children. "We'll take off our shoes." And so they entered…

The children thought that in every library in France and beyond, it was normal for readers to take off their shoes. Years later, when they discovered the library in a nearby neighborhood, they were surprised to see readers entering the reading rooms with their shoes on. But this practice didn't bother them in the slightest; on the contrary. One former patron told us that it was of great help in gliding across the floors. Some visitors who were ready to admire all that we did thought this was a rule we had worked out in advance. According to them, the children could get weak from reading so much, and it was good for them to feel the ground beneath their feet. We simply kept it as a practice because the children had no problem with it. They would come to the library out of breath, remove their shoes, and feel a little bit as if they were at home.

And so they entered the library in their stocking feet. How could I forget their amazement as they discovered this world of joyful colors before them, so different from the sad, ugly, and slapdash buildings of the school where they spent a good portion of their days. The library's architecture served as a symbol in the *cité*: a symbol, in the heart of everyday life just a stone's throw from the shopping center, of something different. The beautiful light gray color of the concrete walls stood out against the red of the brick houses. This building was a visible gesture, an invitation to enter another reality, something that offered a change from the regular day-to-day: the place was simultaneously new and familiar, and central to a form of community life. And with reading, it could open itself up to a person's innermost core.

There were a thousand ways to approach this place, many of which had not been anticipated. There was the pleasure of scaling the library, as if climbing a tree, with the added pleasure of transgression. Yet another possibility was offered by reading: the unpunished transgression. "I want a book about children who do a lot of stupid things. Things we don't dare do in real life."

It was wonderful to witness how the children responded to this unexpected gift—their joy, surprise, astonishment, and pride. This beautiful, round, bright, and warm home offered itself to them with open arms. As soon as they stepped inside, they drank it all in and felt encouraged to explore the riches of a whole new world.

At the library's opening, the children came in droves, restless and jostling each other behind the door. Surely all the kids from the *cité* had come. The door was finally thrown open and they rushed into the entrance hall, quickly removing their shoes so they could head straight to the reading rooms. And there, their attitude changed. There was no shouting, no fussing; they were apparently quite moved, and I'm tempted to say they were showing their respect and admiration for this place. There was a certain level of commotion, of course, but no shouting: a kind of quiet reigned, as is normally expected in a library. From the start, they had the right attitude. The children were touched by how welcome we'd made them feel, as if they were guests we were happy to have brought into our home. We'd given them beauty and we'd given them our trust; they were eager to show their parents, and some went to fetch them, pulling them in by the hand. "Quickly, quickly! Come and see how beautiful it is. And it's for us."

Everything Is Beautiful Here

The shelves were finished with light-colored wood and filled with books of all colors. Meanwhile, in the girls' school and the old municipal library, the few books grouped on metal shelves were covered with paper or had dark bindings; they were all the same. There was no comparison with the Bibliothèque des enfants in Clamart, where everything was beautiful and simple.

Here, the furniture was not graceless; but rather, it was made of nice-smelling pale wood, with seats and tables in muted colors, plus chairs in large, medium, and small sizes, as if to accommodate Goldilocks' three bears. There was also the option to stretch out on the honey-colored cork floor. In this library, which was the size of a house, everyone could make themselves comfortable.

The furniture was Scandinavian, from Finland. It was designed by the famous architect Alvar Aalto. Anne had made this decision, together with the architects from the Atelier de Montrouge. Designed in 1935, this furniture fit in perfectly with our library, and fifty years after the opening, it's still there and in good shape. It's withstood the visits of many children, including some who were quite boisterous. At the architects' request, Aalto even designed some of the furniture specifically for Clamart. I later had the opportunity to admire libraries in Finland and Germany that he'd designed and furnished. I went to Rovaniemi in Finland, which is very close to the Arctic Circle and has such short winter days, to admire this luminous architecture. At home, in Clamart, I also enjoyed the natural light that illuminated the library from all sides, as well as the refreshing green of the foliage in the garden. The library was especially attractive when it was all lit up and viewed from the street at nightfall. It made passersby want to enter this place where life seemed to be so good. They could see children and adults alike, all busy in their own way, and imagine joining them. It makes me think of a wanderer in a fairy tale who, having lost their way in the forest, sees a well-lit house amidst the trees and takes hope. They dream of stopping there, of rapping on the window so someone will open the door; of enjoying the solace of a warm welcome and finding a place amidst generous, convivial company. The wanderer would then regain their strength to continue on their journey. This is more or less what the library was all about.

This was the first time a library just for children had been created in France. Every architectural detail was designed to create a place for reading. The clever alternation between the thick walls and the large windows overlooking the *cité* evoked reading itself: there was interiority, silence, and reflection, but also a view onto the world. Children had complete freedom to move from one room to another. They could wander, make chance discoveries, be surprised. The arrangement of the rooms facilitated this fluidity, encouraging children to walk around, open to new possibilities; this is what was needed to discover a book or a subject that could unexpectedly capture one's attention.

The materials were beautiful and honest. There was no infantilizing cuteness but rather pale wood, concrete, flooring made of terracotta and cork, and solid, elegant Finnish furniture. This solidity was welcome. It provided a secure base for diving into fascinating books that took readers on distant journeys, like Leon Garfield's *Black Jack* or John Meade Falkner's *Moonfleet*.

Madame Pêtre

We quickly realized that we needed someone to greet the children as they left their coats and shoes in the entrance area, so we posted a small announcement in the bakery: "The library is looking for a mother from the *cité* to greet the children." The woman who came was Madame Pêtre, a grandmother.

And so for decades children and their parents were always sure to find Madame Pêtre at the entrance. Generations of children got to know her, and she'd remain a fixture in their memories. She was there faithfully every day when school got out to greet the children and assist them. She had an important role. Since she lived in the *cité*, everybody knew her. People ran into her at the shopping center. For parents, it was reassuring to know that she was in the library. For children, it was wonderful to have someone who was ready to listen and tell stories to them after school, like an attentive grandmother. She came from North Africa, where storytelling can be a great source of pleasure. She didn't mind getting them into line, like in the good old days. Occasionally, she would sew on a button or mend torn clothing. She was also happy to talk to the parents when they'd take the time to sit and talk. In winter, Madame Pêtre was always there in the dimly lit hall. There was a lamp on her table that provided light for the odd jobs that kept her busy. It was the very image of comforting intimacy, as in a home. The children felt expected, welcomed. It was a simple pleasure. Coming back from school to find the house empty can be hard to bear, and children will automatically turn on the television or switch on a tablet or video game in order to feel less lonely. There at the library, it was different.

We would sometimes get visits from former readers who'd undoubtedly come to revisit something from their childhoods. One afternoon, I saw a few young people in their twenties arrive. As they came in, they were jostling each other a little, giggling, and seemed somewhat unruly. I was on my guard. So often today, we worry about groups storming in, determined to "mess things up." But this wasn't the case. They asked for news about Madame Pêtre, Wahed, Zaima, Aline, Juliette... It was as if they were reuniting with their family after a prolonged absence. They also talked about the stunts they'd pulled: "We gave you a really hard time," they said, with a touch of regret. Then they shyly asked, "Could we look at the books we loved when we were kids?" And then these big guys quietly took their places around a big table to leaf through some of their childhood storybooks, including *Goldilocks and the Three Bears, Sylvester and the Magic Pebble, Good Friends, Zeralda's Ogre,* and *Where the Wild Things Are.* These were positive memories of childhood that remained, through thick and thin, within reach. It's amazing to see how a child's first literary experiences, as they should be properly called, remain precious to the very core, no matter what difficulties one has encountered in life. There is true culture there. It reminds me of the old peasants I've met who, at the end of their lives, have taken great pleasure in reciting the fables of La Fontaine and other poems they learned by heart during their brief time at school. This is the power of these childhood readings, in all of their simplicity, their complexity, and their immediacy.

Do As You Like Here

At the library, children could count on having all kinds of interactions with other kids of all ages, but also with adults who welcomed their questions and requests. Where else in the *cité* could they get this kind of reception and stay as long as they wanted, enjoying the pleasure of not being alone, of being free to do nothing amidst people who were reading, bustling about, or chatting? And if they felt like it, they could join a small group or dive into a book.

Children could stay for hours if that's what they wanted: to read entire novels, to get lost in dictionaries, to explore large atlases, to read tales, to group around comic books and mangas, to look at beautiful art books or works of non-fiction, or to do research for school. And today, they can also access video games or consult the Internet in countless different ways.

With the Littlest Ones

From an early age, children would make themselves at home there quite naturally, and could find their way around with ease. I would see them making their way towards the books. First, they'd find the beloved storybooks they already knew. In this respect, they had a kind of culture from very early on. Then they'd ask, "Can you read me a book?" I'd start to read with one of them and others would take interest and approach. Many listened with a storybook tucked under their arm, waiting their turn to offer up their suggestion. They would in fact worry that the time for shared reading would end too quickly. It was then up to them to decide who would sit closest to me. Most children wanted to sit in my lap or snuggle up alongside me. This was so they could see the pages better but also turn the pages, make a comment, or point out something that was surprising, amusing, or similar to something from their own life.

The youngest of the children, new to this world, would tell me in their own way, with innocence and intensity, how much pleasure they took in the smallest things. The extreme concentration on their faces as they attempted to decipher the images was a sight to behold. They would bend over a page to closely examine a detail that they found interesting or intriguing. They wanted to savor every detail, no matter how minute it might have seemed to us, of this world they were exploring. Gaston Bachelard referred to these as "immense details."

Because toddlers don't yet know how to read in the usual sense of the word, I had to pay closer attention to them. I would take the time to suggest books, read to them, listen to them, and observe them. Forcing their development was the farthest thing from my mind. On the contrary, it was a matter of letting them savor the wonderfully gratuitous pleasure of their first encounters with books, pictures, and stories to their heart's content, before the stress of early schooling set in. Of course, the youngest children don't read like we do, but they certainly do read. In place of the typographical characters, they proudly identify the clues that give meaning to the story. Adults, on the other hand, seem more attentive to the structure of a story. When adults and children read together, this can only make for a more enriching experience.

Regarding this matter, I always like to refer to *Mouse Tales*. In this little book, Arnold Lobel presents a beautiful metaphor with the walks that Very Tall Mouse and Very Short Mouse take together. As children and adults, aren't we like these two mice going for a stroll? As they are out walking, the two mice share their respective discoveries with each other—what's high in the air for Very Tall Mouse, and what's low to the ground for Very Short Mouse. "Very Tall Mouse would say, 'Hello Birds.' And Very Short Mouse would say, 'Hi bugs.' When they passed by a garden, Very Tall Mouse would say, 'Hello flowers.' And Very Short Mouse would say, 'Hello roots.' [...] Soon the storm was over. The two friends ran to the window. Very Tall Mouse held Very Short Mouse up to see. 'Hello rainbow!' they both said together."[11] Then, for the first time, both of them saw the same thing at the same time.

I liked the idea of these two friends following the same path, each receptive to what surrounds them, attentive to what the other one sees and says, and then looking both looking through the window, contemplating the world with amazement. It's a beautiful vision of what it means to read together. It shows the importance of the exchanges between the child who listens and the adult who gives them their full attention and thus helps them to rise up and learn about the world. As an adult, the child's gaze awakens in me a forgotten childhood and, for the time being, puts me at the child's level, "on the same page" as them. The child enjoys the pleasure of having an adult who is ready to take an interest in and even be moved by what comes from the child's world—an adult who can be silent at times so as not to disturb the thrill of the discovery with untimely interventions. It is truly a wonder, this confluence of two perspectives that delight in the richness of the world around us. Isn't this the expression of authentic cultural experience?

This confident and reassuring intimacy is part of the enjoyment. In the library, there were no children sitting quietly in rows or circles. To really dive into a story, you have to be able to settle in comfortably. How wonderful it is to be lulled by the voice of the adult who is telling the story. I was reading *Rasmus and the Vagabond*, a novel by Astrid Lindgren about an orphan and a kind-hearted vagabond, to a small group of enthralled children aged between eight and ten. A four-year-old girl was sitting comfortably on my lap. She seemed to be listening with pleasure. What could she possibly understand about this story for grown-ups? I asked her, "Is this interesting?"

Her answer was clear: "I like grown-ups' voices."

This was often how the little ones would become acquainted with the library-home, an exceptional place where they belonged, where children of all ages were mixed together, and where their curiosity was on the

---

11. Arnold Lobel, *Mouse Tales*, Harper Collins, 1978, 26–31.

alert. Reading can truly blossom when there is simplicity and trust. The little ones knew they could do just as the older ones did, and liked it when they'd take the time to be with them and read them a story. They saw them participating in all kinds of activities, all kinds of events.

A Place of Beginnings

To borrow a book, a child needed a library card, which required registration. Children needed to perform this act themselves, even if it required the parents' authorization and, whenever possible, their presence. The child was the one who made the decision to become a member of the library. This meant that there was no group registration for a whole class or for a summer camp. The process was not an impersonal administrative formality carried out in a near-mechanical fashion and was never rushed. The child was not a "customer." This unpleasant formula did not apply at the Clamart children's library.

For the registration process, we'd meet at a table in the lending room. We'd get to know each other, and I'd take my time as I spoke with the child one-on-one, quietly and attentively. We didn't ask intrusive questions about whether the child was a good or bad student or a strong or weak reader. We weren't interested in labels or a child's reputation. This was a place of beginnings.

During the registration process, some of the regulars would approach and listen, like curious spectators, embracing the opportunity to add some comments for the newcomer's benefit. Once the formalities were completed, the regular would sometimes offer to show the new child around. In this way, a new arrival would get a personal introduction and feel welcomed by the community of children.

When they signed in for the first time, the child would read aloud a somewhat solemn sentence written in the register: "By writing my name in this book, I become a member of the library. [...] I look forward to participating in the life of the library." Then, the child would write down their name and sign, and they'd be given their reader's card. In a way, this was their first act as a citizen. The card had the value of a contract.

Some learned this the hard way; on occasion, a card was temporarily confiscated. But how many times have former readers passed through and confided that they'd held on to their reader's cards?

During their first interview, the librarian would ask the child: "What do you like? What interests you? What would you like to do in the library? You know we can help you." Right away, the newcomer understood that the librarians were fully available to assist them on an individual basis.

I am endlessly amazed by what interests children. I'm thinking of a mother, one of my close friends, who told me about her little boy, Frédéric, being outraged that his younger sister Florence didn't want to go to school. "But if you never go to class, how will you know who the druids are?" Had this convinced her?

Librarians Always on Their Feet

"I like the library," a child confided to his mother, "because the librarians are always standing." This was a visual reminder of the adults' availability, and it was true: we were always standing, ready to advise with the necessary discretion, to help a child find their way, or to simply listen. We didn't sit behind desks because this would have created distance, whether we wanted it or not, and the library would have run the risk of looking more or less like an administrative unit.

This is what had most impressed me when I discovered the first L'Heure Joyeuse in the late 1950s. I saw Madame Gruny and Madame Leriche standing there, talking to the children and giving their time freely. This relation was precious because it was simultaneously personal and discreet, and centered on reading. It was a matter of working with the child to determine what best matched their experience and their needs and to help them find their way around. Thus, we fostered the awakening of the child's sensibilities and intelligence, their emerging tastes, and they felt the kindly attention of someone who was trying to understand them. Children were acknowledged and deemed capable of appreciating what was beautiful, great, funny, surprising, subtle, and "worthwhile."

Recalling his years spent at the library, a former reader named Dominique confided, "Nobody had ever paid so much attention to me before. Nobody had ever been so interested in me. Thanks to these exchanges, I felt like I existed. I felt important." Our place was always right alongside the children. I can still see Lise or Zaima by the stacks, listening to a child attentively. They'd take all the time required to make reading suggestions and would tell the children a little about them. When a child had finally made up their mind, the librarian would hand them the book in a lovely gesture of offering.

Our small team always tried to break down any barriers that could have complicated interactions. As we were making plans for Clamart, I visited many libraries and noticed that the librarians often worked in their offices or behind the circulation desk, not having any contact with their readers apart from stamping their cards, checking if they had returned their materials on time, or issuing them with a fine if the books were late. Today, tasked with making reports, drawing up statistics, and performing other administrative tasks, some supervisors primarily interact with their computer screens and pay little attention to what the children are experiencing—their questions, their findings, their suggestions.

The Library, a Second Home

In all honesty, there were a thousand ways to experience the library. Some children were just passing through. They'd come to check out materials and enjoy the service that had been made available to them. They wouldn't stay for long. They generally lived far away, in the lower districts of Clamart, and had to rely on their parents to drive them. Others simply didn't feel the desire to participate in the life of the library or didn't have the time. A lot of them had busy schedules. A parent might say, "My child doesn't have time because he's involved in so many activities." On the other hand, there were many others, especially those from the *cité*s, who liked to stay in the library for a long time. It was, in a way, their second home. They felt good there and were happy to find their friends there.

This wasn't just a place to borrow books from, but a place to personally participate in community life. There was a relationship with the children based on reciprocity and this helped build self-esteem, which was needed to venture into reading and discover oneself, others, and different worlds. What a joy for the child to hear: "We need you, your ideas. We are listening to you."

Becoming Curious

The commitment to involve readers in the life of the library was one of the major legacies I got from the first L'Heure Joyeuse. I had been especially fond of this unique form of coexistence. It naturally fosters connections, exchanges, and questions. This is how people get curious; and that is what matters. Without curiosity, how can anyone be interested in reading? How can life be worth living? "I remember," said Michel, a former reader, "that we could come with our ideas. You always tried to realize them in one way or another." Now the director of a theater troupe, he reminded me that he and a few others had suggested putting on little plays based on folk tales, and this had given rise to a theater workshop, which had made a great impression on the children.

Meanwhile, a child named Frédéric had mentioned his passion for geology and mineralogy. On his first visit, he'd sought out books on these subjects and had immediately offered to help complete this area of the collection by suggesting "more scientific" works he'd come across during his visits to the natural history museum. Other children asked to display their own collections. I also remember the contribution of a child of Lebanese descent. After visiting Lebanon on vacation, he returned with a voluminous file he'd made himself, and it found a place among the document files available for the children.

When readers' interests are taken into consideration, the library comes alive. I remember a very simple experiment I conducted when I was in Cali, Colombia. I was leading a week-long course for librarians from different Andean countries who worked in French schools. It took place in a dreary room in a middle school resource center that really just seemed like a storeroom where broken machines and large, faded geography maps had piled up. I seem to recall that there was also a life-size human skeleton. A few students certainly used it occasionally to consult resources for their homework, but nothing beyond that. The librarian had long since given up. I suggested doing something that to me, was just common sense: to hand out blank sheets of paper to the students so they could write down questions and explain what they wanted to find in this place. I still remember how eager they were, and they appeared to be happy and enthusiastic as they were writing. I admired the variety of their questions. One of the teachers I remained in contact with for a long time told me that his students started to behave differently after this simple act revealed that the teachers were open to their questions.

"Can We Help You?"

Right away, the children in Clamart felt responsible for "their" home. Encouraged by the trust we showed in them, they offered to help the library operate smoothly. As soon as it opened, they would come up to us and ask, "Can we help you?" And so, under our watchful eye, they immediately started to run the lending desk, which is so vital to the life of the library. This remains one of the children's cherished responsibilities to this day. It makes them feel very important. It is, as one might suspect, a coveted position. Children would also ask that we give them training, and they demanded a follow-up review; the assistant librarian card had to be earned, just like the job itself. Back then, there was also the delight that came from using the rubber stamps. Because of the Internet, it's different nowadays, but it's still necessary to be welcoming and to punctually observe the "service hours" indicated on a sign.

I remember the surprise of the teachers from the *cité* we'd invited to explore the library shortly after it opened. They were surprised to be greeted by children running the circulation desk. Other children had, with the help of one of the librarians, created a beautiful exhibit on *Around the World in Eighty Days*, which provided an opportunity to follow in the footsteps of Phileas Fogg on his journey. They'd used materials from the library to create "visits" to the different countries. The readers had a little passport with a stamp for each of the countries they traveled to. They also made a model of Fogg's house, based on the descriptions that Verne provided in the book. We displayed the names of those who had collaborated in this beautiful work. This amazed the teachers even more: with a few exceptions, the children were far from the top of the class. Several teachers were delighted to see them there. They were happy, they said, to see their pupils in an unexpected light. These children who were usually at the back of the classroom, were in the forefront there. The library provided them with other ways to give the best of themselves.

Many years later, in a difficult and even violent suburb near Cordoba, Argentina, I admired the attitude of an elderly librarian who had excellent relations with the young people. Most of them had bad reputations in the neighborhood and spent the bulk of their time hanging out on the street. They had taken to this place because they were listened to there, and they felt welcome to contribute, in one way or another, to the life there. These teenagers, whom many people preferred to avoid in the street, received full recognition here. The library news, posted in the entrance hall, always featured the names and photos of those who had been in charge or had simply chipped in. They had found their place in this establishment. They knew that their individuality, their interests, and their questions were all valuable. Can the desire to know, to read, and to participate really arise in those who don't seem to exist for anyone?

Today, in the new libraries, readers are completely autonomous. Thanks to a machine located near the exit, they're able to check out the books and other documents by themselves. With barcodes, it couldn't be easier. To tell you the truth, I miss the good old circulation desks, which have tended to be replaced by these modern devices. They reminded me of French cafés where people take the time to talk to each other while enjoying their morning coffee and discussing the headlines from a newspaper that's spread across the counter. I loved the spontaneous conversations children around the circulation desk, and I learned a lot about their tastes and what could enrich their lives as children or adolescents. There were also the adults who would accompany their children or simply bring back the books borrowed by their children. Their comments also enlightened us.

Charlotte's Web

I remember what a father said to me when he brought back *Charlotte's Web*, E. B. White's veritable masterpiece. He was an academic, and therefore a serious man. He had been personally moved when he'd read it to his children and had been unable to conceal his emotion. He had gotten choked up. I could only imagine how happy the children must have been to have experienced such a story with their father, with someone who had such a good understanding of what moved them and who was also capable of being moved himself.

Charlotte's Web is the amazing story of a deep friendship that develops over the course of the book between a spider and a pig. It begins with a terrible revelation: "'Where's Papa going with the ax?' said Fern to her mother as they were setting the table for breakfast. 'Out to the hoghouse,' replied Mrs. Arable. 'Some pigs were born last night.'"[12] "A rough start for a children's novel," the father had said. It was, indeed, drama erupting into the peaceful happiness of everyday life, a threat of death overshadowing the joy of birth. The little girl and then the unusual spider try to save the pig with the help of their intelligence and their strength.

I'm always happy to see adults who are interested in some of their children's reading material. I remember a mother coming to return a book her daughter had borrowed. "I read it," she told me. "My daughter had insisted that I experience this book that had touched her so deeply. I was also very moved."

---

12. E.B. White, *Charlotte's Web*, (1952; repr. New York: Harper Collins, 2012), 1.

The Infinite Steppe

The morning it happened—the end of my lovely world—I did not water the lilac bush outside my father's study. The time was June 1941 and the place was Vilna, a city in the northeastern corner of Poland. And I was ten years old and took it quite for granted that all over the globe people tended their gardens on such a morning as this.

This is how Esther Hautzig's beautiful autobiographical story begins. Esther is sent to Siberia together with her family. This was where she was to live—or rather, survive—as a deportee, from 1941 to 1945. Every day was a struggle against hunger, cold, and intense heat. But there was such tenderness in her family, courageously keeping its dignity, that Esther faced the difficulties with confidence.

This mother told me that some of the passages had had a profound impact on her. One of them, for example, described the arrival of the vagrant Vanya, with whom they had to share the cramped space of their dilapidated hut.

He was the village beggar and people said he stole. Now the bum was going to live with us? [...] Perhaps this man has a worthy *reason for begging? [...] The next evening, Vanya the bum stood at our open door.*
"May I come in?"
"Of course you may." Mother stood up.[13]

I told this mother that I'd had the opportunity to meet little Esther, now a grandmother living in New York. I'd met her through our friend Emma Cohn, whom the children in the library knew well.

---

13. Esther Hautzig, *The Endless Steppe: Growing Up in Siberia* (1968; repr. New York: Harper Collins, 2018), 135.

Clean Hands

Most of the children took their various commitments seriously. We saw evidence of this a few months after the library opened. There were large patio doors that opened onto the garden. It was a pleasant garden for reading in the summer. They could sneak in through the door or climb over the wall—the children entered the library in all sorts of ways. It was a game for them. But in the evening, everything had to be closed, and this took time. One Saturday night, one of the many doors was accidentally left open. The next day, a Sunday when the library was normally closed, some children noticed and simply pushed the door open. They settled in as usual. Then they went to tell Madame Pêtre, who lived in the neighborhood, about the open door. They knew she had the keys. She came and locked the door and everything was fine. For the children who told us about it, this all seemed to have been a matter of course.

They saw themselves responsible for the library to such a degree that some even offered to clean it up. We put a stop to that right away. The parents were outraged and complained, "Why don't they start by getting their rooms in order!"

Many visitors have expressed admiration for the spontaneous respect the children would show for what they'd been given. To look at the books, for example, they had to have clean hands. That was the rule. The mayor of the town even felt the effects. He told me that when he wanted to look at books his children had borrowed, they demanded that he wash his hands first.

At first, the children accepted the library as a gift deserving of respect. Then they got used to it. When the library was no longer brand-new, we had to find ways to offer something surprising, to create unusual and joyful experiences, as in the earliest days. In the late 1990s, the library welcomed the Japanese artist Katsumi Komagata. Elisabeth Lortic, the librarian who had helped establish his reputation in France, organized his visit. His delicate storybooks were displayed in the library where the children could leaf through them at their leisure, though they were asked to wear white gloves while turning the pages. In Japan, it was common for cab drivers and railroad workers to wear such gloves. I was impressed to see how easily and quickly some of the children from the *cité* adopted this Japanese-style protocol. I saw them turning the pages slowly, carefully. In a kind of reverie, they respectfully contemplated these exceptional works. There was no doubt: this surprising opportunity made the children feel respected. In a public interview, Tomi Ungerer, a free spirit if ever there was one, spoke at length to praise respect in its many forms. For him, it was essential. With Komagata's works, these children were given such an opportunity for admiration.

There are many other experiences that come to mind. In the spring of 2008, we had a beautiful exhibition of old and contemporary Korean publications. The man behind the exhibition, a publisher and connoisseur of the art world named Ho Baek Lee, had come with one of his main artists. For one week, they devoted themselves to setting up the exhibition, which was arranged on beautiful board displays. Everything was rather fragile and yet everything was within reach. The library was going through a difficult time due to a threat of permanent closure. The older readers were occasionally aggressive. These young people, who usually came as troublemakers, were attentive and full of respect for what was being offered. Was it because they had enjoyed the presence of the artists at work?

Savoring Silence

Respect manifests itself in many different ways. In the early years of the library, a small sign on the door to the room for the older children warned that it was "reserved for silent readers." We thought that silence would be truly appreciated in a place for reading. It is a real pleasure to read while being surrounded by others who are focused, absorbed in their own books.

In the library, the children actually observed a form of silence spontaneously. Of course, in the circulation room there was always some chatter and occasional chasing, but nobody really yelled loudly. Former readers tell me how much they appreciated the fact that the librarians never raised their voices and how they liked the absence of noise and commotion. There was no need to shout—what mattered was just being able to talk to each other. People spoke quietly, and that was enough to be heard. The world of reading is not one of a domineering order. It is in the realm of privacy and of trust.

Everybody of all ages always liked the toddler reading room. Why was this? Was it because it was at something of a remove, and cozier? Because it was the place for storybooks, which everyone enjoys exploring? Because it was possible to shut oneself away in there? Doors had to be added in order to protect the little ones from invasions, occasionally noisy, from the bigger kids. A lightweight curtain protected them from prying eyes. All this was in the purest tradition of reading, its necessary privacy, and even its hidden side. It was the dream of the small, secret room where the imagination could run free of disruptions, hidden from others' eyes thanks to the curtain you just had to push aside to enter into a world of make-believe, like C.S. Lewis's Narnia.

Bringing together Books and Theater

The library regulars knew they could visit the basement, a labyrinth with multiple doors leading to the librarians' offices as well as to a studio where the children could work. Most importantly, there was a beautiful storytelling room with a fireplace. There were all kinds of events and shows there. Sometimes there were intimate gatherings with an adult who would animate a discussion. It could also become a theater in the round for shows the children would put on with help from artists. This began shortly after the opening in Clamart when Catherine Dasté, granddaughter of the great Jacques Copeau, had come as a friend. She had just staged *The Magic Tree, Jerome and the Turtle* (*L'arbre sorcier, Jérôme et la tortue*), which was the only play written by children to be produced by Le Théâtre du Soleil. We'd been there. That was in March 1968, at the Cirque de Montmartre. This outing had not been like the usual school outings. No big groups. We'd gone as a family—better yet, as a big family of willing participants. It was a dream for the children to leave the *cité* and go to Paris, which was actually not that far away. Yet most of the children in our city had never seen the Eiffel Tower. Taking the bus was a production unto itself. Until December 2014, the *cité* was served poorly by public transportation. Now a tramway connects it to Paris. This is fortunate, because in these suburban *cité*s, which are too frequently isolated, there is the risk of just going around in circles, of getting stifled, of lacking perspective.

The theater workshop made an impact on our young readers—one that was really strong, judging by what some of them have said about it. I'm thinking of one in particular, Michel Albertini: the library had awakened in him his lifelong vocation. As had been the case with some of the children in the library, it began with the simple desire to act out certain Grimm or Perrault tales or even some stories from the novels of the Comtesse de Ségur. But there was no need to stop there. At the library, we acknowledged children's desires while helping them to take it one step further, to distance themselves from the clichés, from what is commonly found on television and elsewhere. It was important to give them a taste for truth and beauty.

Reading and theater were thus a good mix at the Clamart library. Looking at some of the old photos from a theatrical performance at the first L'Heure Joyeuse, I could make out a young Jean Anouilh next to a little Charles Aznavour. As with our dear Michel Albertini, was that was where they had discovered their vocation, where they had taken their first steps as artists?

I remember my meeting with Jean-Louis Barrault. His theater was in the old d'Orsay train station, which I would drive past every day in my little 2CV. I suspected that some of the large spaces at the station were unoccupied, and since I was looking for somewhere to house our Parisian offices, I decided to meet the owner. I went to see him with Simone Lamblin, who had been the one to organize the meeting. It was absolutely unforgettable. First we enjoyed how beautiful it was on the top floor of the station, and the magnificent view over the Seine. I told him about our work and of my desire to find a place there for La Joie par les Livres, which at that time occupied a dilapidated room on the Rue de Louvois that belonged to the BnF. He was immediately captivated by the idea. I can still hear his words: "Yes, we're going to get married. We're going to marry the theater and the children's book." When I returned, Madeleine Renaud was there and this idea of marriage did not please her at all. It was an impossible marriage. So I had to leave again in search of another place for us to establish ourselves.

Ulysse, Alice, Oh hisse

As a consolation, the Cultural Intervention Fund (Fonds d'Intervention Culturelle) offered me a great location: the municipal bathhouse and the building next door on the large square where the Centre Pompidou was to open. Its general management was enthusiastic about the idea. For me, it was a dream location with popular, high-quality art accessible to children and families, and books from all over the world that were easily accessible. What more could I have asked for? It seemed that all my efforts were going to pay off, but unfortunately with a change in minister, I had to forget about this possibility. There was confusion at the Centre Pompidou. Jean-Pierre Seguin, founder and director of the Public Information Library (Bibliothèque publique d'information), suggested that I organize a comprehensive exhibition devoted to children's books. It was inaugurated in 1978 with the name "Ulysse, Alice, Oh hisse." The Pompidou Center had just opened, attracting great crowds, and I was told that there were more than 200,000 visitors for our exhibition. It took place in an enormous space, a large pit at the very entrance of the center that has since been covered over. Organizing a guided tour of an exhibition of books was not a simple matter and would have required an army of librarians ready to present the books on display. This wasn't feasible, so I made do with a jukebox. A beautiful one in a local restaurant had caught my eye and gotten me thinking. So we had our jukebox and I asked our storytellers, Bruno de La Salle and Muriel Bloch, to use it to record the book presentations we had prepared.

The little ones had a place of their own at the immense Centre Pompidou. At the entrance to the exhibition, there was a huge, illuminated image of Hulul, Arnold Lobel's little owl, to greet visitors. He set the tone. Hulul in his bed, distressed to see that there were there were two strange bumps under his blanket. They scared him, and Hulul couldn't sleep. From the outset, it was clear that to fully enjoy the exhibition, it was necessary to return to one's childhood.

Stories were given pride of place. Bruno de La Salle was working on his masterful interpretation of the *Odyssey*. Muriel was in the early stages of her storytelling career. Members of the Golden Age association (association L'Âge d'or)—retired people with grandchildren I had presented storybooks to sometime before—were making their debuts as storytellers in our exhibition. I admired those who had no fear of telling stories amidst all the noise and bustle. There was a very dignified gentleman in his 80s wearing a three-piece suit who was strolling through the rather impersonal space. He appeared perfectly comfortable telling a story to anyone who would listen. In the "House of Telling," one could go to listen to storytellers such as Nacer Khemir, who had just published *The Tales of the Ogress (Les Contes de l'ogresse)*, stories of horrible witches who devour their daughters in a Tunisian setting and that is not so different from that of Shakespeare; or Pierre Gripari, a genius storyteller and the author of the unforgettable collection called *Tales of the Rue Broca (Contes de la rue Broca)*, with includes the hilarious story of the witch of the broom closet, which continues to delight children to this day.

Nurturing Children with Stories

In those days, there wasn't much storytelling in libraries. Now, in all the libraries' annual reports, storytime has its place. A storyteller is invited, and it's a celebration. It has its rituals. Like a show or a painting one is invited to admire. It takes place in a separate room, where the children are asked to sit quietly and listen. Storytime has its specific setting. I always thought it was good to take it further, to wander through the library and go outside to rejoin the world of the suburbs. Then it would take on a different tone. We had to have a thousand stories up our sleeves. Librarians would come up with impromptu stories, almost as if they were making rapid sketches, all throughout the library. In this way, children were given unexpected stories, and they took great pleasure in them. Nurturing children with stories was one of our tasks.

This was why the library decided one year to organize a weekly storytelling hour with the entire team. Storytelling was everyone's concern, no matter what role they played in the library. It was just as it had been in certain households long ago, when everybody participated in the sharing and exchange of stories. The principle of this initiative was based on emulation: as more stories are listened to and more stories are told, the desire to know more stories and to know the stories better becomes stronger. Thus, every Wednesday at lunchtime, librarians, secretaries, storekeepers, and service personnel were all invited to tell and exchange stories that they wanted to share with the children.

Telling Stories Anywhere, at Any Time

When we would leave the library, storytelling and reading aloud quite naturally found their place in areas where there were a lot of people. Wahed Allouche was an excellent librarian-storyteller and was familiar with many tales, including those of the *Thousand and One Nights*. He would often accompany me alongside the sandbox or, when the weather forced us to, right into people's houses. We'd take the time to tell a story, just as we had out on the street, but this time in someone's home.

The repertoire of another Clamart librarian, Marie-Isabelle Merlet, was also very extensive. I liked the way she'd go about it: she'd tell a story at any moment, especially Grimm's tales and tales from the Jewish tradition as exemplified by Isaac Bashevis Singer and the French storyteller Ben Zimet. She'd tell a story because the occasion seemed appropriate, or because she had just discovered a story and felt like telling it. She could be standing in the middle of the room, around a table, or anywhere else. She'd start with one listener and others would soon follow, like curious passersby driven by curiosity and the desire to listen, even though some didn't attend the traditional storytime because they thought they were too old. This was an especially rich experience for the teenagers who were sometimes reluctant to read but who could develop an appetite for stories in this way.

This informal way of telling stories was similar to the approach taken with younger children around picture books; at any time, and depending on their availability, the librarians would take the time to sit down and show or read a storybook to one or two little ones, and a small group of interested children would form very quickly.

A librarian must be a storyteller. The author Daniel Pennac firmly believes this and tells librarians how good it would be to hear them tell visitors lost in the "forest of possible reading choices" of their favorite novels, that in so working their magic, the books will fly off the bookshelves into patrons' hands.[14]

I've seen this mode of presentation, both informal and enticing, practiced admirably in New York, at L'Heure Joyeuse, and also in Clamart, by librarians who were happy to share a good book. It is, after all, the very basis of our profession. In the morning, as the members of the team arrived, sometimes I could see that some of them were excited: They'd just discovered a masterpiece and were eager to share it with us and, of course, with the children. I remember one of them hadn't even taken off her coat before starting to tell us about the book she'd just finished reading. It was *The Silver Crown* by Robert O'Brien.

> *She had known all along that she was a queen, and now the crown proved it. It was the first thing she saw when she opened her eyes; it lay beside her on the pillow, shinier than silver [...] She got out of bed, stood in front of the mirror, and put it*

---

14. Daniel Pennac, *Comme un roman*, Gallimard, 1992; published in English as *Reads Like a Novel*.

on her head [...] It did not occur to her to wonder from whom it had come; she was merely aware that it was hers by right.[15]

A Corner of the Garden

In Clamart, there was a fireplace, like in the good old days. We would recreate the atmosphere of hearthside gatherings and intone the magic formula: "Once upon a time..." The librarians told stories, as did visitors. I remember one friend of the library, Denise Basdevant, who had lived in Romania for a long time and had written a collection of Romanian stories. In the finest tradition of Central Europe, she told enchanting tales of devils alongside the crackling fire. She was accompanied by the Polish illustrator Josef Wilkon. With broad strokes on white sheets of paper, he created demons that leapt before the children's eyes.

The storytelling room opened wide onto the garden. The rustic door of the large surrounding wall irresistibly evoked the mystery of Frances Hodgson Burnett's *Secret Garden*. Here, there were magnificent changes in season, with the gold of the gingko in autumn and sometimes snow in winter. Former readers remember how much they loved to sit in the garden over the summer vacations. There were luminous moments, they tell us, when they completely forgot the *cité*, which was dull during the summer months because there was nothing going on there. For them, the garden further accentuated the sense of homeyness. The Japanese look of it encouraged calm; the niches in the wall made it possible to sequester oneself to read undisturbed. There was even a small corner of the garden for some vegetables. Parents and grandparents originally from rural areas had given their advice, all too happy to contribute to their children's second home. That summer, I saw children leave with books and lettuce under their arms. This was culture in all its forms! Today, children still tend this corner of the garden. They take it very seriously and go to see what's being done in the community garden in

---

15. Robert C. O'Brien, *The Silver Crown*, (1968, repr. New York: Aladdin, 2001), 1–2.

a nearby neighborhood, Pavé Blanc. And later, they celebrate with their parents over soup made with vegetables they've helped to grow.

Aline Antoine's Workshop

Every week after telling a story, Aline Antoine, an artist turned librarian, would lead a workshop so the children could create their own pictures of what had sparked their imaginations. It was a proper workshop, with Aline discreetly advising each of them how to best express themselves. It wasn't a matter of simply coloring on white sheets of paper—they could have very well done that at home. Each time, she'd suggest colors, materials, and techniques that fit best with the story. Once the children had completed their works, they were displayed on a large panel in one of the reading rooms for a week.

Our library has always provided opportunities for real workshops. There were theater workshops, puppet workshops, and workshops for other kinds of creation and expression. The adult's role is essential, both to acknowledge the children's expectations and ensure they have the best experience possible.

Before the introduction of computers, children used to come to the library after school to print their own "literary creations" or the library newspaper, since they had a real printing press at their disposal. There were also some old typewriters—less glamorous than the press, admittedly—that some visitors had generously donated. Thanks to the presence of these machines, the shy children became more confident and started to make up little stories, write poems, or describe events from their lives and then print out what they'd written. Today, the printing press and typewriters are long gone and children save their writing on computers. The printer has taken the place of the press, and I do find this to be something of a shame. There was real teamwork with the press and we'd move around the characters made out of lead. I liked the atmosphere of the studio. I remember how diligently those in charge of the newspaper worked. I can still see Martine Sonnet, who later became a well-known writer, and Patrick Boivert, one of the pillars of the theater workshop, making the final corrections to the newspaper before it was printed.

We'd keep ourselves busy in this large space—always with the children's help, of course! From time to time, the older children would prepare audiovisual montages and recordings for the younger ones, often bringing some of our foreign storybooks to life. They'd create puppets and stage the show using the techniques of shadow theater. This was how they presented Remy Charlip's madcap storybook, *Mother, Mother, I Feel Sick*. The book is just as dizzying as the theatrical adaptation the children had made of it.

Aline, who was always attentive to the stories and books the children loved, helped to develop the workshop. She'd help them unobtrusively, and just as she did with the workshop after the traditional storytime, the techniques she introduced would vary from project to project. These included engraving and painting, sometimes on slides, for audiovisual montages to go along with soundtracks they would make themselves. I noticed that the children who'd been in such workshops would then pay particular attention to the storybooks, audiovisuals, and art books that Aline brought in, as well as those in the lending room. After trying his hand at zinc engraving, one child mused, "Hey, me and Rembrandt did the same thing..."

Teryl Euvremer

I really appreciated the presence of Teryl Euvremer, a subtle and quiet artist who shared her pleasure of storytelling and creating with the children at the library. She would come specifically for a lively collaborative project with the children that progressed for several weeks all throughout the library. She refused to call it an "event." This term sometimes evokes a pre-packaged theme or program, useful for reports to be transmitted to authorities: it risks not giving the unforeseeable, the spontaneous word of the child, its fair share.

The child psychiatrist René Diatkine made fun of other tired phrases like "My child has a lot of activities." For him, this evokes some leisure programs and courses chosen from a box to ensure that the child will later be a "performant" adult. With Teryl, there was none of that. What she made with the children emanated from the very life of the library. Her simple way of telling stories naturally encouraged children to tell them as well. Over the course of a simple conversation, there would suddenly be a digression.

"By the way," she would say, "this reminds me of a story." And then she'd tell it.

"In your story there's a wolf," the child would then say. "In my house they tell a story almost the same, but it's with a fox." And so he'd share that particular version. This was how connections were made and a community developed.

I remember the wonderful weeks when Teryl dreamed up a project with the children's help. Sometimes it was hard for everyone to live together at the library. It wasn't easy for young teenagers to make their way through the strollers and baby carriages as they entered. Nor was it easy for the little ones to be with the big kids or to deal with how abrupt they could be. So Teryl played with the notions of big and small to show that both were necessary and that coexistence could be a real asset. She brought the tallest and the smallest from folk tales and literature into the library. It was necessary to think about making very small objects to hide in the room for the older children and very large figures of giants to place in the room for the younger ones. Jack and his magic beanstalk took over the entrance. Little bugs the children had made scurried across the shelves. Teryl and the children prepared all of this in the workshop. And in a workshop, there is a lot of storytelling. There's nothing like active hands to loosen the tongue and get people talking and telling stories, just like bygone evenings spent by the hearth: people would tell stories while shelling peas or peeling chestnuts, and this would bring all the generations together, with everyone enjoying each other's company. "Here," said Teryl, "in this house of books, doing is essential and it takes all sorts of forms. Adults are not content with giving out things to do. They want to do things with you." This was very different from school, where the teacher would give out assignments.

Marie Saint-Dizier

I still remember some friendly visits from Marie Saint-Dizier, the author of books beloved by children and adolescents. The library was sometimes overrun by groups of older children who'd storm in noisily to meet friends, take over, and make a mess. Marie was there one time this happened. There were some novels lying around on a table and she picked up *Holes* by Louis Sachar. She had read it before and started talking to them about it in a personal way. I saw these young people, usually so rowdy and even sometimes aggressive, fall silent to listen and participate in the discussion. Each one wanted to take a turn reading a page aloud. They read very well, in fact, and I could sense that they were moved.

The book begins in a rather harsh way: young delinquents find themselves in the camp at Lac Vert, a place where they are locked up and subjected to horrible forced labor. The hero winds up there but he doesn't know why. Was it some kind of curse? Wrongly accused of stealing a pair of sneakers, he has to choose between prison and this camp. *The Passage* is a novel of rare subtlety and is full of sympathy, friendship, and hope. Marie told them about other books that she loved and that had touched her. She talked about herself, too. It was really a beautiful moment, with everyone being able to relate to one another and wanting to share.

Another time, in a similar way, I heard her talk about her love for Jack London. She also shared with these young teenagers how much she loved reading about Martin Eden, who was none other than London himself. She praised the author's genius in describing how much suffering and embarrassment there is for Martin—a penniless young man—when he visits the rich family of a genteel girl who graces him with her attentions.

> *He knew that he must stand up to be introduced, and he struggled painfully to his feet, where he stood with trousers bagging at the knees, his arms loose-hanging*

and ludicrous, his face set hard for the impending ordeal. The process of getting into the dining room was a nightmare to him.[16]

We all were moved by the sensitivity of this writing and by Marie's generosity in sharing her emotion with us.

Taking Time for the Unexpected

Like many large suburban *cité*s, ours suffered from being isolated and closed off. These visits from artists or strangers passing through, improvised or not, were all the more precious for the children, especially when these kind-hearted adults graciously agreed to speak with them. They came from the neighborhood, the neighboring towns, and other countries. In the library, thanks to these encounters and random conversations, the children discovered that everyone had something to offer.

For example, there was a librarian from New York who visited Paris often, Emma. She worked at the reception desk for teenagers at a library in the Bronx and was perfectly up to date on what young people were into across the Atlantic—not just books but also movies, since she was a film librarian. In return, she would ask the teens of the *cité* to let her know of anything that the young people in her own neighborhood should know about.

At the library, time was freely offered, with a sense of fluidity that was not locked into restrictive schedules or "canned" events with rigid structures. To tell the truth, like Teryl, I don't really like the word "event." At the very beginning, we were tempted to overly structure every hour the library was open. It had provided a sense of reassurance. We were so anxious to do well that we set up programs back-to-back, but this left no room for finding out about each other, for plain and simple interactions. Administrative authorities and donors would often demand reports and

---

16. Jack London, *Martin Eden*, (1909, repr. New York: Modern Library, 2002), Martin Eden, 14.

statistics that proved to them that the library was functioning properly, at least according to their criteria, with many activities that could be accounted for. Classes and groups were developed with a vengeance. But what about individuals' unique interests? It was important to allow the unexpected to find its place, to take root, and to develop. "Surprise us," the library's regulars would sometimes say. How good it was to be surprised by unexpected readings, by chance interactions!

When I think back to the first days, I am amazed. Right away, without any particular instructions, the life of the library organized itself and everything fell into place in the most natural way. Yet for the children, the library was something new: mixed ages, boys and girls together, experiencing and building projects freely with others, having time to read, to talk, or to do nothing. All of this was unusual in an establishment for children. For me, these developments provided evidence of just how right the librarians at L'Heure Joyeuse, and then at Clamart, were in their notion of collective life. Because it is flexible and simple, it can adapt to all situations, all cultures, other climates, and other times; the library's easy adoption of the Internet provides yet further proof.

The children quickly felt at ease among the books in the library and with our help, they easily found their way around. As soon as the library opened, I saw children drawn to books that "weren't like the others." Pascale, who was just six years old, told me that what he liked best were the books that were "in foreign." "Will you read me a book in foreign language?" This was a frequent question. These books' covers certainly suggest that there are many wonderful things inside. We'd take the time to sit with the children and introduce them to these books from other lands. For books in Japanese or Swedish, we'd rely on the English synopses sent by our foreign correspondents. These works were often whimsical, playful, and sometimes even serious. They were different from the books then available in France, where it was impossible to find anything like them. I saw little Pascale and some other children imitate us by "reading" these storybooks aloud and trying to capture the right tone. Like us, they would pretend to perfectly decipher these texts written in a foreign language, and some children would come closer so as to listen.

Masterpieces from Elsewhere

I've always introduced the children of our cité to masterpieces from other countries, but I wanted to introduce them to French works, too. I could tell them which books other children had particularly enjoyed. Some of the foreign books were not yet available in French translation, but the images and the rhythm spoke for themselves. They had the dizzying humor of cartoons, probably because some of their authors worked in the Disney studios. They bore the felicitous traces of this. Children would hit the ground running with books such as the Berenstain Bears' hilarious *The Bike Lesson*, which had not been translated yet, with the son who watches delightedly as his father struggles to maneuver his bicycle. There was also *Are You My Mother?* by P. D. Eastman. A bird that has fallen out of its nest embarks on a wild quest. He has never met his mother, since he was still in the egg when she left. So how would he recognize her? He asks all kinds of animals he encounters along the way and even asks a construction crane the same question: "Are you my mother?"

In the 1960s, with a few happy exceptions, most French publishers seemed quite timid. I'm thinking of the French reception of the great Astrid Lindgren, whose works of wacky, kind-hearted whimsy have long been recognized throughout the world. At that time, her masterpiece *Pippi Longstocking* was passed over in France in favor of some of her less innovative works, such as the Kati series, which was published at the time by Éditions Nathan.

Fortunately, L'Ecole des loisirs soon started to publish children's books that were funny, or spooky. Tomi Ungerer was a great success. He recognized the child's right to live childhood to its fullest, uninhibited and free from heavy-handed didacticism. It didn't matter that *No Kiss for Mother (Pas de baiser pour maman)* was in black and white. We'd peruse the book at our leisure so as to savor all the details of this rascally cat's countless pranks. Children inevitably identify with this cat who tricks his parents, making them believe he's in the bathroom brushing his teeth and washing up whereas he's really sitting comfortably on the toilet reading comic books. I can still hear the sound of the children laughing as we looked at these books together.

During my stay in New York, I noticed that some publishers were extremely open-minded. Was this due to the vitality of the libraries? Or the artistic sensibilities of those who were running them, and the trust they placed in children? It seems that at that time, there were fewer taboos there than in France. I think of *The Dead Bird* by the great Margaret Wise Brown and illustrated by Remy Charlip. For decades, I kept recommending this little book to some of our more open-minded publishers, but to no avail. When one of them, much to our delight, finally decided to publish it, they changed the title. The word "dead" was removed and replaced with a more commonplace and all-purpose title: *Un chanson pour l'oiseau* ("*A Song for the Bird*"). It seemed that adults were afraid to talk about death with children. This book was about finding a dead bird in the garden, collecting its body, and holding a sacred burial ritual. The slow procession extends across the pages of the book, which is in landscape format. There is an alternation between spreads that have facing pages in muted colors and facing pages that are all white except for very spare text. Everything encourages contemplation so as to experience the gravity of the event. Everything is done with the necessary dignity. The bird is buried and life then resumes with joy and dance.

The Guest Book

As soon as the Bibliothèque des enfants opened, people from all over the world came to see it. They were delighted and surprised to discover this place of culture where children could make good use of the freedoms they were given.

To jog my memory, I went through the library's magnificent guest books, now kept in a storeroom at the BnF, and I was deeply moved.

What happened there from the very outset, with our desire to awaken children's curiosity, had seemed entirely natural—and yet it had been entirely new. As I turned the pages, I considered these astonished, admiring comments written by visitors from all over the world. For them, the creation of this library in the Parisian suburb marked was a major event in the world of children and pedagogy.

The writer Jean Schlumberger opened the guestbook with the encouraging words, written in his lovely handwriting: "How lucky the children of Clamart are! Who knows what vocations will spring forth here? Everything to enrich young minds will be within their grasp or before their eyes."

I turned the pages of these beautiful guest books that were covered with all kinds of exotic characters, Japanese ideograms, and messages in Arabic, Korean, and Thai. I read the testimonials, one after the other, with great relish. Many of the best-known artists in the world of children's books such as Maurice Sendak, Ezra Jack Keats, Arnold Lobel, and Laurent de Brunhoff had also left their mark.

There were countless testimonials. "The realm of dreams? No! But faith in the children? Yes! And the opening of these young minds to the reality of the world that is given to them." Some librarians saw in it "the death throes of bureaucratic and utilitarian libraries." Vladimir Jankélévitch noted with a touch of malice that the children's library of Clamart was "much better than the Library of the Institute (Bibliothèque de l'Institut de France)." I discovered that my mother had also written something in the guestbook. Her sentiments touched me in particular because they were so similar to my own. She thought that the happy times the children experienced in this library would "stay with them all their lives and bring light to them in difficult times." Today, though, for many children in the *cité*, the future is rather bleak. Unemployment is constantly on the rise. It's difficult to find one's place in such a society. Yet it is certain that at the library, our readers will have enjoyed full recognition as unique, irreplaceable individuals in a world of beauty and trust. At least that is my wish.

Marcel Aymé

I always spent a lot of time with visitors who come to Clamart specifically to explore this library they'd heard so much about. I liked to give them a taste of the subtlety and depth of certain children's books. Often, I couldn't resist reading or narrating a few passages from great masters like Marcel Aymé. As a child, my bedtime book had been *The Wonderful Farm (Les Contes du chat perché)*. I'm still attached to it. For those who love books, some of these tales like "The Bull" and "The Elephant" are like manna from above. The bull loves learning and takes to reading with great enthusiasm. And there is a little hen who transforms herself into an elephant just in time to find her place in Noah's ark.

I also like to share "The Donkey and the Horse," a work that I consider to be particularly profound. It starts off as a game between Delphine and Marinette: "If I were... We would be." One evening beneath a full moon, they make reckless wishes—to be a horse and a donkey, respectively.

> *Early in the morning, Marinette opened her eyes and it seemed to her that between her eyelashes, she saw two big hairy ears moving on the pillow in her sister's bed. Delphine, also sleepy, took a quick look at her sister's bed. She found it quite voluminous, strangely rounded, and went back to sleep nevertheless [...]. Not without difficulty, they got down from their beds and stood on all fours. [...] The poor big horse didn't think of running. She looked at her little girl's dress thrown over a chair next to the bed, and at the thought that she might never fit into it again, she was miserable.*[17]

The parents were surprised and annoyed at first, then faced facts and made good use of these animals for the hard work on the farm. They were heartless; Delphine and Marinette would be useful, profitable. Little by little, the youngsters forgot their human origins and how comfortable their lives as human children had been. Fortunately, thanks to advice

---

17. Marcel Aymé, *Les Contes du chat perché*, Éditions Gallimard, 1939.

from Uncle Alfred, everything turns out well in the end. What just seems to be childish tale in fact invites us adults to deep contemplation.

It was a particular pleasure for me to present Tomi Ungerer's very first storybooks to my visitors in the mid-1960s. If I hadn't read them out loud, they would probably have passed them over. *Zeralda's Ogre* and *The Three Robbers* were considered cruel books, not for children, and many wondered how anyone could publish such frightening books. All I had to do was open them, read them aloud, and tell them how receptive the children were to them and what parts they found to be moving. Then, their perspectives would change—their perspectives on these books and, perhaps just a little, their perspectives on children and their tastes.

A Climate Hospitable to Creativity

The Clamart library emerged and developed in a promising context. The time was undoubtedly ripe for it. I've already mentioned the work of Robert Delpire, who cleared the way by upsetting the established order of children's publishing. He had called upon excellent French artists who were free of ideological and didactic intentions. In 1965 he established the École des loisirs, which very quickly published foreign storybooks of exceptional quality. This brought in a powerful wind from across the Atlantic and, later, the Far East. This swept away the sanctimonious, stuffy, and often dull image of the publishing world of the time. The principal authors—Ungerer, Sendak, Lobel, Lionni, and Spier—recognized the true nature of children. They remembered what it had been like to be children.

There was also Pomme d'api, which was the first magazine for children and adolescents published by a press group. It would continue to grow in importance, both in France and abroad. From the first issues, what struck me most of all was the quality of the images. There was well beyond comparison with the mediocre illustrations that children's magazines are usually overrun with. As with the best storybooks, the art of storytelling through words, images, and rhythms was on full display.

This press was a real laboratory. A new illustrator was enlisted for each issue, and for many it was their début. The editorial team solicited the help of a linguist, Laurence Lentin, to address the important matter of readability. I also appreciated the attention given to parents. From the outset, this press presented reading as a family matter.

Soon after, the publisher Harlin Quist arrived from the United States. With his two associates in France, François Ruy-Vidal and Patrick Couratin, he gave a new face to children's publishing. They involved some of the great names of French literature such as Eugène Ionesco and Marguerite Duras, as well as artists such as Nicole Claveloux. These sophisticated works got a lot of attention in certain circles.

At the same time, Isabelle Jan, who like me had trained at L'Heure Joyeuse, introduced remarkable works of fiction from abroad to France. The "International Library" ("Bibliothèque internationale") that Isabelle created in 1967 began with the French version of an American work published in the 1930s, *The Little House in the Big Woods* by Laura Ingalls Wilder. This was the first in the long series known as *The Little House on the Prairie*, which another French publisher picked up. Many decades after their first publication, these novels are still loved by children.

When Isabelle was preparing her collection, she was also thinking of publishing the adventures of Moomin the Troll. She asked me, "Could the adventures of Moomin, born in the snowy and harsh lands of Finland, resonate with the children who live in France's mild climate?"

We'd had some unforgettable times in that small office in the Montparnasse district, thrilled to have been involved in the start of something big. Edwige Talibon-Lapomme, who regularly wrote a double-page spread on children's books in the national daily Combat, would come to reflect with us. His articles were not a simple collection of reviews and provided readers with keys to enter the complex world of children's literature. Sometimes booksellers like Véronique Lory, who created Chantelivre, also joined our meetings. Just a few years later, children's bookstores started cropping up all over France.

The early 1970s were especially fruitful. This is when Gallimard Jeunesse, under the leadership of Pierre Marchand, came into being. It was quickly considered the best children's publisher at the international level.

Jack Lang asked me much later, in 1981, to organize the first commission at the National Book Center (Centre national du livre) to support the publication of books for children. This is how the ministry of culture came to fully support this branch of publishing that had seemed so stagnant in the early 1960s, with a few happy exceptions.

Within just a short period of time, the children's book received full recognition in France. Today, the Montreuil Children's Book Fair (Salon du livre jeunesse de Montreuil) is a real event that attracts many foreigners.

Distinguished Visitors

We had countless visitors. I'll just mention a few that were remarkable in one way or another. Agna Barto, president of the Union of Writers for Young People (Union des écrivains pour la jeunesse), came with a whole Soviet delegation, for example. These countries had a very real interest in literature and libraries. Anne was there for the occasion and, as a token of their appreciation, the visitors immediately pinned a small brooch bearing the effigy of Lenin on her jacket. And so she wore it as she showed them around.

In 1993, Her Majesty Michiko, Empress of Japan, also honored us with a visit. This was quite different, as one might imagine. I knew that she was interested in children's literature and especially in poetry. A few years earlier, I had received a fine book by the poet Michio Mado, Animals, which she had translated into English and that had illustrations by our friend Anno Mitsumasa.

Welcoming the empress was not a simple matter, but this was not her fault. Though she herself was highly approachable, the obligations dictated by the Japanese and French authorities were very complicated. I had been invited to the Japanese embassy on the day prior to being presented to the Imperial couple. My friend Leena Maissen, secretary general of the International Board on Books for Young People (IBBY), was also invited. That evening, Emperor Akihito approached us, said a few words, and shook our hands. Shook our hands? According to my friends, this was an incredible gesture. Leena and I, meanwhile, admired him for the fact that he seemed to be perfectly up-to-date on our activities to support children's books.

That day, I'd had several bundles of children's books sent to Empress Michiko. She was going to meet some of these works' authors the following morning. They were entirely surprised when she spoke with each of them individually about their books. Needless to say, her visit was quite an event for the cité. But Michiko had asked that nothing be changed on her account. This had not been easy! But the library remained open as usual to toddlers accompanied by their mothers or their babysitters. The empress went to the younger children's room and knelt down near the children to look at a storybook with them. All of this was very brief, of course—it had not been on the itinerary. She was so friendly that people from the *cité* wanted to see her again. "When is the Japanese lady coming back?" the children would ask. Since then, our ties have remained strong, and I've had several opportunities to meet with her during my missions to Japan. I have always admired her genuine attention to everyone. Her presence amidst the audience members during a lecture I gave in Tokyo both surprised and emboldened me.

But what touched me the most was a visit from some children who had come especially from Cuneo, Italy. The person in charge of their city's library had offered to accompany them to Clamart to get ideas for the development of a children's section.

Interns, students visiting on fellowships, and many foreign librarians came to Clamart for long periods. In the early years, most of them came from Northern Europe and the United States. For a long time, librarians in Scandinavian countries who were preparing to visit France for a little vacation were reminded, "Don't forget to contact the Clamart library. Go and visit it! It's worth the trip." They liked the freedom we enjoyed.

Meeting with All Together in Dignity (ATD) Fourth World

Joseph Wresinski's visit marked the beginning of a true collaboration with ATD (All Together in Dignity). He knew that in our *cité* of La Plaine, in Petit-Clamart, there was a development built to accommodate families facing dire poverty and various forms of exclusion. Our library was in alignment with his commitments. Since the late 1950s, his movement had been fighting for the recognition of the poorest families' aspirations for dignity. Reading was a natural part of this. When he discovered the destitution of the *bidonville* of Noisy-le-Grand, his first reaction was to create a kindergarten and a library. There was even a hairdressing salon. All of these elements, in their own way, promoted social integration and gave people a real sense of self-worth.

Very soon after the opening of our library, Père Joseph Wresinski visited Clamart. He was moved, he told us, by the presence of such a beautiful cultural facility in a neighborhood like that. He was aware that we were constantly striving to make the best books available to children and to inspire their curiosity. He invited me to speak about my experience at one of the monthly meetings held by the ATD in their "cellar," near the church of Saint-Séverin in Paris. By way of introduction, he recalled his first visit to Clamart, which had been one of the most moving moments of his life. His involvement was, from the very beginning, a source of inspiration for us.

Cooperation between our library and Père Joseph was quickly established. He often invited me to meet with him in his distant banlieue and we'd talk a lot. A member of his team would attend each of our meetings, frantically taking notes on all the topics we discussed. Notetaking was no small feat, as ATD's activities were always meticulously observed and documented. Interactions with children and families gave rise to scrupulously documented observations that facilitated our understanding of these places. I was impressed by this almost scientific rigor, which is so often absent from humanitarian work. It made it possible for us to avoid making generalizations.

Père Joseph asked me to encourage public libraries to welcome people living in marginalized situations. This was a matter of justice as well as strategy. With Anne's support and the city of Créteil's agreement, a librarian from Clamart named Claude Gilbert was going to open and run a library that would become an annex of the municipal library. This library would be open to the populations who were usually absent from our cultural institutions. ATD's founder was counting on Clamart to lead our profession in this direction.

It was thanks to the ATD activists that I introduced some original initiatives likely to be recognized by our profession, such as the street library I would have the opportunity to set up later on in our cité.

ATD's "cultural hubs" were of particular interest to me. Out in the street, children were offered all kinds of entertainment: paintings, puppets, and other forms of expression and play. What most of these children preferred, I was told, was books and reading. Though I'm a librarian, I was surprised. How could this not delight me?

Approaching the Outskirts

Inspired by ATD, we decided to work beyond the confines of the building and reach out to those on the margins, in the outskirts. We had noticed that children living in the more poorly regarded *cité*s often had trouble finding their place in the library. When our library opened, a mother was quick to warn me: "Whatever you do, don't let in the children from the 'Million' *cité*. There are some really undesirable families there. They're all hooligans."

In the administrative spheres, this was referred to as the cité of "hardship cases" ("cas sociaux"). With such labels, it was no surprise that these children had trouble being accepted anywhere. They were often tempted to come and cause trouble or not to come at all. And so we'd have to go to them, adapt to their way of life. Since they spent their time outside, on the streets or in playgrounds, that was where we 'd reach them.

In the early 1980s, we decided to offer the best of our services in this underprivileged neighborhood, all year round. We would read aloud to the children and also offer book lending services, just like at the library. All of this was outside, in places where children would play and the inhabitants would pass by, looking on curiously. For me, it was important for this to be in full view of everyone, both to encourage the element of surprise and to help everyone feel welcome.

This unusual library was set up in the morning every Wednesday, which at that time was a day when children did not attend school in France. It was always at the same time, in the same place, near the sandbox. We'd set out our two baskets of books on a low wall, arranging about fifty books—the most beautiful, the best loved—in these flat bakery baskets as if they were croissants and rolls. Since the inhabitants of this *cité* were mostly of foreign origin, we also put out beautiful photo books about the countries that some of them had come from, books they couldn't afford but that we were happy to show them and lend out to them. There were those who wondered in disbelief: "What? You lend them books and they're not registered at the library? You don't even know their address!"

It was true that most of them didn't have a reader's card, but that didn't matter. With their help, we quickly wrote down the borrowers' names in a notebook. That was enough for us. They would bring the books back next time, or maybe to the library. We always trusted them and we were never disappointed.

Lending books out so people could take them home was important. It established a line of continuity between what the children experienced with us and what they'd invariably want to share with their families or simply re-read to their heart's content. I loved to see the children after reading time, selecting one or two books that they'd particularly enjoyed and wanted to keep for a while. They'd go home, clutching these books to their hearts and delighted by our trust in them.

Showing up late for this weekly event was out of the question; the children would be on the lookout for us. As soon as they saw us, they'd abandon their games and everything would quickly fall into place. Some would spend a long time rummaging through the baskets, deciding on their selections. Others would isolate themselves to read, and others would listen to a grown-up or a librarian read a storybook. We told stories and shared our impressions of the books: what we liked and what we didn't like; what made us laugh or cry. Everything was natural and free. The librarians were there to read, share, and converse with them.

"It's Like Me, But It's Not Me."

I really enjoyed these moments. Like when I met with Tatian, a four-year-old boy with jet black hair, for example. We were outside and we were both looking at a Japanese storybook. It had no text and depicted a day at the beach, with people gradually appearing on the sand, one hour after the other, one page after the next, to then empty itself gradually until nightfall. It was necessary to carefully inspect the images that spread out across the double pages. In this way, Tatian discovered that there was something to see, to understand. There was a new world hidden between the two covers of the book that revealed itself to him. I shut the book after we were done. Deeply touched, he punched the book with his fist and said repeatedly, "I've never seen anything so beautiful." This very young boy had suddenly discovered what reading meant, what books could offer him. He left with this storybook clutched to his chest.

I think of the amazement of the Puerto Rican children I'd read to in the library in the Bowery. I would share in their jubilation as they exclaimed, "How beautiful!" Before that, nobody had taken the time to read with them in a family setting. They were experiencing a kind of birth, an entry into literature, as the child psychiatrist René Diatkine called it. They told me in their own way that these were intense experiences of beauty: the beauty of a relation, of a discovery, of a book.

I also remember Benjamin, a five-year-old child to whom I was reading Russel Hoban's *Say Goodnight, Adele*. It's the story of a little badger who, like all the human children across the globe, comes up with various pretexts to delay bedtime. Benjamin was moved, and interrupted me. "It's like me, but it's not me," he said. In just a few words, he defined the very act of reading. He was becoming aware of himself, his own existence, and wanted to let me know. Even though he was a child, he could "read between the lines," an ability that is characteristic of true readers. He related life—his own life—to the book. To use a beautiful image from Emmanuel Levinas, the book is like a bird with folded wings waiting for the reader's breath so it can spread its wings and take flight. This explains some great literary successes like *Willy the Champ*, a moving character created by Anthony Browne. Even though Willy is a chimpanzee, enthusiastic readers also see him as a kind of brother. I know a Nicaraguan child who asked to wear clothes that were exactly like Willy's: the same sweater, the same sneakers.

At the street library, it was the essentials that brought us together: the pleasure of each another's company, of sharing ideas, of speaking, of a story that was read aloud and listened to; this was, in short, a genuine encounter. The children would join us as they liked, gathering around to hear a story, taking a look at a book, and then leaving if they preferred to return to their games. The teenagers—the big brothers on their little motorcycles—would pass by, come back again, look around, stop, and sometimes join in and lend a hand by showing the youngest ones some of the storybooks. They'd read to them and would clearly have a lot of fun.

The parents would watch what was going on from their windows. They'd see their children waiting for us to come and throwing themselves into our arms as soon as we arrived. "So, our children are interested in books!" And they'd thought they'd been doomed to failure! This offered them a new way of looking at their children and at reading as well.

It wasn't easy to interrupt these moments of grace. At noon, the parents would call out to the children. "Come on, it's time for lunch."

"We can't. We haven't finished the story."

But it was time for the library to pack up. I reassured the children, "Come this afternoon to La Petite Bibliothèque Ronde. It's open every day, even on Sunday. You'll find your books, as well as many others, there. We'll help you choose. You'll meet other children and have all the time in the world. There are even computers. We will be there. Come, we'll be waiting for you." Before long, these children showed up at the library, and any shyness or hostility they might have had before were gone; they felt acknowledged and accepted there.

Going Door to Door to Share Our Books

Consistency was a golden rule that we had made for ourselves. This was, after all, a public service. Our visit was a sign of respect for a population that was frequently marginalized. It was a comfort for those who had experienced the drama of displacement and precarity. But what would we do when it rained or snowed? As winter approached, I saw that as the children came to the street library, they were shivering from the cold. We had to find a solution. Maybe set up in the stairwells? No, that wouldn't do. It was cold, dirty, and noisy, and we'd be disturbed constantly.

Why not go door-to-door? I went with Wahed Allouche, a member of my team, to share something joyful—joyful for all of us who had the desire to share what we loved, and for the children and their parents who delighted in these discoveries.

"What do you talk about with the parents?" the mayor of the town asked, a little worried.

"About books. It just comes naturally," I replied.

In keeping with the hospitality that is traditionally valued in the countries to the south of France, we were welcomed warmly. The parents knew that in going door-to-door, we expected absolutely nothing in return. In all senses of the word, everything was free; everything was joyful.

And so every Wednesday, when the weather wouldn't permit us to stay outside, we would go up to the buildings and knock on doors.

"Who is it?"

"This is the library," we'd say, and the parents would then open the door with complete trust. They knew us and had seen us with their children. At first, books would get lost and it would take a while for them to be located. But routines soon developed and the books would be waiting for us on the table. The conversation naturally started with the parents. A number of them started reading to their children on a regular basis, or leafing through the books with them.

"I read this one to him and he liked it; this one made us laugh. And next time, could you bring a book for me?"

I loved visiting a particular Roma family, a grandmother who had custody of her grandson. At the time I'd drop by, she would be preparing lunch. Her grandson always wanted the same book, *The Rolling Galette (Roule Galette)*, but we'd suggest other storybooks and read them to him. The grandmother couldn't read, but she would readily come in from the wonderful-smelling kitchen to get a glimpse of the book. She seemed to enjoy it and I like to think that after we left, she perused it over and over with her grandson. Perhaps, in her turn, she had the desire to tell him stories. I later learned from a city councilor in charge of cultural affairs that this child had become an avid reader and was planning to start a magazine.

All these families were all grouped under the category of "hardship cases." But under this one single heading, what diversity there was! Some parents would wait for us and offer us mint tea and homemade pastries, but unfortunately, we couldn't linger too long in just one place.

The vast majority of the families we met had immigrant backgrounds. There were, however, a few rare exceptions. One encounter in particular was unforgettable: the door opened, and the man standing there warned us, "We don't have children, but we have books. I'll show you one that you won't find anywhere else." From his library, he took out a small, handwritten book dedicated to him. The text was by Jacques Prévert and the illustrations by Picasso! He explained: "When I was little, my mother was a cleaning lady at Prévert's house and I often went there on Thursdays. He gave me this gift." One more reason to admire the great Prévert.

The Countess of Ségur in the Cités

Wahed and I would visit a large French family from time to time. They were apparently very poor; the children were pale and scrawny, as if they'd stepped out of a Dickens novel. We always received a warm welcome and everyone got to choose a book. I'll never forget how the father picked up some of the books and caressed them. We had put a novel by the Comtesse de Ségur in our basket. The edition we had was a magnificent facsimile of one of the very first editions published in the 19th century and reissued by Jean-Jacques Pauvert in the 1960s. It had embossed red silk binding and gilt pages. The father was visibly moved. What we were loaning out to them with our complete confidence, the works we wanted them to experience, were of exceptional quality. Nothing was too good for his family.

So, yes—sometimes I'd put works by the Comtesse in the book baskets we'd bring to the families of this transitional *cité*. I knew how much the children of our library loved her works. This may seem surprising, given the social context. But this was indeed the case. With Madame de Ségur, they got to live in castles, and this gave them the opportunity to dream. It did not bother them in the slightest. They would step right into a world that seemed far removed from their own reality, and reading would transport them through time and space. Children, like all true readers, know how to see beyond appearances. Ségur perfectly mastered the art of the story, the details, the dialogues. There is never a dull moment, and there is even sometimes violence. These novels are not romances—far from it! This pleases the children. I've heard some say, "I would like a book with children who make a lot of mistakes and are punished." The Comtesse gives them what they want.

Every Wednesday morning for twenty years (until 2001) I had many good experiences like this. Never during our visits had we been the target of ill-will or aggression. Children and families always respected their commitments, just as we did, with unwavering consistency and loyalty. Then, because it was unsafe, the *cité* was destroyed. A new neighborhood with a more affluent population has since replaced it. The codes required to enter the buildings now make it difficult to visit, which is a shame. But momentum has gathered. My young colleagues continue to leave the library every week to reach out to those most in need. They meet parents and young children at a Resto bébé du Cœur that sets up their displays nearby, telling stories and showing storybooks that are likely to touch them both.

Our open-air libraries are like branches of the neighborhood library. It's a way to send out feelers. What we consistently offer in Clamart alongside the buildings or by the market is, in my opinion, a standard library service. For struggling families, it's an initial form of contact. Then, they can join what may, through relationships with other children, become their home, their concern: the public library in their neighborhood. This link is vital.

A Shared Table

Sometimes we'd invite our visitors to eat with us. I have wonderful memories of such moments we'd share, relaxing. Juliette, the cleaning woman, would prepare some delicious dishes from her native Auvergne, and we'd all contribute something of our own. A former reader confided to me that when he'd arrive on Wednesday mornings, he always enjoyed the good smells coming from the kitchen. For him, he said, the library was like a real home. Some visitors passing through became friends of the library and sometimes helped us to explore new directions. This was the case, for example, when we were visited by Bruno de La Salle, "the storyteller in love,"[18] in the early 1970s.

He had just returned from a long trip around the world. He'd heard about our library and wanted to meet us. Over the course of the meal, he told us about his travels, his discoveries, his interest in oral storytelling

---

18. Bruno de la Salle, *Le Conteur amoureux*, Casterman, 1995.

traditions, and in other cultures. He told us how, barely more than a child, he'd discovered some great texts such as the *Odyssey*. These texts, he said, had always stayed with him and he wanted to share them with others. For him, our library was the ideal place to give new life to storytelling.

Bruno offered to help make this happen. He would come in from time to time to tell stories, accompanied by a crystal organ made by the Baschet brothers, but he'd always insist that the librarians share something, too. The traditional story hour at Clamart and a few other libraries usually involved just reading books to a whole group. Storytelling, on the other hand, was a different animal. It required real personal commitment and was really an exercise in memory. In Clamart, with Bruno de La Salle's encouragement, new seeds were sown for the revival of storytelling not just in libraries, but other places as well. The time for such a revitalization had come, as evidenced by the fact that the enthusiasm for it went well beyond the walls of our library. This encouraged Evelyne Cevin, a librarian at Clamart, to find her own path. She has since become a recognized expert in the art of storytelling.

We also had some great children's book artists at our table. This included Fran Manushkin, who wrote the witty storybook *Baby*, which we successfully promoted in France. It is the story of a baby who does not want to be born. He resists all enticements. He feels fine in his mother's womb and does not want to join our world. What finally convinces him to be born is the promise of a kiss. We loved this book so much that we dreamed of seeing it published in France, but this wasn't easy. The book also seemed to have some troubles of its own being born. Many of the people we showed this storybook to rejected it for various reasons. Some protested that this was a delicate issue and could possibly warp children's minds. Others said it wasn't scientific. Some editors refused to publish it, claiming that the black and white illustrations practically doomed it to failure. It took a preface by Frédérick Leboyer, who had written *Birth Without Violence (Pour une naissance sans violence)*, for this book to see the light of day in France, where it continues to delight children and adults alike.

Arnold Lobel

I also remember our visit from Arnold Lobel, who made a stop in Clamart on his way back from the Biennial of Illustration in Bratislava. I was delighted. I find that his work, thanks to his subtle understanding of the spirit of childhood, is exceptional. He had insisted on giving me his latest book, *Uncle Elephant*, a strange and endearing book about the friendship between an elephant and his grand-nephew. Every morning, the young elephant accompanies the old uncle elephant as he blasts his trunk to greet the new day and all that nature offers in abundance: the flowers, the insects, the birds, the sun, and the clouds. What a pleasure it is to join in this ceremony! Like Toad, the little hero of *Frog and Toad Together* and *Frog and Toad Are Friends*, we also liked to make a list in the morning of the good things that awaited us. I also think of the "tear-water tea" from *Owl at Home* and how solemnly the little ones responded. We discovered all of this with joyful complicity. Yes—for us, his visit was truly an event. "The Nobel for Lobel!" as we liked to say.

Maurice Sendak

We also had a memorable meal with the great artist Maurice Sendak. The news of his visit to Paris in 1978 had circulated like wildfire in the world of children's books. Sendak, no less than a god, was going to be among us. He'd heard about our library and readily accepted my invitation to lunch. We had a lot to talk about. We discussed some of the Grimms' tales. He had illustrated two volumes that had just been published by Gallimard, and he told us that his favorite was the magnificent and difficult tale of the juniper tree. In it, a boy is killed by his stepmother, and she cooks him in a stew. She then serves it to the father, who unknowingly eats the flesh of his son. We happened to be serving stew that day, which provided some impetus for our conversation. In a way, reading is like eating words, an almost Biblical image—and can at times be quite literal. An American child had, in accordance with a common practice in his country, written to the author of his favorite storybooks to express his admiration. Maurice answered him in spite of the copious mail he received every day, and the child was so happy to have received a personal letter from his beloved author that he literally swallowed it.

Yes: children eat words—they feed on them and make them their own, often at the most opportune moments. I can still hear a five-year-old girl opening the door to the garden and announcing in the most natural way that she was walking out into the morning. What an elegant way to express herself! I later found the same phrase in the mouth of Lobel's Toad as he started his day. "He opened the door and walked out into the morning." *Walked out into the morning* sounds so lovely! How it rolls off the tongue! This child had spontaneously spoken like the great poet Lobel.

Tomoko and the Kamishibai

To our great delight, we were often joined at our table by Tomoko, a longtime friend. She was sometimes accompanied by one of the greatest Japanese illustrators, Seichii Horiuchi, who unfortunately is not known in France and left us far too soon. With long hair that he kept gathered under the cap he'd always wear, he didn't look like the Japanese tourists we usually encountered in town. He'd been living in France with his family for several years but did not seem to know French, and would participate in everything without ever speaking. He was a fine connoisseur of children's books from all over the world. It was doubtless thanks to him that Japan became aware of some of our greatest artists like Léopold Chauveau, whom France seemed to have forgotten at that time.

Tomoko also helped introduce the Japanese to French folk tales, such as those by Bladé. This was also the case for *The Wolf and the Woodcutter* (*Le Loup et le Bûcheron*), a true masterpiece of motion. It's impossible to forget the wolf rushing like a whirlwind and the woodcutter attempting to escape him by hurrying to the top of a tree as fast as he can go.

Both Tomoko and Seichii shared with us the art of *kamishibai*, a form of folk art that was relatively obscure at that time, though today it has a place in all the libraries of the world. Seichii generously made a *butai*—a small cardboard theater that presents stories by way of large images in a wooden frame—for us, and sometimes I would set it up outside next to a building. This was very much like the way the *butai* had originally been used: During the crisis of the 1930s in Japan, men would set them up on the frame of their bicycle out in the streets or in public parks, then tell stories and attract passersby, collecting a few coins by selling them sweets.

In our open-air library, the children were the ones to decide who'd get to present these little Japanese performances to the others. The children were emboldened as they hid behind these big boxes. Those who could read well would have the text of the story, translated by Tomoko, before them. The Japanese leave nothing to chance. Precise instructions described how to read, the rhythm of the narration, how to move from one picture to another, and the intonations and the silences to be observed.

The Pleasure of Meeting New People

The children would tell us to surprise them. For this reason, I liked to organize spontaneous events around people who were ready to come in and share with the children. They were always welcomed, and some would stay for a long time. Their contributions were sometimes unusual, and this was probably what made it so special: the surprise of unexpected events, readings, and encounters. We were lucky to be able to introduce them to the children. It was different from a school in that we could invite whomever we pleased with no administrative authorization required. Everything was simple and natural.

In particular, I remember a man who was passionate about soccer. I was making arrangements with France Telecom for the installation of a new telephone line and the man I was talking to, intrigued by the library's name, wanted to know more. He spent his spare time running a soccer club for children. We spoke for a long time. He offered to give us a list of carefully curated magazines and books and said he would be happy to meet the children and show them videos to explain all the nuances of the game to them.

Inviting Artists and Scientists

The children enjoyed these encounters and were proud to make recommendations. "I know a veterinarian who lived in Gabon with the chimpanzees. He got to know them well. Not in a zoo, but in real life, in the jungle. He also studied wolves in Canada. Can we invite him? I'm sure he would come. He's got a lot to say."

When everything is virtual, it's wonderful to have a real encounter with people who make the effort to show up! These aren't courses or conferences. What the library prefers instead are person-to-person encounters, which can foster awakenings, beginnings. A child's intelligence is first and foremost affective. Children are responsive to adults who give it to them straight: how a vocation is born, the learning that is required, the trials and tribulations, the surprises. This is how the thirst for knowledge is transmitted. These approaches are similar to those of Célestin Freinet's pedagogical model: having children meet with people who have rich experiences they've agreed to share. For many years, the Clamart library benefited from the generous help of Pierre Guérin, friend and long-time collaborator of Freinet, who created audiovisual materials designed for students in Freinet classes. Passionate about science and pedagogy, he had chosen to be a teacher and had always preferred classes for developmentally challenged students. Up to the end of his life, he was constantly filled with wonder and able to share his discoveries with others. I would sometimes see him arrive with an old leather satchel full of audiovisual materials and a few books—sometimes even with his beloved Nagra equipment, if he needed to make an audio recording. Whenever he visited, he'd always share some of his recent discoveries with me. He fostered remarkable encounters between the children of the library and people with rich experiences of all kinds who were willing to share. And so it was, thanks to him, that the older children interested in the fate of the dinosaurs were able to talk to an astrophysicist and a paleontologist, each with their own hypotheses to explain the phenomenon. Pierre trusted the children to come to their own conclusions.

After such encounters, a child wouldn't necessarily walk away with the sense that they'd grasped everything intellectually—but they would feel moved. Receiving information in such unpredictable ways, they'd come up with questions that had real meaning for them. In this way, the library's offerings stimulated curiosity and, as such, were truly meaningful. When searching the Internet, on the other hand, there's a purpose, and it's a lot harder to get lost.

"Real Scholars Come to See Us"

All areas of knowledge have a story to tell. Passionate specialists eager to share with the children would bring different disciplines to life and give them a personal dimension. Today, we can glean some information using the Internet, but real-life encounters remain more crucial than ever. In our cité, a priority education zone, the children were moved by visits from those who took the time to come and meet with them personally—to talk with and listen to them. "Real scholars come to see us," they'd say proudly. "They come especially for us." The visitors would establish a common thread, just like in a vivid story, while describing the pathways, the trials and the errors, the questions—in short, the mind at work.

In the library, trusting relationships developed between children and the "experts" they'd grown close to: artists, artisans, travelers, explorers. Under these conditions, children could express their genuine curiosity, and the resources offered by whatever channels of information they'd used would take on a new meaning. They would listen attentively and ask questions. They were heard. The great dinosaur specialist, Philippe Taquet, once director of the natural history museum in Paris, told me how important it was for him to listen to the children's ingenious and often fundamental questions.

Such dialogues—such mutual discoveries, such encounters—are the true essence of life. More now than ever, with the presence of the Internet, human mediation is absolutely indispensable. This is how we move from mere data collection to the realm of knowledge.

A Trip to a Luxury Hotel

I met a longtime friend of ours, Laurent, in the 1970s. At the time, he was working on the Paris-Florence line as a ticket inspector. His children were young then, and he was interested in the storybooks for readers of their age. I admired him for his subtle, extensive knowledge in this domain. Fascinated by artists such as Bruno Munari, he'd bring me books back from Florence—masterpieces that were not yet available in France. He especially liked the *Eloise* books by Kay Thompson and Hilary Knight, which were no longer in print. Once they were available for purchase again, we wanted to suggest having a conference dedicated to them.

Eloise's story is about an insufferable little girl who lives in a big New York hotel, the Plaza, where her mother works. She is intrepid, fears nothing, and is quite a handful for her governess, Nanny. There's never a dull moment. The lively images of the book take us with her making her merry way into the elevators and through the kitchens, the bathrooms, and everywhere she causes trouble.

Laurent immediately proposed a program for the Clamart children that would be a sort of literary pilgrimage in Eloise's footsteps. In addition to the scholarly conference on Knight and Thompson's work, why not have them discover a grand hotel and walk in the footsteps of Eloise? Laurent, who was a chauffeur in his spare time, seemed to know all the great hotels of Paris. He suggested that we go to the Plaza Athénée, just like in New York. I called the manager, who immediately agreed to my many requests. He was ready to put a room at our disposal where the conference could be held, and also to welcome the children from our suburban *cité*. And what a welcome we got! The children were treated to a delicious, velvety hot chocolate. The waiters in white jackets bowed to the children and served them deferentially. In a hallway there was an elderly woman playing the harp, an instrument our fascinated young visitors hadn't seen before. The director of the Plaza thanked me warmly. He was happy, he told me, to receive such guests. They livened it up, much like Eloise in her New York hotel.

There was also a costume designer from the Opéra de Paris who came to tell us about her process for imagining a costume—the way she would draw it, how she'd choose the colors, the materials, and the shapes—in short, how she did her job. At the library, the children were able to watch *Donkeyskin (Peau d'âne)*, the film directed by Jacques Demy. This was all a part of a library program called "Tales and Costumes." At the entrance to the library, children and parents were greeted by a tall mannequin wearing a lovely costume our friend had made. It truly did justice to the princess of Demy's film and the tale by Charles Perrault.

Madame Kowaliski

And so, in the heart of our neighborhood there was a home open to encounters of all kinds, a place where guests were happy to have very informal exchanges with young people. The library really had its share of friends, starting with the parents and teachers of the neighborhood. Many of them went out of their way to support the library when it was threatened with closure. Others, deeply interested in this place where it was so easy to meet children and young people, would simply stop by for the joy of conversing with them. Some of the children and adolescents shied away from formal programs but were at ease with what seemed like a regular conversation amidst the hubbub of the lending room.

For many years, there was an elderly woman from Clamart who would visit us on a regular basis, Madame Kowaliski. She lived in the *cité* and would come every Wednesday to spend the day with the children. She was very pretty and refined. For years, she was really part of our team. She looked just like Babar's old lady friend, the one who takes our elephant to the pastry shop to enjoy brioche and chocolate eclairs. Madame Kowaliski was passionate about science and photography. She was a friend of Robert Doisneau, this master of depicting everyday realities, and had worked with him for a long time in her youth. She liked to look at non-fiction books with the children. It was not just reading. For her, everything served as a pretext to tell them about her experiences, her discoveries, her surprises. The children were enthralled. This woman was an event unto herself. She had fans who were still writing her when she was almost a hundred years old.

Tana Hoban

At the library, there were sometimes also "work sessions" with authors and children that could be very inspiring. These truly creative workshops made it possible to experience the wonderful master-apprentice relationship.

I'm thinking, for example, of a friend of mine named Tana Hoban, a great American photographer who was living in France. Her books were published in the United States and not very well-known elsewhere, though they were highly appreciated by the followers of Jean Piaget. They were as much loved by children as by art enthusiasts.

I first met Tana when I was a visiting professor at UCLA, then saw her again in Paris at a book fair being held at the Grand Palais. She had just moved to France with her husband John Morris, one of the founders of the Magnum agency. We've been friends ever since.

The photographs of scenes and ordinary objects in Tana's storybooks offer children the exciting opportunity to explore concepts, and it's a delight for all to discover these photo books with no text. They propose a kind of game to see who will be the first to find what's hiding —geometric shapes, colors, spatial positions, volumes—amidst the busy images, depending on the particular book's theme. These books provide rigorous training in the power of observation.

A true artist, Tana offers a fresh and sensitive perspective on things in our surroundings that we can't see or, out of habit, have lost the ability to see. These are humble things, simple street scenes. All this, she says, can be learned, and this learning is all the more necessary in an environment that's considered ordinary. It takes the help of an artist like her to learn to rekindle our interest, through simple actions, in what sometimes seems so unworthy of stopping and photographing.

When Tana came for several days to lead a workshop, she first explained to the children, using books and photos, why she might choose a particular subject and a particular angle. She shared the considerations that go into all artists' work. The children learned how to frame subjects, how to isolate a detail, how to admire "unimportant" things by looking through a cardboard tube or through their hands after positioning them around their eyes. Then she suggested they get to work. She gave them some guidelines to help them make their choices, and with the Polaroids at their disposal, they went hunting in small groups in the library, outside, at the shopping center, and at home. Tana and a few adults went along with them. On their return, they all looked carefully at what they'd come up with, and she gave them some suggestions and feedback. She congratulated them on some discoveries that would never have occurred to her. And to finish, the children made two small books.

Christophe Gaessler

Christophe Gaessler, a friend from the neighboring *département* of Seine-Saint-Denis who was a kindergarten teacher would also come in to lead workshops. On several occasions he presented books and works of art, like those in Paris's Dapper African art museum, that had made an impression on him. He'd do this for the sheer pleasure of it. He involved some of the children in activities that allowed them to explore some of the creators' worlds from the inside. With just kraft paper, black markers, and some strict ground rules, they collaborated to create a cave in the style of Jean Dubuffet. I remember how impressed the parents were by the imposing work presented in the entryway and how proud the children were.

Christophe wanted to whet their appetites before introducing the children to the library's books on African mask art. The books were just one part of a whole program he'd organized. He would tell stories about masks, explaining the significations and rules according to the various ethnic groups. He then encouraged the children to create their own masks before he introduced them to the Vouvi and Boa masks in the Kitadi picture books. When he finally shared the books with the children, they were especially attentive. They were touched.

Moomin the Troll

I would have loved for the children to have met our beloved Tove Jansson, author of the remarkable Moomins series. Unfortunately, taking them to Finland was not a possibility. But they met her in another way in Clamart, thanks to her incomparable translators, Pierre and Kersti Chaplet.

In Finland, Moomintroll is a national hero, just as Astrid Lindgren's Pippi Longstocking is in Sweden. Both of these heroes' sphere of influence extends far beyond the borders of their respective home countries. Children all over the world enjoy reading about them.

Is Jansson's work really all that simple? You can judge for yourself. This series opens us up to that realm so familiar to children: the world of magic. All dreams can come true there, but there's always a certain logic. This is what Moomintroll experiences, along with his family and friends, when eggshells fall into the magician's hat and turn into clouds, like comfortable little cushions that can be used for travel.

> *The clouds bounded wildly about until the Snork discovered how to steer them. By pressing a little with one foot you could turn the cloud.*[19]

Tove knew how to give the simple pleasures of everyday life their due credit, just like our friend Arnold Lobel. Following a storm in Moomins' land, what does the sea bring ashore?

---

19. Tove Jansson, *Finn Family Moomin*, trans. Elizabeth Portsch, 2010, 16.

A little farther away, amongst the birch-bark, floats and seaweed, he discovered a raffia mat, a broken dipper and an old boot without a heel [..], a glass ball and shook it. Then up whirled a mass of snowflakes inside settling gradually to rest on a little house with windows of silver paper.

"*Oh!*" *said Sniff.* [...] "*I don't know which I like best, the lifebelt or your snow storm.*"

Wonderful treasures stolen from the sea!

The boat was indeed heavily laden when she sailed away from Lonely Island after the storm.[20]

Here is the pleasure of collecting, which children are familiar with: think of the treasures that they bury at the bottom of their pockets. As for the purse that Mama Moomin has consistently at her side, it contains "nothing but things you might need all of a sudden. Spare socks, candy, wire, aspirin, and things like that." There is a reassuring joy in listing these little things that make you think that Mommy Moomin really does have an answer for everything, that she can solve any problem.

I was invited to Tampere for the celebration of this great artist's eightieth birthday. When I returned, I told her fans about this unforgettable event, describing how beautiful she was as she crossed the city in an elegant flower cart. She'd been dressed all in white and, like a queen, her head had been crowned with exquisite white flowers. I'd been very impressed.

Lovers of children's literature and philosophers alike had come from all over the world to Tampere. The long distance hadn't deterred those who were so attuned to the spirit of childhood and the philosophy reflected in this series of works about a simple troll. A Japanese philosopher I met in Tampere told me she'd learned Swedish in order to read Tove's own words, to avoid possibly losing anything in translation. She also told me that she'd learned French so as to read the philosophical works of Simone Weil in the original version. So, in her mind, Moomin

---

20. Ibid, 79–82.

was in good company. I think Tove Jansson will go down in the history of children's literature alongside another Scandinavian: nobody less than Hans Christian Andersen.

Back in France, I contacted the Finnish ambassador. He knew Tove well and said, "Our two islands are neighbors." Together, we organized a small party in Clamart. Adults and children of all ages gathered there to listen to the magnificent texts read aloud by a fellow librarian, Jean-Pierre Radenac, a skilled reader who was especially fond of Tove's work. Some children had already read and reread the Moomin stories, but they enjoyed hearing them again alongside others who were discovering them for the first time. I experienced the shared response to her works at this gathering like a kind of enchantment.

These were stories from *Tales from Moominvalley*, texts of a rare poetry tinged with humor. Kersti and Pierre Chaplet, who had translated them masterfully into French, had come to join us. The librarian revealed with delicate restraint how the musically-inclined Snufkin was going to compose his spring melody. He then took us through uninhabited, solitary landscapes. We could hear the cries of migratory birds and the song of the stream, which sings in a minor mode like the mosquito.

> *"It's the right evening for a tune," Snufkin thought. A new tune, one part expectation, two parts spring sadness, and for the rest just the great delight of walking alone and linking it. […] "I must have the brook in my tune also," he thought. "In the refrain, I think."*[21]

When the Library Goes to School

When I was a fellow at the NYPL, I worked with a librarian from Amsterdam, Janetje Daane. She told me that in her neighborhood she would go from school to school and from classroom to classroom with a big bag full of books that she liked to share. She knew they could reach a young audience that way. She was jovial and exuded a true *joie de vivre*. An

---

21. Tove Jansson, *Tales from Moominvalley*, trans. Ernest Benn, 2010, 4–5.

excellent storyteller, she knew how to draw in students, who comprised her primary audience, but also their teachers. I'd seen her at work in New York. She would read aloud from books, but just a little—enough to give them a taste so that, when they left school, all they wanted to do was run to the local library and find its treasures. Then this place could play its true role by responding to individual interests and by offering children not just books, but also the opportunity to become a part of a home that was rich in interpersonal encounters and therefore special.

And so Janetje had brought stories into the classroom. This was no doubt a break in the routine, and it was good for students to have visitors from the outside enter their enclosed environment and bring some endearing characters with them, too! It was an opportunity for the children to go on literary journeys and enjoy them together as a class.

William Steig

I like recommending the works of William Steig, which I find irresistible. There is, for example, the story of Dominic, a dog like no other. It's easy to get the teachers I know to share this story with their classes and check in on him day after day not for any pedagogical reasons but for the simple pleasure of reading Dominic's stories aloud and giving children the chance to be moved, to laugh, and to dream. Dominic "was a lively one, always up to something. One day, more restless than usual, he decided there wasn't enough going on in his own neighborhood to satisfy his need for adventure. He just had to get away." He follows the directions given by a witch-alligator, who seems to have "many more teeth than were necessary for any ordinary dental purpose." But it doesn't matter! "I'm going wherever my fortune tells me to go." He prefers the risks of adventure to knowing his fate in advance and he takes his life as it comes, fully enjoying every moment.

Dominic is good company. He's fully human, but with his loyalty and sense of smell, he's all dog, too. His sense of solidarity allows him to free those he meets over the course of his travels from the terror of the Doomsday Gang. He saves the life of a goose destined to be eaten by these heartless men. "Imagine! To be hanged, to be hanged by the feet while on the way to market! And me a widow with children to look after!" Dominic always gives treasures that would have only weighed him down, and is rich in the friendships he makes along the way. Good humor, generosity, a love of life, and freedom course their way through the pages of the book, as we follow him from one day to the next. The playful illustrations are masterful—William Steig was a long-time cartoonist for the *New Yorker*—making you want to go along with the dog, who makes his way with nothing but a bindle and his story.

Storytime in the Morning

I advise some teachers to start each school day by telling or reading a story. My advice is based in particular on the experiences of Serge Boimare, a former teacher who works in classes with at-risk children and pre-teens. A story awakens the child first thing in the morning to the heights of the imagination, the depths of their emotions, and the magic of their teacher's performance. Students then feel alert, capable of focus, and ready to absorb something new. This does not involve any exam, request for a summary, or intrusive questions. The child is just carried away by the story—a pleasure for its own sake.

As René Diatkine reminds us, music must come before music theory. This story first thing in the morning is thus the music. With it, we leave the passivity of being, to use a lovely expression from Gaston Bachelard. Students are the recipients of images that make them think and dream. They can approach their various learning experiences and disciplines in a different way.

For the students and the teacher, being moved collectively connects them to each other and is a valuable form of shared experience inside the classroom. But it's important that the teacher offer these stories without any strings attached. Elzbieta, a magnificent children's book artist, regrets that some of her storybooks have been transformed, against her will, into exercise books for schoolchildren. "It goes like this: 'Has Little Grey found a shoe, a letter, or a sponge? Put a cross in the appropriate box...'" And she asks us adults: "When you read *In Search of Lost Time*, do you want to be asked if little Marcel eats a madeleine, a croissant, or a doughnut?"[22] But is telling stories to children really useful, if you can't use them pedagogically?

The famous British storyteller Marie L. Shedlock liked to quote Charles Hermite, a great French mathematician, from his address to the members of the French Academy of Sciences (Académie des Sciences): "Cultivate the imagination, Gentlemen, everything is there. If you want mathematicians, give your children fairy tales to read." The usual arguments that there's not enough time, that the students are restless, do not hold. To quote Bachelard again: "To imagine is to launch out towards a new life." How can we turn down such a beautiful invitation?

I suggested to Mathilde, who has a difficult class of CE2 third graders in the Paris suburbs, that she start her day in this way. She told me how much this gesture now brightens up her school days. Still, it's important to choose the right story. Her students, she tells me, know right away the difference between true works of art and flat, conventional texts.

Filling Up One's Inner Theater

In kindergarten and elementary school, the same group of children who are the same age spend all day together, every day. These are ideal conditions for diving deep, over the course of weeks or even months, into books that can only be fully appreciated when there's enough time to really inhabit them and move through their captivating universes that have all the complexity of real life. The characters of the stories have such a presence that they become cherished friends, and children bring them up spontaneously. This gives them the opportunity to develop a familiarity, quite naturally and joyfully, with a work of literature. Their own emotions are transfigured. They are responsive to the beauty, strength, and subtlety of language.

---

22. Interview in *Télérama*, November 29, 2014.

Adults reading aloud to the children are moved, too, and discover that these works represent something invaluable. It wouldn't occur to them to "employ" these texts for disguised grammar, vocabulary, or morality lessons with test questions, requests for summaries, or other such exercises. A perceptive adult spontaneously refrains from this and is careful not to compromise the quality of such experiences. It is special for the children and also for the teacher. It creates a kind of opening in the life of the class. Then life resumes in a different mode, with the focus on instruction and its necessary exercises. But the spirit has been invigorated.

The imagination is fueled by stories. "To fill up one's inner theater" is an expression that was used by the psychoanalyst Colette Chiland during a seminar held in Tours in 1973. In her address, "Various Ways of Not Reading," she distinguished the *liseur* from the *lecteur*. The *liseur* knows how to decipher the typographic signs but does not go beyond this. *Lecteurs*, on the other hand, go in search of characters who move them and leave an impression on them, and their imaginations keep getting richer in this way. Little by little, the characters start to inhabit a *lecteur*'s private life. The story resonates within and nourishes them. This is why it is necessary to tell stories, again and again, tirelessly. How can one develop a taste for reading, for stories—how would it be possible to even get interested—without a real inner life?

Unpacking the Library

It is important to choose wisely. But where to begin? I still have some reservations about these anonymous lists sent out to teachers, even if they suggest quality works. Such lists can be found everywhere on the Internet along with comments and reading guides. They have their place, of course, but these aren't enough to make our choices clear. In my eyes, person-to-person conversations based on meaningful experiences are invaluable. This is how a community takes root and develops. This is where collaboration among the school, the bookstore, and the library really comes into its own. A love of reading, for teachers and students alike, is not decreed by a series of compulsory readings. Readings are chosen, they're desired.

Daniel Pennac evokes a teacher "whose passion for books was infinitely patient and even gave us the illusion of love. Did he have to favor us—or respect us—his students, to give us to read that which he held most dear?"[23] I think of the teenager who was locked up in a reformatory, a kind of prison for young people, in a small town in Mexico called Guanajuato. She would always express her gratitude to Lirio, the librarian facilitator I worked with for many years, telling her: "I know you always want the best for us."[24]

There's nothing quite like the meetings where librarians, teachers, and sometimes parents share their experiences and favorites informally. There is a sense of trust and tongues are loosened. Everyone "unpacks their library."[25]

Elisabeth, the director of our neighborhood preschool, told how "her" five-year-olds were moved by a Tomi Ungerer storybook, *Otto: The Autobiography of a Teddy Bear*. But what could they possibly have understood about this story without knowing anything of the tragic events of World War II? David is a German-Jewish child whose playmate is Oskar, also German. David's family is deported. David, sad to leave Oskar, entrusts him with Otto, his teddy bear. What follows is Otto's incredible odyssey through the war and the bombings. He unexpectedly finds himself alongside both Oskar and David, who are finally reunited thanks to him.

---

23. Daniel Pennac, *Comme un roman*, op. cit.

24. Comments noted by Lirio Garduno, my usual interpreter in Mexico.

25. An expression employed by Walter Benjamin in his essay "Unpacking My Library" ("Ich packe meine Bibliothek aus"), written in 1931 and included in *Illuminations: Essays and Reflections*, trans. Henry Zohn, Houghton Mifflin Harcourt, 1968.

To Give the Love of the World

Otto is a story of violence, wars, and racism. But it's also a story of friendship, and children respond to this. It's possible to talk to kindergarten children about painful subjects without causing them to lose hope. I think of the philosopher Elisabeth de Fontenay who, in response to a journalist's questions, maintained, "Even when you are a pessimist, there is a decency to be maintained. As Hannah Arendt said, we don't have the right to transmit criticisms of the world to children before we've passed on a love of the world."

There are also philosophical picture books that make you think. Wolf Erlbruch's *The Big Question* is an example. A cast of twenty or so characters answer the question "Why are we here?" with humor, wisdom, and poetry. There's also *Reflections of a Frog* by Kazuo Iwamura, a Japanese book of vignettes that is both funny and profound. Some see it as an illustration of the philosophy of Emmanuel Levinas, because of the importance given to the face of the other! Thanks to the discovery of these books and to the conversations we've had at our meetings, there have been nothing but surprises and questions about the children's interests and how best to address them.

The Adventures of Hermes

To all children, even to those who have little inclination for reading, I suggest *The Adventures of Hermes* by Murielle Szac. I also recommend it to teachers and parents. The book begins, "The sun was only barely beginning to rise when Hermes came out of his mother's womb. He stretched himself, yawned, and leapt right away to his feet. Then he ran to the entrance of the cave where he had just been born, in order to admire the world. 'How beautiful it is!' he murmured. It was indeed a very strange birth."[26]

---

26. Ibid

I would have barely uttered these words in the library before some of the children would, as a matter of course, start to approach. Having stopped whatever they'd been doing, they'd draw closer, eager to discover Greek mythology in one "episode" after another, along with all the seriousness and complexity of human relationships as depicted in the myths. Essential questions are addressed there in a simple, pictorial language. Each chapter ends with a question, for example: "How was Hermes going to steal those cows without being spotted?" It was absolutely irresistible. The children would come day after day to find out what Hermes was up to. In a beautiful preface, Serge Boimare writes that by encouraging children to "follow mischievous Hermes, children couldn't ask for better company as they grapple, joyfully and light-heartedly, with the questions fundamental to the human spirit." It's a fascinating read! The young listeners couldn't wait for the next day to satisfy their curiosity. They read the book at their leisure to find out the fate of "the divine scamp."

Reading Aloud and Its Treasures

I like to introduce teachers to wonderful contemporary works such as those by Michael Morpurgo, François Place, and Timothée de Fombelle. These are works which children might not discover on their own. Reading aloud makes it possible for the children to enjoy them and to be moved together.

This has included, for example, Richard Adams's *Watership Down*, an epic about rabbits. These rabbits overran the Clamart library for a time, touching all generations in a unique way. I've introduced teachers to the story of these animals who, trusting in the intuition of the frailest and most fearful among them, have to leave their native rabbit warren. In this book, there is an entirely natural interweaving of the concrete reality of rabbits' existences and the richness of human experience. The human interest is revealed through the rabbits' mythology, but also through the political and social problems, the problems of life and death that they must solve.

The same is true of Timothée de Fombelle's magnificent works—in particular, *Toby Alone (Tobie Lolness)*. It is particularly rich: the language is magnificent and the illustrations by François Place are subtle and witty. Children enter easily into the story day after day. Toby Alone is seven years old and only a millimeter and a half tall, "which was not very big for his age." He ends up on wild flight inside the world of the tree he is trying to save. He takes the reader with him into a surprisingly lively and complex universe. Toby is distinguished by his courage, clear-sightedness, and goodwill as he confronts evil in the form of a dictator who keeps an entire population enslaved. These long readings can be delectable. Salman Rushdie compares reading a moving book to an amorous encounter: "When we love a book, the sensibility that emerges from it combines with our own, and we see the world through the eyes of the novelist. [...] It's like falling in love [...] I know when it happens to me because my reading suddenly starts to slow down: I don't want it to end, I want to stay in this relationship."[27]

Boimare observes that his unruly students, usually unable to concentrate, fully enjoy the scientific and technical descriptions in the works of Jules Verne that many readers—myself included—usually prefer to skip. There is, then, a kind of silence among them, a pause, consideration given to the understanding of the real.

I also like to share the work of Michael Morpurgo, a great writer beloved by readers of all ages. At times, he simply tells the story of something that really happened. *Christmas Truce* is a masterpiece for all. It is a true story that takes place in the trenches on Christmas Eve 1914 when, spontaneously, English and German soldiers decide to fraternize, to talk to each other, and to celebrate the holiday in their own way. The brevity of the tale, with its great solemnity and understated tenderness, encourages it to be read aloud. Morpurgo's language is beautiful, simple, and dignified, in keeping with the event. One reads this book slowly, meditating on it quietly.

---

27. Interview in *Télérama*, December 17, 2008.

I also like to suggest *Kensuke's Kingdom* by the same author, which takes place against the backdrop of a nuclear war. The novel affirms that it's possible to have a different world today. Fiction or a true story? The boundaries between the two blur in this little book that bears the marks of a great story, illustrated subtly by the remarkable artist François Place. It is a beautiful tale of friendship between a young English child stranded on an island and an old Japanese man who is there because he chose to live in solitude after the Nagasaki disaster. The language is simple, superb.

I also suggest non-fiction works such as some of the storybooks from the "Children of the Earth" ("Enfants de la terre") collection, now classics, in the Père Castor collection. They may be old, but they have stood the test of time. These take the form of authentic, insightful stories, with a subtle and profoundly honest presentation of the lives of real people. Children can identify with the people in these books while gathering valuable information. Relationality, emotion, and the joy of understanding come together in the world of anthropology. Isabelle Jan, who worked alongside Père Castor, states that here there is "no vain didacticism, no dry intellectualism; on the contrary, there is the awakening of sympathies, the discovery of differences and similarities [...] For a child, it is interesting and enriching to see how a foreign brother is cherished or punished, how he addresses his parents, how they address him. This is what it is to understand others."[28]

I also like to share a book by Paul-Émile Victor, an explorer who lived for long periods of his life among the Eskimos: *Apoutsiak, the Little Snowflake (Apoutsiak, le petit flocon de neige)*. Children are still interested in reading this classic, which was published in 1948. It is truly a work of ethnography. The author took children's desire to understand very seriously, with everything described very precisely. Moreover, he had a gift for storytelling. There is no sentimentality—he just tells it like it is.

---

28. Statements published in La Revue des livres pour enfants and cited by Michel Defourny, *De quelques albums qui ont aidé les enfants à découvrir le monde et à réfléchir*, L'école des loisirs, 2003.

I remember the questions asked by a very young child who had just read the story of Apoutsiak in the library. The reading had provoked real metaphysical reflections in him and he wanted to share them with me. For example, he asked, "At home, they told me that's not what it's like after death. So, what is it really like?"

Around King Matt

I participated in some memorable sessions discussing one of Janusz Korczak's major works, *King Matt the First*. When his father dies, Mathias becomes king. He is ten years old, a child-king who cannot read or write, and he runs away from the palace. He wants to become a reformer king. It's not easy to give children democracy. He experiences success and failure, war and peace, friendship and betrayal, but remains faithful to his commitment to the end.

In our library, this classic aroused the passion of our young readers and gave us a lot to talk and think about, so we would get together with the children to discuss it. Former readers still talk to me about it. When talking about the book, they discussed very serious matters such as the notion of responsibility, which had great importance in their eyes. Other issues included the difficulties of understanding between parents and children, the fragility of democracy, and the powerful role of the press. The children's readings would have been incomplete without these free discussions. These were in keeping with the spirit of the author, a great Polish pediatrician who was also a principal at an orphanage in Warsaw and who died with his orphans in the Treblinka extermination camp. These discussions were in perfect keeping with his idea of a children's republic embodied by the orphans who were in his charge. It just so happened that these debates took place in Clamart a few days before May 1968...[29]

Many years later, in Crépy-en-Valois, an elementary school teacher invited me to his class when he learned of my interest in the Polish

---

29. Ibid

pediatrician who had authored this coming-of-age novel. He had decided to read it to the children.

I then witnessed the entrance of King Matt the First into the classroom. With the teacher's guidance, the children took part in debates about the book while adhering scrupulously to the guidelines. The way the room was organized helped: as soon as I got there, we all sat in a circle, so as to set the tone for our meeting. There were no good students or bad students, and everyone had the right to speak and to be heard. The teacher played the role of moderator discreetly, which added to the seriousness of the discussion. It was impressive to see how these meetings stimulated a taste for debate in these children. The conversation was very rich and astonishingly mature. I was impressed, as were the students.

What remains of such moments? The time for reading and discussion came to an end, and everyone left their spots in the circle. The children returned to their desks and the teacher to his. The children felt acknowledged and listened to, intelligent and perceptive; something had changed in the way they acted with each other. They had learned to express themselves, to listen to each other, and to discuss. In order to conclude the Mathias event, the teacher had reserved an auditorium for the children to have a *real* debate in public. Students from other classes were also invited. It reminded me of the French National Assembly.

For several years in a row, these children from Crépy-en-Valois came with their teacher to spend a day in Clamart. They took a long trip on public transport, then had a picnic in the garden and reunited with some of the library's regulars. For them, the trip was entirely worth it. I fondly remember my collaboration with this teacher who knew so well how to engage children's minds.

Mint Tea and Croissants

There are sometimes unforeseen successes when classes come to see us at the library. For example, an original initiative was carried out in a very poor district to the north of Paris where many people were living in squats and thus in a state of precarity. I'd been constantly spreading word about it because it struck such a chord with the neighborhood's inhabitants, most of whom had recently immigrated to France. At the time, the person in charge of the library in this neighborhood was Blandine Aurenche. She had a trusting relationship with the teachers and wanted parents to find their place in the library, this place open to all, and to be able to discover with their children the richness of what it had to offer. In agreement with a school principal, she had the idea of occasionally inviting a whole class of young children and their parents.

These visits would take place in the morning. There was mint tea, hot chocolate, croissants, and brioches to set the tone. The visitors were welcomed as friends. The little ones were already familiar with the library, but for many parents, it was a revelation. During these morning visits, they were amazed to see how comfortable their children were among books. They saw how their children easily locating the books they wanted to show them and sometimes pointing out a picture they found especially moving or asking them to read a story.

The librarian presented some of the books that both children and adults found to be irresistible. She would read them out loud and display the pictures. Everything was easy, frank, and warm. All of it was free, in every sense of the word. Parents now knew that they would always be welcome in this place and that the joy of reading could be shared as a family. In a neighborhood like this one, parents often didn't dare come in through the door of the library. But here, they knew they were welcome. I'm always pleased to promote, both in France and abroad, this splendidly conceived project that was accessible to all. These were wonderful encounters.

I also remember interesting class visits to the library that involved a lot of questioning and debate. These were in fact rather rare, which I find to be rather regrettable. It would stimulate children's minds when students' questions around a given topic were addressed by the teacher, then made part of a broader discussion. The children were then eager to find out more, to understand, to know. As Célestin Freinet said, "You can't make a horse drink if it's not thirsty!"

There's no doubt in my mind that the discussions they had afterwards, once back in the classroom, were very valuable. Such investigative visits also led to the development of some materials that later found their place in our library. I remember that a survey a class did on our neighborhood was published, and we included it in the documentation resources provided for the children. There was nothing else like it in our library. These young researchers were proud to see their work recognized and provided for the community's use.

Such experiences were rare. Each year, in search of an interesting solution, we'd call the previous system into question, only to arrive at the certainty that it was necessary for schools to have their own main libraries. No matter how valuable scheduled trips to the public library may have been, how ready the librarians were to help, and how willing the teachers were, they could not replace a school library as a reference resource that students and their teachers could access at all times.

Libraries in Schools

Anne Schlumberger, upon listening to my thoughts, decided that an experiment was needed. What she had in mind was a village school in Le Muy, located in a *département* she knew well, Le Var. Her suggestion was for a librarian from Clamart to create a library within the school and get it up and running, all in close cooperation with the teachers there. Claude Gilbert was a good librarian for the job: dynamic and open, she had proven her mettle in Mont-Mesly, a neighborhood in Créteil, while collaborating with ATD Fourth World. Thanks to her enthusiasm, she worked effectively with both teachers and parents. A team effort was then put in place. This was the early 1970s.

I think I can safely say that this was the very first main library within a French elementary school. All the features of a real library immediately came together in this little town. The influence of Clamart was obvious. Freinet had a presence there too, and Claude could count on a few teachers who were a part of this movement and weren't scared off by teamwork.

A Freinet teacher, Colette Marchand, had spent a long time in our library. She was fascinated by the creative life that flourished there and helped us with her insights. She saw how a school library could be a collective resource. With students having access to a variety of resources at all times, a school's approach to teaching would thus undergo a radical transformation. Under such conditions, children would learn to select and compare information and to communicate their discoveries. In short, they would learn how to do research, to debate, and to think. Supported by their teachers and the librarian, students would feel collectively responsible for their knowledge and the library would become a place for discussion.

For the experiment in Le Muy, the team had complete creative freedom. There were no directives imposed from above, and we conducted our experiment in the field with our eyes wide open and critical faculties on alert. This is how the school came to consider giving children freedom of movement. Students could go in pairs at any time to fetch materials, even when they were in class, if necessary. They'd read, they'd consult documents, and this would spark debate. Freedom of movement? But what about security issues? This wasn't a problem. There were no incidents. Another novelty: parents were welcome, not to cover the books in paper or for repair jobs as a way to save money. No, they were invited to take part in what was going on in the library and some of them, without interfering in any way with the teachers' objectives, had a real place there. This included Germaine, a vintner's wife who had become, thanks to the library, one of the school's true allies.

Transforming Schools

What is the situation like today?

Pierre Guérin took me to a rural village, Aizenay, in the Vendée. This Freinet school was to be the subject of one of our audiovisual reports that I'd be taking with me on all my missions in France and abroad.

Talking about a school library, this new resource, wasn't enough. It was necessary to see how to set it up, how to bring it to life. These videos astonished teachers and got them interested as they observe the new types of relationships that formed between teachers and students. For example, we'd see the school principal on the playground. She was sitting on a rug, kindergarteners crowding around her as she read a storybook that seemed to fascinate them. Then she listened to them read. She looked like a mother surrounded by her children. Upon seeing this scene, one teacher told me that this had been unthinkable before. She said admiringly, "What a change in attitudes!"

It was exciting to see the children fully participating in the life of the library. A small girl presented a book, Janusz Korczak's *Glory*, to a group and expressed how moved she had been. "I even cried," she said. One boy made fun of her and she answered, "You're jealous." Here, reading became personal and a source of real exchanges. It was not like the traditional book reports, read in a rushed, monotonous voice.

I received a report from the principal of the Aizenay school, Anne Valin, and her successor Joël Blanchard. They participated in and witnessed the school's transformations. I was impressed: the library quickly became the very heart of the school and was "organized together with the children (weekly library meeting); it is in constant interaction with the classes. The students can access it on their own at any time, if they feel the need to do so for their projects. [...] They also go there to prepare a news review, to read to younger students, to meet adults other than their teacher. They can also send faxes to schools in the network seeking materials or information."

How many schools in France have embraced such a plan? The libraries that look to Aizenay as a model are still rare. It seems as if the way French schools are currently run does not easily allow for it.

While I was in Sweden for a conference, I noticed that there was a school nearby. This would be a good opportunity to see its library. I made a spontaneous visit, dropping in around lunch time. The library was nearly empty, but one of the few people there offered me a quick tour. He seemed to know everything about the place—how it was run, how frequently it was used, what treasures it held, the classification of the books. I asked him, "Do you work in the library? Are you a librarian?"

"No, I'm the school dentist."

Clearly, everyone there had an interest in the library.

René Diatkine

The child psychiatrist René Diatkine liked to return to the significance of genuine encounters. My own encounter with him was, in fact, decisive. In my professional life, there's a before Diatkine and after Diatkine. This doesn't just apply to the Clamart library but others throughout France and now also abroad. In projects that I take on and support in different regions of the world, particularly in the countries of the Global South, I mention him constantly. My methods have been enriched by his comments, and he's also suggested new ones to me. He brought my perspective into focus. Our interests converged on the same concern of creating conditions everywhere that encourage access to reading for everyone, while giving priority those who are usually farthest removed from the world of books.

We met in 1979. The French Ministry of Education (Ministère de l'Éducation nationale) had organized an important symposium about reading and the conditions for teaching literacy. I was the only librarian who'd been invited to speak. All the other speakers were teachers and/or researchers. By speaking concretely about the kids' lives at the library in Clamart, I revealed the unsuspected wealth of our activities to these pedagogy specialists. Immediately after my presentation, René approached me in the hopes of combining our actions and discussions. As a librarian, how could I not be delighted? I was aware of the work he did as a child psychiatrist in the 13th arrondissement of Paris. I knew that he was particularly interested in the world of books and stories, in the pleasure of reading, "an essential psychological activity, allowing the subject to become the narrator of his own story, thus giving him great inner freedom."[30]

In France, René is one of the great figures of psychiatry, especially child psychiatry, following in the footsteps of Freud and Winnicott. At the Alfred-Binet Center (Centre Alfred Binet), located in the heart of a district of Paris that is home to many immigrants, his practice brought him into direct contact with the problems of assimilation and exclusion. He met "destitute parents, teenagers who no longer know what their history is made of, very young children who are unable to build it."[31]

What I learned from Diatkine is, for me, essential: under the age of five, in the period when their language is being structured, children all have the same appetite, the same interest in stories, the same taste for books, no matter what their environment might be. These observations are based on his own experiences and research as a child psychiatrist and psychoanalyst, as well as the work of Emilia Ferreiro, a disciple of Jean Piaget. When all very young children have access to books while also getting the attentive and discreet guidance that is so very vital, inequalities in reading may no longer be inevitable. This is what moved me to action.

A dedicated researcher and practitioner, Diatkine was keenly interested in what was happening at the Clamart library. From time to time, he'd invite me to speak at his seminars, which were for doctors, child psychiatrists, psychoanalysts, psycholinguists, and health care workers. I would simply explain what made up the life of the library, a place where children could personally experience the joy of reading in complete freedom while discovering an original form of coexistence; where they learned to live together and collaborate as they chose.

I would mention the discreet and attentive place of the adults, their way of helping the children orient themselves in this vast world of books, their roles as intermediaries and onlookers who were close to

---

30. Florence Quartier-Frings, *René Diatkine*, "Psychanalystes d'aujourd'hui," PUF, 1997.

31. Ibid.

the children. I explained how everything we did was simple and natural, free and joyful, so that when we would sit among the children, who would circulate amidst the books at their ease, it was like being with family, informal and marked by a kind of intimacy. Reading was thus experienced in the company of others in a spirit of freedom and trust.

These were simple acts that could take place anywhere—in the library but also outside next to buildings, as we'd made a weekly practice of doing. Passersby would stop and marvel, with parents and older siblings sometimes sitting next to the children and reading a book with them, just like the librarians. We were all together in the world of books and relished these moments. All it took was a few carefully-selected books and making the time to sit down with the children. Then it was possible to experience the very essence of reading there in the open-air library.

This was of interest to Diatkine: "Not only are the most disadvantaged children ready to discover the pleasure of books, but the parents who are most in difficulty are also moved by this unexpected interest and, in turn, take responsibility for the books. What seemed irreversible is changing: isn't this a compelling reason to abandon conventional wisdom?"[32]

Go Where You Are Not Expected

It was necessary, therefore, to leave the library to reach parents and children who would otherwise risk missing out on such riches. We had to rally the people where they were and create a movement. This is what Diatkine was doing with two other psychoanalysts, Tony Lainé and Marie Bonnafé, and I immediately became associated with their project. In their eyes, it was important that these actions, which ought to be able to take place everywhere, be developed in close relation with the public libraries. An association was established that brought together librarians and figures from the health sector. It went by the acronym

---

32. Preface to the book by Marie Bonnafé *Les Livres, c'est bon pour les bébés*, Calmann-Lévy, 1994.

ACCES (Actions culturelles contre les exclusions et les segregation, or Cultural Actions Against Exclusion and Segregation) and was quite an undertaking. Other associations were to follow the same path with much intelligence and openness, such as the When Books Connect (Quand les livres reliant) network, itself also quite an undertaking.

Diatkine advised librarians: Go where you are not expected, where you do not think you will find books. Wisely, and with humor, he insisted that we choose unusual places, places that at first glance didn't seem suitable. The people we wanted to reach didn't come to the library. Not yet. They were intimidated by such institutions and often had negative memories associated with reading. We'd have to meet them elsewhere, surprise them; then they might discover that books could speak to them.

He told us to look for places where people had time on their hands, where they were bored, because then they would be receptive and ready to explore. There are places that are essential because people have to go there, like health centers, like mother and child protection centers. We could set up in waiting rooms, take the time to settle in with our baskets of books amidst the parents and the young children. The same applied to early childhood centers, day-care centers, nurseries, and social centers, too.

By opening up the health community to us, Diatkine encouraged us to have a presence in places where we could reach the little ones in the company of their parents. We had to be able to meet parents and young children together. Reading is something that is shared and that can be experienced fully as a family. Parents, therefore, had to be able to figure out what role they played in these exchanges.

"Offer books of real quality," Diatkine urged. "That's how you'll reach the parents. They themselves will appreciate the beauty and imagination of the books they discover. Let them see what astute readers children are. They'll be amazed. For the parents, this is certainly a new way to understand their children, to relate to them, to enter discreetly into the world of their imaginations, at their level."

Demonstrating how to do this helped to avoid many misunderstandings. It was also the best way to interest all those who were close to the children like babysitters, medical service staff, those working at the early childhood centers, and of course parents. A book is not just an unimportant object that merely serves to keep the child occupied. It is a site of interactions that is available to everyone. Would the adults be able to participate in these exchanges with the necessary delicacy and discretion? If they saw us at work, then they certainly would. It was important for them to witness these happy moments experienced together. Then they would be able to take it from there in all simplicity and with respect for the child. Diatkine always preferred the term "sensitization" to "training." For the adults, it was not a question of conforming to a more or less restrictive model dictated from on high. It was necessary to feel comfortable. This was how connections are made, and what made individuals ready to give and to receive.

But how could we have a presence everywhere? Did librarians have the time? Diatkine told us to grow our partnerships, to propose collaborations everywhere. He suggested that we be willing to listen and work together with those who knew children in settings other than own. They'd have a lot to say, too, and could enlighten us. Then we'd have people who could fill in the gaps. We'd meet up and think together; then, all over, moments of reading with the children and parents would find their place.

Diatkine proposed that we all discuss the matter together. He told us: You, the librarians, have a special place alongside these young children. They come to you freely and ask to sit by your side to enhance these moments of sharing. They need your attentive and reassuring presence as they are moved by new experiences; but you also read the story to them. You are right there and able to watch them take ownership of a book, a story, with its words and images. You can pace yourselves according to the child's rhythm. You take the time to do so and get in sync with the children. You see how they read and this interests you deeply. You come to better determine what it is, in the quality of the story and the image, that gives them pleasure.

Observe, Write

As a researcher and therapist, Diatkine considerably enriched our practices. The seminars he organized for us reinforced our interest in observation. He passed on the desire to take careful note of how children and parents experienced these moments and how bonds developed between them. Observe. Write. Don't leave out the details. They're significant. This will allow you to fully review the moments you've shared with them and will give you a lot to think about. Observation enriches your way of being. It sheds light on your practices. It places what is fundamental—mediation—at the heart of your work.

The child is happy to be the object of your unobtrusive attention. It's reassuring. You are there by the child's side: sympathetic, free of judgment, and without any interest in tests. You leave the young readers with their multiple interpretations, even if they disconcert you, even if they do not seem to be "in accordance with the author's intention." This is precisely what you are interested in. The child who reads or listens to a story is a subject and is, in their own way, an author. They are free to experience the story as they wish, as they need. "It is not the author's intention that counts, but what the readers read," Paul Ricœur reminds us.[33]

Children spontaneously give themselves the right to their own interpretations. Interpretations are as numerous, as unique, and as personal as each reading, as Marc-Alain Ouaknin, philosopher, rabbi, and expert in Talmudic readings, evokes in his beautiful book, *Bibliothérapie*. His rich conception of reading corresponds perfectly to reading as it is spontaneously experienced by young children.

Young children read and express themselves with their entire bodies. I notice how a child will peruse a book, stop at a picture, then come back to it. I see a child pick up the same book over and over again, and this prompts me to take a closer look. What is it that has proved to be so moving? Children's words flow freely, wondering, and I'm amazed.

---

33. Paul Ricœur, *L'unique et le singulier*, éditions Alice, 1999.

Though they are young, they are already astute readers. I also see them rejecting one picture book or another. They want to hear nothing of it and close it with authority. This is the reader's freedom.

Thanks to the teachings of Diatkine and his successors, I and others were learning to decipher children's behaviors and to attempt to understand them. The smallest details helped me to grasp what the child was experiencing at the level of intimacy, interiority, and freedom. They gave me a glimpse of a child's life in all its remarkable, unexpected, and profound dimensions, informing me about these inner experiences brought about by readings that moved them. They were like little seeds that germinated and grew in the mind, like sap that rises and can nourish a whole interior life. All this can take root very early, unassumingly.

The book is a site of personal encounters. We wouldn't dream of painstakingly trying to inculcate certain ideas. This is what makes our job exciting. Anyone who wants to become a librarian should go through this step first. They will know this job is right for them if they can make a personal commitment to it. This doesn't just apply to small children—the same goes for the older children and pre-teens who use the library. Our task as mediator is different, but just as necessary. The librarian's job is not limited to the distribution of books. Listening and observation have an important place.

Of course, I'm not a certified psychologist, but I pay close attention. The notes I've taken make me want to share my experiences, to exchange my observations with others, to expand my knowledge about how children read, and to find my rightful place as mediator.

Over the course of many years, Diatkine was very generous with his time. Every month, we would meet with him just outside of Paris in Evry. The session began with a librarian mediator sharing a detailed and thorough presentation of a moment of shared reading with a child. Then Diatkine would give us his analysis, which provided us with unbelievably valuable insights. Today, such meetings are widely attended. They take place regularly at the Sainte-Anne hospital in Paris in the presence of two psychoanalysts, Marie Bonnafé and Evelio Cabrejo Parra.

At the Heart of the Human Experience

Children remind us what reading is all about. It is an act of freedom. Down with the thematic readings too frequently asked of children! Is literary emotion confined to such frames? In the library, we can free children from these constraints. Long live the freedom of the reader! Far be it from us to worry about profitability and performance. Reading serves no purpose except to live better, to know oneself, to encounter the other, and to discover the world in all its beauty and complexity. Children ask us to help them find a book they'd like, and we try to respond by getting to better understand the child as an individual. Then we take the time to get to know them well enough to suggest a reading that might speak to them.

For us librarians, reflective activity is based on reality, pure and simple, rather than abstract theory. The starting point is what we observe on the job: the daily reality of the children and the discoveries, emotions, and relationships that are created through these shared experiences.

For my part, I've raised awareness throughout Latin America and Eastern Europe of what we discovered thanks to Diatkine: how useful it is to increase sites for reading, to reach out first and foremost to people who live on the margins, to make precise observations, and to reflect collectively. This moves us away from routine practices and from being obsessed with statistics. We are, together with the children and their parents, at the heart of the human experience. Thus, we are driven by a joy of connection, of reflection, and of dialogue. The library is always in a state of flux because at its center it is human. The mediators and librarians that I meet along my way recognize that this new way of doing things has profoundly changed their view of children and books as well as how they do their job. Thanks to shared readings and quality encounters, attentive parents and caring librarians have confided in me that they now look at children in a new way. Alongside the children, we witness something great, profound, and joyful. We see them awaken to the world around them. We are with them at the heart of human existence and are deeply happy.

It's not about "getting kids to read" and bolstering the library's statistics. The project is far broader than that. For a long time, the argument used by many to justify the importance of children's libraries was that they were preparing the readers of tomorrow. Yet this cast childhood by the wayside. Reading can help us to live better—today. It sets the mind in motion and provides fodder for a child's inner life. Will these children be avid readers when they are adults? I do not know the answer to that question. But I do know, however, that they will have experienced happy moments as children.

The Importance of the Useless

What is important is the present as experienced by the child, and that we share it with them. Diatkine has always reminded us, correctly and good-naturedly, that what counts in life is that which is useless, seemingly free, and enjoyed for the mere pleasure of it. This considerably lightens the weight of the "pedagogics" that often gets in the way of discovering the joy of reading and that is so heavy a burden for the child to bear. I remember some teachers' interesting reactions on this subject. I was invited to speak with teachers from the Freinet movement who were meeting for their annual congress. What I'd had to say had been thought-provoking. "It's true," one of them said. "When I see my children playing with Legos, it's useless and yet…" Another said, "I'll have to watch myself. I'm so often tempted to say to my students, 'You might find this boring, but it will serve you later.'" The child's here and now—it counts.

At the library, our task of mediation and observation is not limited to early childhood. It extends to readers of all ages, though of course in different ways. For older children, it is experienced through the conversations that take place about favorite readings and fascinating subjects they sometimes return to persistently. If they remain silent, the quality of our observation and respectful welcome support them in a different way. There, too, there is always something to note, to exchange, to consider.

With Sarah Hirschman, Beauty for All

The first time I met Diatkine, I also met Sarah Hirschman. This likewise had a profound effect on me. I immediately saw that, in many ways, the course charted by Diatkine converged with hers, even if they were interested in different age groups. ACCES focuses on babies, toddlers, children under the age of five, and their parents. Diatkine had actually always had an interest in preteens as well, but he left us far too soon. Sarah primarily focused on adults, with teenagers occasionally included in the mix.

Both gave priority to populations that, for various reasons, were usually removed from the world of books. They were committed to introducing them to high-quality works. In this way, they demonstrated their faith in people and in books. They also recognized the importance of working in conjunction with public libraries. For them, mediation was paramount and reading, which helped to create bonds, made it possible for people to live better lives.

Sarah often came to France with her husband Albert, a great economist and sociologist who was respected worldwide. In addition, he was a Nobel Prize winner with honorary degrees from more than twenty prestigious universities. He supported her initiatives. When we were exchanging ideas, she'd often say, "I'll talk to Albert about it. He'll be interested." A librarian in New York had advised Sarah to meet me, convinced that with our initiatives and experiences, we'd find common ground.

During her frequent visits to Paris, we used to have lunch together near the Centre Pompidou in one of those small restaurants near the Stravinsky fountain, alongside the works of Jean Tinguely and Niki de Saint Phalle. We would stay there for hours talking, and when we left we'd both be brimming with ideas.

In 1972, Sarah created the program *People and Stories, Gente y Cuentos*[34] in the United States. It all started very simply. She approached a woman

---

34. See Sarah Hirschman, *People and Stories/Gente y Cuentos: Who Owns*

sitting on a step in front of a building in a Puerto Rican neighborhood in Boston. With a book in her hand, she asked her if she would listen to a story with other people from the neighborhood and talk about it. The woman was surprised but saw this as a chance to break from her daily boredom. She said yes and set out to find five or six people to form a small group. The first session was a reading of *La siesta del martes* by García Márquez. The participants had little formal education, but they knew life with all its disappointments and joys. Through Márquez's words, they experienced the emotions of the mother and daughter in the story, and suddenly they discovered not only the pleasure of listening to this complex text, but also their own capacity to speak about it. The enthusiasm was so great that there was a second and then a third session around other stories.[35]

This scene, relayed by Katia Salomon, communicates the spontaneous and simple nature of the meeting, the surprise that ensued, the originality of the comments it elicited, and the richness and complexity of the work proposed. Sarah's book is entitled *People and Stories: Who Owns Literature? Communities Find Their Voice through Short Stories,* and the subtitle states the purpose clearly.

The original idea has remained intact over the years. Sarah Hirschman has never stopped fighting to bring the beauty of great texts to people who do not normally have access to them. She has never given in to attempts to hijack these groups and turn them into social inclusion sessions, even though this may be fashionable. She has always maintained excellent criteria in the choice of texts.

Sarah had to overcome many obstacles since it's not the norm to think that literature of the highest quality can speak to everyone, especially adults who have had little schooling and have led especially difficult lives that have kept them removed from the joys of reading. Not very many people believed in this project. Wasn't it elitist? Wasn't it presumptuous

---

Literature? Communities Find Their Voice through Short Stories, IUniverse, 2009. In France, this movement is called *Gens et Récits*. It is directed by Katia Salomon, Sarah's daughter.

35. This is recounted in a presentation leaflet by Katia Salomon.

to suggest complex works? Today, these literary encounters facilitated by *People and Stories* have found their natural place in certain public libraries in the US.

Sarah Hirschman worked with Paulo Freire, the Brazilian educator and philosopher who coined the term "conscientization": a continuous process of learning and moving forward together through concrete actions to free oneself and create a society desired for the long term. Sarah participated in this movement in an original way by turning to literature. This was totally new, even revolutionary. The participants, presented with authentic masterpieces, discovered their ability to connect with a literary text. Sarah's daughter, Katia Salomon, drew inspiration from this when she had similar sessions over the course of several years with inmates at the Fleury-Mérogis prison. I followed her activities and admired her selections. She proposed short stories by García Márquez, Hemingway, Borges, Maupassant, Selma Lagerlöf, Naguib Mahfouz, Raymond Queneau, and many others. The readers became aware that their life experiences helped them to appreciate these works—that they gave them new meaning.

At these weekly meetings, the participants would volunteer their feelings and ideas in response to what was often a very complex text. They knew they could approach these texts with a critical mind, engaging in a kind of sensitive dialogue. Each then realized that they could apply the ideas elsewhere, understanding that their own lives were unique as well as a part of something larger. This, in turn, could be a source of strength and dignity.

Participants discovered that they did in fact have things to say. It was important to create a situation where the readers/listeners could feel comfortable and free to express the ideas and the images the words evoked for them. Katia noticed that there was a joy that developed over the course of the discussions. The participants were awakened to how enriching a lively exchange could be, with their opinions and experiences allowing for particular interpretations of a word, a sentence, or a described emotion. Once the session was over, many felt the need to converse about various themes and often about the text. Certainly not all of them, who then returned to the solitude of their cells, would become readers who'd devour such books. But at least they would have enjoyed exceptional moments with others.

Katia continues to initiate and organize such meetings but in other contexts, like in the countryside of the Occitan region of France, with people from different generations coming together to discuss literary works.

Revisiting Age-Old Stories with Serge Boimare

Certain teachers were of enormous benefit to me as I determined which books to choose and how to present them. These include Pierre Guérin, the aforementioned Freinet teacher who had opted to work with developmentally challenged children. There was also Serge Boimare, who had been a teacher for a long time and had always chosen "problem" classes with children and preteens who had dropped out or were seriously failing at school and refusing to learn. When working on the margins, attentiveness and inventiveness are key. I've been impressed by Boimare's creativity, and I owe a lot to him.

His experiences and reflections have interested me because they've developed over time. Given the chaotic backgrounds of his students experiencing serious difficulties, he has come to radically question pessimistic generalizations, especially those regarding such students' tastes and judgment. His choices are daring. He takes a fresh look at the unavoidable question of mediation. What he says flies in the face of the somewhat simplistic idea that explains the vogue for a certain kind of young adult fiction. As well-intentioned as these works may be, sometimes they offer a condensed version of social issues like drugs, violence, incest, and homosexuality. Harboring general ideas about adolescence, the authors and proponents of such works forget that these books can sometimes be limiting rather than freeing. Often, they are mired in stereotypes and they unwittingly communicate a misunderstanding of young people's experiences, both the personal and universal They also forget that a true literary work with ambiguity and depth leaves readers free to forge their own paths. I've observed many times that young children sense this instinctively. Surprised to find themselves identifying with characters, they are familiar with the joy—I would even say the necessity—of the journey, of the detour, to discover themselves, to find themselves. Michèle Petit, an anthropologist who is particularly interested in reading, recalls that "We need the faraway. When we grow up in a confined universe, these escapes can even be vital."[36]

What Boimare says, meanwhile, dismantles our preconceptions about the possible—or impossible—paths charted by these young people who violently reject all learning, especially reading. Are they condemned to remain at a remove from real literary experiences? What he describes is not limited to children with serious challenges. These extreme situations served to shed light on my reflections about reading in general and helped me choose which books to recommend to children— to all children. Boimare explains, "Most of the children I was in charge of teaching had been expelled from several schools in the neighborhood for serious violence and lack of discipline. [...] After fifteen days of classes, I had no more students. Most of them were outside, busy playing or else provoking me if I was so bold as to try to get them to return. As for those who stayed inside with me, there was no question of learning. I had to be content with distracting them or keeping them busy. Otherwise they'd join the ranks of those taunting me from beneath the windows. I would have switched jobs if I hadn't found a book of (Grimms') fairy tales left on a shelf in the classroom. [...] One day, I started to read some of the tales to the three or four children who were still with me and, as if by magic, I saw my students coming back, one after the other, to listen to the tales. Unexpectedly, I saw these tall, volatile preteens curl up in their seats and suck their thumbs to listen to stories that, to me, seemed to be at the kindergarten level [...]. After about six weeks, I started to see encouraging signs. First, I saw the group finding some cohesion, becoming a forum where it became possible to exchange words other than insults and verbal provocations. The children

---

36. Michèle Petit, *Éloge de la lecture, La construction de soi*, Belin, 2002.

began to talk together about the heroes of the stories I read to them, and they no longer threw their family issues in each other's faces."[37]

Boimare tells us how children who violently refused any kind of scholastic education were able to become passionate about works that are ranked among the great works of our literary heritage: the Bible, the Odyssey, the great classical myths, the Grimms' tales, and works by Jack London and Jules Verne. "We should not make the mistake of believing that the most underprivileged are put off by cultural themes. It is often these age-old stories that are closest to the internal concerns of these children, who are ever so deprived on the cultural level." There are these powerful literary works and then, at the other end of the spectrum, the bland, thin texts "for struggling readers" that, Boimare notes, students angrily reject.

It seems that the more challenges children have, the more they prefer and even need strong, colorful texts, even if they dread them at first. In contrast with what they can expect from current issues that are flatly integrated into certain works of fiction, it is these encounters with metaphor—with the literary, these far-flung travels, these detours encouraged by coherent, universal texts—that can allow them to think more clearly. The portrayals and images presented by the tales, by the poetry and the myths, are conveyed with true art and presented with the necessary distance.

Boimare's numerous, carefully-analyzed examples were truly illuminating for me. The students classified as "non-readers" in his class "didn't understand what they read, couldn't put images or ideas to sounds." He therefore suggested that they explore reading based on cultural representations of the fears that usually pushed them to withdrawal or dysfunction. He didn't use big general theories but looked candidly at the realities of these children and adolescents. His proposals were unexpected and merit close attention.

---

37. Serge Boimare, *L'enfant et la peur d'apprendre*, Dunod, 1999. All the quotes that follow are excerpted from this book.

He recounts what happened when he presented these kids with, for example, the powerful Biblical story of the divine punishment of the arrogant Balthazar. His students, he tells us, plunged right into the palace of the king of Babylon: "Balthazar, while indulging in debauchery, used the sacred vessels looted from the temple in Jerusalem by his father, the famous Nebuchadnezzar. [...] Under the influence of drink, Balthazar ordered that the gold and silver vessels his father had taken from the temple of Jerusalem be brought in so that the king, his lords, his wives, and his concubines could use them for drinking [...] A bloody hand moving on the wall and the joyful assembly, suddenly sobered by this nightmarish vision, descended into a nightmare of horror and terror. [...] Then the king changed his tune as his spirit was struck with fear." If children were interested in this text that Boimare read to them, "it was essentially because this king Balthazar [...] was in the grip of emotions like those they'd had themselves, or that they could have had [...] It's necessary to look beyond appearances [...], there are many similarities between what is experienced by a class of at-risk children and what happened in the big palace of Babylon. Excitement, feelings of omnipotence, triumph, greed, envy, contempt for the rules are, in our group too, ways of not recognizing the law, of refusing dependence, of keeping doubt and questioning at bay." Curiously, these children who rejected all rules and discipline were spontaneously shocked by these desecrations and determined that they deserved punishments commensurate with the seriousness of the offence.

"This seemingly complicated, anachronistic story held their attention because it spoke to them of feelings they were familiar with, feelings that were certainly comparable to those that confused them and kept them from thinking." They entered into this story because it offered something more than just a reflection of the kinds of family problems and fantasies they encountered daily. It was important for "the theme underlying the intellectual work to be distant, in terms of both time and space, if the representation of anxiety it offered was to be negotiated mentally." With these powerful texts, "what had been blocking these children for years was overwhelmed and swept away by the essence of the message."

Listening to Beautiful Texts

What the best texts, classical or contemporary, offer us is something other than a flat and faithful reflection of the prospective reader's concerns, which is a clearly-demarcated path. We do not enter a literary work head-on, but rather by way of the fictional world and the images it creates. They take us down indirect paths and get us to experience our concerns in all their power, subtlety, and depth. Unconsciously, without even realizing it, we discover ourselves there. "This brings to life the desire to know, which has become stronger than the fear of learning," says Boimare.[38]

Of course, the work of a teacher like him is exceptional—as was the magnitude of the difficulties faced by his students—and he was also remarkably patient; such mastery takes time. Is this work solely for psychologists and psychotherapists? No, for him, "cultural mediation, whether literary, scientific or artistic [...] must be able to play its role. It must be able to give a form the mind can manage to the anxieties that keep someone from flourishing."

Boimare's observations, by enlightening me about those who are classified as "non-readers" or "struggling readers," encouraged me to propose quality works—great texts—to everyone, without exception, and to take the time to read or reread these books that expose them to the wide-open sea, that ask the universal questions with their great ancient myths and cosmogonies. His reflections have encouraged me to take the time to personally rediscover works that are often misunderstood because they are called classics, though this has not deprived them of any of their power. It also helps me to be discerning in my choice of contemporary works that should not be dismissed or ignored.

---

38. Serge Boimare, *L'Enfant et la peur d'apprendre*, op. cit.

Whether they are books from the past or the present day, it's important to propose readings that are worthwhile. We don't need to limit ourselves to them exclusively, however; without question, we need books that are easy, too! But it would be a real shame not to discover books that are "too good to miss," to use the expression of the very first librarians in New York at the beginning of the 20th century—works so beautiful that it would be a shame to never know they existed. This is where, as mediators, we find our place.

And we all need to hear beautiful texts. For the person who is reading out loud and the person who is listening, a sensitive, sensual reading can be a real treat. After reading Boimare, I was inspired to take the children on a journey "twenty thousand leagues under the sea" or "to the center of the earth," or to cross the wilderness of the Great North. I also feel like inviting them to follow tiny heroes like Toby Alone. These books address origins, death, and sometimes archaic fears. Everyone always comes back for more.

I also think of Bruno de La Salle, our storyteller friend, and the great texts he chose to share in all of their power and beauty. I've often listened to him and I know how his artful storytelling will suddenly transport me to a world of infinite richness. I could listen to him all day. Bruno narrates, sings, and chants the *Odyssey*, which he knows by heart, from his heart. He tells me that sometimes young people are deeply touched and come to him to ask, "But where did you find all these stories?" They are well aware that they've just experienced a great work. I find this encouraging. I'm sure that, whatever one's culture or aspirations, we are all capable of loving such works that have traveled across the centuries and enlightened humanity. It's up to us to introduce them to the children and young people of today!

The Intelligent Heart

René Diatkine, Sarah Hirschman, and Serge Boimare—men and women with intelligent hearts, to use Hannah Arendt's expression— have, each in their own way, inspired me a great deal in terms of what is at the very core of my profession. They are avid readers and have a very positive view of the library, provided its functions are not limited to simply distributing materials. They all share the same conviction: the encounters that the library offers can help transform the most difficult of lives by opening up new avenues through reading. They believe that the diversity, depth, and joy of reading can help to reduce determinism. In giving rise to self-awareness, knowledge of the other, and a unique voice while freely nourishing the imagination, reading makes it possible for us to live better here and now. I've gained a lot from these people whose humanity I admire. In everything they've done, no great material means were required. All that has counted is open-mindedness, generosity, and sensitivity. There is a real personal commitment. This has always informed my actions in France and the rest of the world, especially in the countries of the Global South, where librarians want to breathe new life into their institutions.

Opening Up to the World

From the outset, Anne wanted the Clamart library to be open to the world. The children of this suburban *cité* needed access to the most beautiful books on the planet, so that they could grow up with them. Giving children the opportunity to wonder is a magnificent gift! This was why, as I mentioned earlier, she gave me the task of building a first-class collection of books loved by children in other countries. She knew that these sensitive and beautiful books would open up the minds of our budding readers in a natural, intimate way to the art, science, and culture of others, and that they would soak them up.

Julien Cain, emeritus director of the Bibliothèques de France, was honorary president of La Joie par les Livres. According to this important figure in the world of libraries, it was essential for Clamart to find its place at the international level. He strongly encouraged me to participate in the conferences held by the IFLA, the International Federation of Library Associations. I followed his advice and attended the 1967 conference in Toronto. I was intimidated. Most of the French delegation was, in fact, made up of fine representatives of the profession. Most of them held leadership positions at the BnF or in large, listed libraries. What was a children's librarian doing there? Were French public libraries represented? They were not, with two exceptions. These two librarians were especially dynamic, and I had the opportunity to talk with them afterwards. As for the children's librarians participating in these congresses, they were mainly from the Scandinavian and Anglo-American countries. Did I really belong there? I didn't know then that, a few years later, this international federation would ask me to be a permanent special adviser, a position that was quite exceptional at the time and that I would hold for twenty-five years.

The functioning of this international body is particularly slow and complex, and it's not easy to get one's bearings. In Toronto, however, the most dynamic of its active members were showing interest in Clamart's activities. Harry Campbell, director of the remarkable City Library of Toronto, confided that he wanted to create a kind of invisible network of particularly innovative public libraries. That was in 1967. Little did I know that I would later be called on throughout the world to share my experiences—and I still am, to this very day. In the early 1980s, I received an invitation from UCLA's library school to teach there for a year as a visiting professor. In France, unfortunately, the ministry did not approve such a long stay, so I was only there for one term. However, it gave me the opportunity to convey to the American students what had enriched my professional life through various experiences around the world, especially in certain developing countries. I'm convinced that such information can also prove useful in countries where libraries have had a long tradition, as in the United States. The young students' enthusiasm attested to this. They even asked that I come back every year.

Projects abroad have always been an important part of my professional life. As early as 1973, I received an invitation to the Algiers Book Fair (Foire du Livre d'Alger) from the director of the Institut Français, Pierre Comte, who asked me to give some lectures in the Algerian capital.

The Clamart experiment showed him an unexpected side of children's libraries. I didn't offer any grand theories about the benefits of reading; rather, what I proposed was simple. I told the story of the library and shared my thoughts about what was happening there. I described a simple, harmonious life where children became, quite naturally, responsible participants. I talked about the workshops and the books. All of this surprised and amazed him. Who would have thought that there were such riches to be found in a children's library? Pierre was enthusiastic. As director of the Institut Francais, he was sometimes called upon to take residence in other countries. He went to Kenya and then to Egypt. He invited me each time, but because of my schedule, I couldn't go.

My Experience in Brazil

My experiences in Latin America had a profound impact on me. In 1977, I was invited to Brazil for a two-month assignment. Leny Werneck, an active member of the Brazilian section of the IBBY, knew about Clamart. It was her idea to ask Jean Rose, director of the large network of the Alliances françaises in Brazil, to organize and take charge of a project that would allow me to help prepare librarians to work with children. It was my first long trip to a country that was, for me, exotic. I was in for quite a shock. On the day of my departure for Brazil, in the rush of preparations, I handed in the manuscript of my book *Laissez-les lire! Les enfants et les livres*,[39] to the publisher, Éditions de l'Atelier. I took a plane to Belém and early in the morning the next day, I was traveling the Amazon River by boat. Everything reminded me of Lévi-Strauss's *Tristes tropiques*. On the banks of the river, men and women, natives with copper skin, were swinging in their hammocks. In the city, I was struck by the extreme poverty, by the number of beggars, and the children and adults with severe disabilities. I was told that some of them had intentionally maimed themselves to elicit pity and collect money.

---

39. It has been reissued by Gallimard Jeunesse with the subheading: *Mission lecture*. The English translation is forthcoming.

At this time, the Alliance Française was also hosting Alain Robbe-Grillet, who was giving lectures on the New Novel. *Alice in Wonderland* forged an initial bond between us. It was the only experience of reading as a child that he could remember. During the two months of this project, we followed the same itinerary from city to city, from north to south, from Belém to Porto Alegre, passing through Recife, Salvador de Bahia, Belo Horizonte, Rio, São Paulo, Curitiba, and Florianópolis. I gave classes and conferences all over about my conceptualization of the librarian's job, about reading to children, and about how I choose books for them, drawing upon my experiences in Clamart.

In Belém, I was shown around some schools. It was a shock for me. Was it possible to teach in such conditions? Everything was noisy and the heat was suffocating. There were noisy fans, open doors and windows, drafts, incessant traffic, commotion, classes left to themselves, absent teachers. How to hold the children's attention? How could they concentrate? Yet these schools were not chosen at random. I was surely shown the best ones.

Luckily, the Alliance Française suggested that I visit an exceptional school located outside the city. It had been built with few resources. Half of the students were children of air force personnel and half were children from this poor neighborhood. Tuition was free of charge and they had adopted educational reform for the first level, i.e., for children up to the age of sixteen. The library was only in its planning stages. I was sure it would come fully into its own with their very smart pedagogy: a pedagogy of responsibility and projects; a balance between instruction in the morning and manual activities in the afternoon; co-management, with only three supervisors for this school of 1800 children. There were no luxuries, no waste. My visit was low-profile—I was content to observe, and my guide did not ask the students to present their work. They didn't notice my presence and just kept on with what they were doing, completely absorbed by their activities.

I was impressed by the natural science museum, composed primarily of what the children had brought. A *padre* passionate about science oversaw it all. He wasn't there when I visited, but everything I saw in this space suggested an exciting job, especially in a region like Pará, with the school surrounded by the Amazon rainforest. In one corner, there were a few live boa constrictors, and in another, there was a huge spider. Elsewhere, there were animal fetuses preserved in formaldehyde, and all over, there were collections of insects, minerals, and butterflies that the children had contributed. Through the window, I could see some students tending the vegetable garden and others planting trees. It was the end of the day and two children came to feed the boas.

There was also a large workshop containing an actual printing press equipped with real letter cases that were bigger than those used for the Freinet printing press. A child had just printed a prayer in small letters requesting indulgences "for his grandmother who is in pain." This was a far cry from schoolwork! Other children were involved in pottery projects, learning collectively and meticulously. Others were involved in electrical work, with the older children helping the younger ones. There were many workshops: cooking and sewing, with both boys and girls; here, they were dyeing fabrics; there, learning about childcare. The children even assumed responsibility for the cleaning.

The science laboratory was not in operation at the time of my visit, but it appeared to be complete, and, in principle, accessible to groups as well as to individual children at all times. A movie room was in the process of being built, just like the library, and it was to be available to children and adults from the school and also the neighborhood.

In France, I talked about my experience in Brazil with the researchers at the National Institute for Pedagogical Research (Institut national de recherche pédagogique, or INRP), who wanted to encourage the creation of central libraries in elementary schools. When I described this school, Jean Hassenforder and Jean Foucambert hailed it as a model. There was no doubt that within the context of such a pedagogical approach, the library would truly come into its own.

These exceptional initiatives I discovered on the other side of the world were proof that they were perfectly viable everywhere.

Encouraging Reading Amidst Extreme Poverty

With a few exceptions, the public libraries I explored back then in Brazil, as in other Latin American countries, were not very dynamic. The librarians didn't seem to enjoy their job. They were primarily involved in cataloging and other traditional library tasks. The books on the shelves seemed to be lying dormant. In the best of cases, middle school students would be there copying encyclopedia articles for school. I tried to convey a different vision of reading services for children.

I remember the friendly criticism from an Alliance Française director. This was in Recife, a city in northeast Brazil: Why come to talk about readings, stories, and libraries for children in regions that are suffering from extreme poverty? Aren't there more urgent matters? Wasn't this an unseemly provocation? He underestimated the liberating power that culture—especially reading and storytelling—can provide. He forgot that these respond to a vital need, especially in places where living conditions are most inhumane. Why should we keep universal culture and its most beautiful treasures from those who have been stepped on and humiliated? Why not give priority to the children who have been robbed of their childhoods? Throughout my professional life, I've had the good fortune to meet people who were driven by this desire for justice.

For example, in Mexico City I met Cristina, who worked in a publishing house and reached out to street children in her spare time. She wasn't afraid to sit with them and would show them storybooks and read with them or tell them stories. Usually, these children and teenagers would stand at the traffic lights and main intersections. They'd run over to the stopped cars to smear the windshields with soap. After some acrobatics, they'd hold out their hands to collect coins until the drivers would gesture for them to move away, dismissing them.

These children have been deprived of their childhoods and such brief moments shared with books gave them something invaluable. What was offered to these child slaves, these rejected children, was time—a time of free pleasure. Instead of running away from them, she got closer to them. She gave them the opportunity to dream of other worlds, of more just worlds where the weak and the small could defeat the powerful. They lifted their heads and felt loved—that is what this generous woman offered to the children. A subversive act, without a doubt. And so she had to put some of them on hold. She had, in fact, received threats from men who believed they owned these children.

When I explored Brazil in the 1970s, this huge country, like others in Latin America, was on the verge of witnessing significant changes in the field of children's books. My project was very timely and took place at a pivotal moment. Most of the libraries I visited were used primarily for school "research." They were painfully sad. In Recife, I was told about a children's library that was not long for this world: old yellowed books, some that had never been opened, some never borrowed, with the most recent loan stamps showing that many books had not been checked out for almost twenty years.

I stayed longer in Rio where, each morning, I gave a series of talks to a large, welcoming, and warm audience. As usual, I gave my pitch and shared my exciting experiences. I spoke a great deal about Clamart, especially the activities that could be initiated anywhere, regardless of economic or social context. I insisted that the library's value came from the beauty of the works, the simplicity of the encounters, the children's participation in the life of the library, and the indispensable mediation.

A few years later in some of these countries, I had the opportunity to be introduced to some of the loveliest initiatives I've ever encountered. This was the work of individuals who were aware of the urgent need for such transformations and who were convinced of the exceptional role that libraries and reading could play under certain conditions. All this was set up and developed with an enthusiasm for discovery and relationships. I'm reminded of the young indigenous man from Colombia who came down from his distant mountain to Bogotá to attend a course that I was giving for several days. He had become a librarian and had only one thing to say: "The library is magic. It's a miracle." That was in 1995, almost twenty years after my first trip to Latin America.

By 1977 I had met some individuals in Brazil who were really committed to giving children's reading its rightful place. There weren't very many of them, but they knew each other. They were all, in one way or another, connected to the FNLIJ, the Brazilian branch of the IBBY. Most of them had a certain social position in their country and knew how to solicit the help of big companies and media outlets to carry out their projects, which they did with the utmost independence. After we'd all met up, they launched a great project called Ciranda dos libros, which allowed for the distribution of carefully selected books in all of the country's public schools.

In Rio, I'd admired what those in my classes were doing in some of the favelas. They were eager to show me. The project was both simple and remarkable. The children I met were clearly among the more fortunate ones, since their parents had been able to sign them up for different kinds of activities. Walking around this extremely poor favela, I saw these children, so full of life, so happy to sing, laugh, play, and dance. The few books were welcome there. We read to them and told them stories and they loved it. But it would be delusional to think that they and their parents could just start going to the traditional neighborhood libraries. Families needed a real welcome so it was important to promote a certain kind of library.

To Give Humans the Awareness of Their Profound Humanity

In 1985, a few years after this long assignment in Brazil, I was invited to Peru. Jean Rose, who'd been the one to invite me to Brazil, had just left the country after having directed the broad network of Alliances Françaises there to become a cultural advisor at the French embassy in Lima. He invited me to give a few lectures in Peru, and I'd also have the chance to attend a conference about libraries in rural areas. I had already heard about the librarian Alfredo Mirez Ortiz, an important figure in this world. He was at the center of this great meeting. He was and still is the director of the rural library network of Cajamarca, located in the mountainous regions of northern Peru.

As soon as I arrived in Lima, I was struck by the extreme destitution. The road that led from the airport to the city crossed through immense expanses of cardboard shelters where entire families were living. I witnessed scenes of exceptional violence in the city. It was the era of the Shining Path (Sendero Luminoso) and the country was in disarray. It was experiencing hyperinflation, which meant that it was practically necessary to bring along small suitcases full of money just to go shopping.

Our meeting was in Cajamarca. On the way there, in a bus, I had the opportunity to speak at length with my neighbor, a short and lively man who looked like he was from the mountains. Our conversation was fascinating. He was very refined, cultured, and spoke French perfectly. He told me how happy he was to participate in this conference and tell me about the origins of this network of rural libraries and the activist librarians who gave a rightful place to the indigenous populations who make up the majority in this region. I guessed that he was a priest. He told me that he was actually even a bishop, but that he'd had to leave Peru for years. *Persona non grata*! And so, he had chosen France. He'd gotten in touch with Abbé Pierre and the two had become friends. He told me that that when he returned to his country, he found his niche when he chose to be a librarian in the network of rural libraries of Cajamarca. During my short stay, I saw him several times at work in different contexts. Who would have guessed that he was a bishop? He was the humblest of the humble. I learned later that he had been murdered.

Being a librarian can indeed be risky in some countries. I knew that some of those in Cajamarca had been in prison. Awakening people to their profound humanity is in truth subversive, especially if those people are at the bottom of the social ladder.

I was impressed by how these librarians approached their job. This region was predominantly Inca, and the library needed to embrace this population. This meant being in close contact with them, listening to them, giving them a voice, and providing them with access to books and reading so they could situate themselves in a wider world without having to give up the richness of their culture. Some of them could neither read nor write, but they still had things to pass on through their words and their works. The library thus gave oral archives their proper place. In Cajamarca, I was able to observe how the research conducted there on Incan irrigation methods had had an immediate impact on agriculture. I saw it in the fields covering the hillsides. I was told that it was less expensive, less polluting, and more efficient. Moreover, it made it possible to escape dependence on the big groups that were invading this gold- and copper-rich region. It was clear why the leaders feared what was happening at the library.

I was especially interested in one of the flagship projects of these libraries that worked together as a network: it was a good illustration of this principle and demonstrated the seriousness of their approach. Librarians and peasants carried out demanding archival work by creating the *Enciclopedia campesina*, the *Peasant Encyclopedia*, from oral archives. For this, they had to revive the Incas' memories of their roots and their communities. The library was enriched by their connections with the earth and the mountains as a sacred space. It facilitated the sharing and transmission of knowledge for new generations. "It is not enough to learn to read," they said. "We must also produce our own books." The *Peasant Encyclopedia* published pamphlets on subjects as varied as music, techniques for weaving and dyeing, and tools, as well as the great cultural figures who had left a mark on their world. It was based on the work of the Brazilian Paulo Freire, who stated that "no one educates himself, men educate each other through the mediation of the world."[40]

Along the way, I've encountered similar initiatives in different places driven by the same spirit. The people behind them had the same desire to reach out to the margins, to get closer to those who are often not recognized by the educational and cultural authorities. They have a high opinion of reading and libraries and are driven by a concern for justice that leads them to focus their efforts on those who are overlooked.

---

40. Paulo Friere, *Pedagogy of the Oppressed*

Because they work close to them and listen, they understand the value of those who have been victims of exclusion and are able to create meeting spaces where they may fully come into their own and have a voice. Those who have created such initiatives often came from elsewhere or from other cultures. In Cajamarca, it was Juan Medcalf, a naturalized Peruvian English cleric, who had such an idea at the end of the 1960s. Likely because of his enormous respect for the landless Incans, he wanted their voices to be heard; but also because their voice is, in a sense, universal. We all need to hear these profoundly human voices.

Fighting against Injustice

After the meeting in Cajamarca, I spent a few days in Lima. I was anxious to find out about the reality of public libraries there and, in particular, the small reading units emerging in the most deprived areas.

A young French woman accompanied me. She was a wonderful interpreter. When I expressed my surprise that she had chosen to live in such a violent country, she told me that her partner was Peruvian. We became friends and would meet up from time to time during her brief returns to Paris. Then she decided to return to France for good and felt the need to confide in me. She told me that she'd led a double life in Peru. She had, in fact, been a member of a terrorist group. She told me that she had learned how to rob banks and how to kill. When I left, this group had violently reprimanded her for having gone with me. Her eyes had been opened when she'd learned about the rural Cajamarca libraries' activities involving Inca peasants and when she'd discovered the small reading units at the service of those who'd suffered from humiliation and exclusion: There was no need for the group to be violent in rising up and fighting against injustice. She'd decided to leave the group at her own risk. It was an act of courage since, as she told me, she risked being killed. To her great surprise, she'd been spared.

Infinite Respect for People

I've been fortunate in having had experiences that were simultaneously humble and exceptionally rich; and in having been able to share them with people in different parts of the world. I've held responsibilities at the international level, both at IFLA and IBBY. All this has allowed me to participate in networks with valuable contacts.

In order to get to know dedicated librarians working in various parts of the world, I was able to count on the help of people who had closely followed the development of our library in Clamart. They knew of my interest in these small and often unusual organizations that, with such intelligence and heart, put people at the center of their concerns.

Those who worked as librarians in these places of poverty and cultural exclusion were passionate about justice. They were also avid readers. They knew from experience that reading could be a portal, could free people to speak, and offered the perspective necessary for them to take better charge of their lives. Rejecting any ideological influence, they showed an infinite respect for people and their freedom of thought. They were driven by the desire to share the best. The indispensable human mediation between people and books was at the core of their approach, and their practices provided material for considerations that were in perpetual motion.

A Seminar in Leipzig

I was able to keep up with some of these librarians and their activities, their projects, and their thoughts. I tried to put them in touch with each other. All this became even more important when IFLA and UNESCO asked me to organize the first international seminar on reading services for children and adolescents in developing countries. This was in 1981, in Leipzig, then a part of East Germany. There, those who had served forgotten communities made their voices heard. I learned a lot from their initiatives, which were driven by strong convictions and rigorous consideration.

All the participants and speakers invited to the seminar in Leipzig came from developing countries. The floor was theirs! This had been my decision. For the first time, they were in charge of the discussions. At the time, this was a major first. In those days, the speakers at these international meetings came from industrialized countries where libraries had long existed, and in a way, they instructed the countries of the Global South how to proceed. This was not what it was like that year in Leipzig. There were a few librarians who had come to officially represent their respective country's policies, more or less. Their statements were formulaic, primarily just praising the governments that had delegated them.

Those who made a profound impact on this meeting by sharing their ways of thinking and their experiences demonstrated that they'd done real, solid fieldwork. They urgently wanted to connect with populations that public institutions did not usually reach out to for various reasons. Instead of following ready-made models, often too readily accepted as universally applicable, they had decided to get closer to the people and account for the realities of their environment, their living conditions, their culture, and their expectations. These new voices spoke up in Leipzig. There were other such voices in Caen and in Bangkok, where I organized similar seminars—sometimes with the same people. For them, it was important to continue the conversations that had started in Leipzig and to know how the programs had developed, what had succeeded, and what had failed. The participants in these various meetings have told me what a revelation these seminars had been for them: they'd found out that they weren't alone in wanting to reach out to the margins. It was a priority for each and every one of them.

Here and there, we'd discover seemingly modest initiatives that got us to rethink the very notion of reading services for children and adolescents and to imagine new strategies. I was pleased that at the seminars, these voices were heard by some of the leaders of library networks in their countries, training officers, and school library directors. I think they had a lot to learn from these grassroots activists.

These activists carried out their projects with modest means. The sense of urgency encouraged them to start without waiting for hypothetical funds. Moreover, the small scale meant they could put down roots everywhere. Their proposals were not intimidating, and everyone felt like they could participate, regardless of their background, regardless of their culture. Kusum Salgado, who had come from Sri Lanka, reminded us insistently, "Library science can wait. Children can't." She then told us about some of the initiatives she was pursuing and supporting in her country. There was, for example, a network of village libraries that prioritized toddlers. Mothers would decide whose turn it was to be in charge of these small reading units and each mother participated in the life of the library in her own way. The Sarvodaya movement, which was inspired by Gandhi, backed these initiatives. It encouraged village communities to take charge of their collective destiny.

I was aware of other similar experiments. I was invited to lead a training session in Ecuador, near Guayaquil. One of the participants took me to library that had become the very heart of a small indigenous village, with the women—the mothers, the grandmothers—participating efficiently. For all of them, it was nothing short of extraordinary. Their joy amazed me. The readings with the children united them in a spirit of discovery and dialogue. I admired the quality of the books, some of which were probably brought by the woman who was my guide. The village was poor. To buy new books, these women wove bags that they sold in the market. The men were away all week while the women thrived doing something that seemed to fulfill them.

I was fascinated by the diversity of actions that came to my attention over the course of the different seminars I organized. Instead of being dictated from above in accordance with a uniform model, they were inspired by local realities, by the people they met, their cultures, and their living conditions. It was a veritable kaleidoscope of initiatives and achievements. Some were the works of licensed librarians, but not all—far from it—and I would be tempted to say that it actually didn't matter. The important thing was not to be encumbered by too many abstract schemes, to be really attentive to the reality of what was happening on the ground with individuals.

Don't Forget Your Childhood

I had invited Somboon Singkamanan, a professor of library science at a university in Bangkok, to Leipzig. I had had the chance to see her at work in her country. What a woman! She was so lively, so funny, and full of ideas. She was also an irresistible storyteller who delighted in sharing what she loved. She taught children's literature and had a deep knowledge of it. Her first class, as I saw, took place outside in the university's park where the students had gathered around her beneath the shade of a large tree. Everyone was invited to tell a story about a significant event from their childhood. She told them that it was especially important for them not to forget their childhoods, the sorrows and the joys! It was a wonderful introduction to this kind of literature, which can be a source of incomparable experiences for children. She liked to remind them, "Don't stick to the theory, let the theory stick to you."

Somboon was a walking library and an extraordinary teacher. Though many of the children's books she loved were part of a universal canon, they were not widely available in Thai. The only place to find them was in the library at her university. She would share them with her students, taking the time to read them aloud with great finesse and subtlety. In this way, she got them to love the beauty and originality of this literature, and she encouraged them to read and memorize the best works. They would then be responsible for passing them on to the children, since they were not available in Thai. These student librarians were like the "book people" in Ray Bradbury's *Fahrenheit 451*. They travelled through the rural areas of Thailand recounting the most beautiful stories and presenting the most beautiful picture books to those who had no access to libraries or books. They collected tales here and there and encouraged children to do the same by approaching parents and neighbors. This made it possible for the apprentice librarians to enrich their repertoire and for the children to discover the richness of their own culture, right at their fingertips. With Somboon's help, some of these stories were published, introducing a Thai dimension there in a country that was being invaded at the time by mediocre publications from abroad. In the beautiful picture books she gave me, the children recognized their games, both new and traditional, as well as the fauna and flora of their environment.

Portable Libraries

Somboon's students were learning how to present books to children. I attended a few of these presentations. They were absolutely compelling, and the children participated with obvious pleasure. These were children from the streets of Pattaya or schoolchildren from the Hmong villages in the northern mountains. The future librarians traveled around the country, especially to rural areas, telling and sometimes acting out the stories. This is how portable libraries, easy to transport on small motorcycles, were born. They were constructed with three panels that would open up and present books to passers-by, and were set up everywhere: down on the street, in the middle of markets, in pagodas, in schools; in all the places where people would pass by or spend time.

I accompanied Somboon and her portable libraries to modest schools in the countryside. I saw the children rushing up to her to flip through the books or to listen to her read them out loud. It was indeed difficult to resist this exceptional storyteller.

The idea for these small libraries traveled and today they can be found in Egypt, Lebanon, and Albania, as well as in refugee camps, where people gather around them to read and talk. In these camps, they are undoubtedly the surest antidote against the destructiveness of inaction, dependence, and passivity. I invited a librarian from Zambia to our seminar in Caen, organized with the help of IBBY. She delightedly confided in me that she was a Zulu princess. She worked in refugee camps and told me how much it hurt her to see so many people in such dire circumstances, moving only enough to reach their hands out for a few coins. People would meet around the little libraries, like they used to meet around wells. It changed their lives. Women found a place there, as well as true dignity.

In Leipzig, the account given by Ellen Waumgana from Zimbabwe also caught my attention. Ellen was participating in women's literacy programs at the time and was involved in developing the materials. She knew that these calibrated and rather boring texts could not really stimulate these newly literate women to read. Then, she thought about children's books. Mothers could read them to their children and enjoy them at the same time. Reading would then be very meaningful and could help keep the family together. But which books to suggest? At the time of our meeting in 1981, Zimbabwe had just become independent. The few books available, from publishers in Europe or the United States, were mediocre. Ellen then thought of writing some herself, so as to give African culture its rightful place. She drew on oral traditions and published in the country's two majority languages, Shona and Ndebele. This is how her project of small home libraries was born.

Once a week, Ellen would turn her house into a library for a few hours. The children would come at the appointed time and quickly remove the books that had been lying dormant in boxes all week. Then the library was set up. Everyone would look at the books together and tell a lot of stories. Ellen, a mother, had many stories up her sleeve, but she also encouraged the children to contribute some of their own. She believed that all work deserved payment, so she'd give them a little money when they did their job well. Then they'd approach the people they were close to, such as their parents and grandparents, their elders, and their neighbors. They'd listen attentively to their stories so they could pass them on in turn. And so it was that they contributed to the life of this small library and this gave Ellen her inspiration to write.

I closely followed the development of the modest home library that began in Harare, the capital city of Zimbabwe. I told Ellen about similar experiments on the other side of the globe. In Japan, there are the bunko, small home libraries that have a presence all throughout the country, in addition to the public library system. Here too, mothers open their homes to welcome the children of the neighborhood. This makes reading a familiar, simple, and personal matter.

Mini Libraries

Similarly, there was a landmark experiment in Venezuela that was of great interest to me. It was taking place in what is referred to in some places as the *barrio* and elsewhere the *favela*, run-down neighborhoods on the outskirts of big cities in Latin America. Bruno Renaud was not originally a librarian but a social worker. I had the opportunity to meet him many times, in Venezuela and elsewhere, and I was able to follow the evolution of the small library in his barrio. He told me that he'd started with what he'd had on hand: there were two books and two children. Then other children came, and little by little, he acquired more books. This is how La Urbina library started.

After leading a day-long training at the Banco del Libro in Caracas, I left with Bruno amidst the late afternoon traffic. The landscape was both strange and beautiful. The hills of the city were covered with white lights, like little candles for a party. This is what favelas looked like at night, similar to other slums I'd seen in other Latin American cities. The shacks covered the hills with glittering lights that belied the destitution.

When I arrived in La Urbina, I was overwhelmed. I was actually already familiar with this muddy hill and its small brick and cinder-block houses that many of the inhabitants had built themselves. I was in fact holding a storybook by Kurusa, *The Streets Are Free (La calle es libre)*, which tells the very story of this library. It was first published in Venezuela by Ekaré, then in France by Père Castor. But upon arriving, what I discovered there was fear. Everyone was protecting themselves. Doors and windows were hidden behind heavy grates. The grocery store was barricaded. The stores weren't letting customers in—they had to stay outside and the shopkeepers passed their purchases through a little opening.

There was one exception in the neighborhood: the library was not barricaded. It presented a different face amidst the mud and the chaos. The doors were wide open and everything was in impeccable order, though not at all fussy. Amidst the confusion of constantly transplanted populations, it was good to feel welcomed and to be able to find one's way around easily. The library I discovered there was truly alive. There were large displays sharing the children's contributions—the little guitars they'd made, *los cuatros*, were hanging from the ceiling. There were also many books, many of them yellowed and grayish. Then I noticed books that were unlike the rest. These were published by Ediciones Ekare, the publishing house started as a department of the Banco del Libro, which was created by the Venezuelan national library. The first books highlighted the cultures and traditions of the country, as well as the fauna and flora. In these respects, the project was similar to what Somboon had been doing in Thailand. The director, Carmen Diana de Dearden, was actually an anthropologist. Today these storybooks can be found in all of Venezuela's public and school libraries and beyond.

The atmosphere of La Urbina Library reminded me of a visit I made to New York City. I had been urged to visit a library located in a rough and even violent part of Manhattan. After getting off the subway, I looked to find my way, and passersby tried to dissuade me from heading in that particular direction. "Do you know where you're going?" they asked. I persevered. I was expected there. In this messy, dirty, and noisy neighborhood cluttered with toppled garbage cans, I discovered a bright and wonderfully organized library. There were flowers. Young people clearly felt comfortable there. It was a true oasis. I saw this as a sign of the librarians' respect for their readers, who responded in kind.

The library in La Urbina is a symbol. Venezuela is an exceptionally violent country with countless murders every day. The librarians have a special status there: They can go and tell their stories outside at nightfall and make their way in peace. The population protects them. The library represents hope. In this neighborhood, the library's celebrations, its newspaper, the stories shared, the discussions, the workshops, the theater—all are part of a concentrated effort to build bonds and create a convivial atmosphere that gets people to feel included.

The young people who play a role in these small libraries are driven by a spirit of activism. I met some of them and I was impressed by their desire to learn more about the neighborhood, to empower those who use the library, and to get parents involved. Another concern: to not give in to despair. Progress was so slow and there could be major disruptions when people moved on. One of Bruno's major issues was how to avoid becoming a helpless organization that counted on getting help from higher authorities. How could they preserve that initial spark and avoid becoming a place that only loaned out materials? This was an essential question. But La Urbina library is able to foster connections among the inhabitants of these neighborhoods, where many are all too familiar with displacement, departures, separation, crowding, and solitude. Before long, young people from the barrio volunteered to help as the library grew and developed, combining book-lending with multiple other activities.

"The mini library therefore starts from down below, at the ground level, which is the best basis and the best guarantee of a coherent development, of a coherence that can and must exist between the means and the ends. It is created on site, not imported, not airdropped from national offices and plans," Bruno told me.

The life of the library came from the neighborhood, where everyone was recognized for their skills and knowledge. "What counts is the possibility for a community to express itself, to be able to mobilize so as to better assume or direct its collective destiny." This was Bruno's utopia, and it bore a strong resemblance to Paulo Freire's.

Poverty: Wealth of Mankind

What does the library do to get the neighborhood involved? The most common way is to have young people take over a workshop and lead it. There are other simple things as well—the director of a mini-library told me that even though cookbooks were in high demand, the ones they had weren't suitable, either because of the directions or because it wasn't possible to obtain the ingredients. The recipes were fine for wealthy people, but not for the poor. There, you had to cook with what was available. So this librarian asked his mother, who lived in the favela, to dictate some of her recipes to him. He photocopied them and made them available to families. This is just one example.

In what for me was a profoundly influential book, Albert Tévoédjrè asserted that poverty is the "wealth of mankind."[41] How to avoid dependence on external help? How to recognize one's own wealth? Librarians in charge of networks in poor countries told me about the difficulties that were caused when there was substantial financial aid that had be spent quickly, even though development had to be taken step by step. Sustaining the initial spark and the power of their convictions was what mattered to these activists. Working in networks and being driven by ideas on constant alert were indispensable.

Bruno's work received recognition and the national library of Venezuela recruited him. The director, Virginia Bettencourt, recognized how effective and thoughtful he was and decided to give him full support by integrating this small library into the national network of public libraries, while giving him the freedom to use his own approach. In exchange, she asked him to help create similar libraries, *bibliotecas populares*, in other poor neighborhoods. Virginia was aware that large institutions needed to send out feelers, like an insect that was able to use its keen senses to gain detailed information about an unknown environment.

Winning Over the Neighborhood

When I was giving a course in Morocco, I was to have another remarkable experience. I had been deeply impressed by a project that Moroccan librarian Houria Sennaji was leading in the High Atlas Mountains. I'd invited her to the Bangkok seminar and continued to follow her work with interest.

---

41. Albert Téovedjré, *La pauvreté, richesse des peuples*, Éditions ouvrières, 1978.

Her project focused on creating cultural centers in the douars of the High Atlas. These are nothing like the cultural or youth centers that have flourished in France. In the case of Houria's initiatives, the local populations contributed to the different phases of the centers' development and operations, including their construction. This gave teenagers and adults the opportunity to learn how to do different kinds of construction work. The projects were developed progressively, depending on the locals' needs and wants. These ranged from a sewing and knitting workshop, as requested by the young girls, to courses in literacy and accounting management, as well as the organization of day care centers so that mothers would have time to learn.

The library therefore became indispensable for the advancement of knowledge. It was there that people acquired a taste for reading and documentation; this opened them up to other cultures. It was a lively place where people met to discuss ideas, exchange information, tell stories, celebrate festivals, and welcome people passing through. The teachers in the douars were at the heart of these projects and young unemployed people took training courses there. Three of them were able to go to India for six months to learn about renewable energy. On their return, they installed electrical power and heating in these cultural centers and also in the homes of those who asked for it.

For these populations that are all too frequently sidelined, the library offers hope. For this reason, it is deeply respected. Defiling or defacing it would be unthinkable. During all my assignments in developing countries and underprivileged neighborhoods, I've observed this same love for a living institution that encourages free speech and invites all inhabitants to find their place and to work together. Harming it in any way would be out of the question.

When our library was threatened with closure in 2006, local organizations and families in the neighborhood mobilized immediately. They decided to occupy the premises, day and night, for two weeks. The families brought us food they had made. It was a party. Eventually the insurrectionists won their case and the library reopened. I was a part of this movement and was impressed by these spontaneous gestures, this generous surge of support from the neighborhood.

Would that be possible today? In less than twenty years, more than seventy libraries in France, including some of the most dynamic, have been the target of major acts of vandalism, including arson. The has happened at schools, too. La Petite Bibliothèque Ronde suffered from its share of serious abuses in 2015. When considering this matter, we called upon Denis Merklen, a sociologist and author of a book whose title shocked us: *Why Are People Setting Fire to Libaries? (Pourquoi brûle t-on des bibliothèques?)*[42] Why do people turn against places of culture, even though they tend to be very open-minded?

A Shelter for Speech

But let us revisit Africa. I had invited Raphaël Ndiaye to come from Senegal to the seminar in Leipzig. He had been an intern at Clamart and I knew him well. In 1981 he was working in his country as the director of the ministry's books department. He is also a "tamtamologist." This speaks to the commitment he's always had to communication but also the poetry of the griots, of drums. He is also a poet and a singer. I saw him in Dakar on a television program and he was singing. How surprising it would be to hear a senior official from the ministry of culture singing on television in France!

I had invited him to participate in our seminar because I thought it would be interesting to find out what place reading might have in predominantly oral societies. He told us how he had fostered the development of libraries in villages where the adults did not know how to read. There was no intention, he said, of having the library be just for schoolchildren. There would need to be a place for illiterate people there, too. "Illiteracy," he added, was a word to be used with caution: "In our country, this word is not synonymous with a lack of education.

---

42. Denis Merklen, *Pourquoi brûle-t-on des bibliothèques?* collection "Papiers", Presses d'Enssib, 2013.

Illiterate men and women can be highly knowledgeable. It is a type of knowledge that gives them the habit of reflecting and of critically examining a problem that arises in their environment. The experience transmitted by a book or document may be an experience they are able to understand because of the training received through oral tradition."

Raphael continued, "Guardians of various traditions should, for the library's sake, be able to address the areas of knowledge that they are responsible for and that they have mastered. Their very presence would be a symbol with an easily identifiable meaning." For them, the library could be a "haven for speech."

They even exhibited tools and instruments of all kinds. For example, a library displayed a *ban ak souf* ("clay and sand") oven, which makes it possible to reduce the consumption of wood, so villagers could learn how to guard against the destruction of forests.

In Mali, as I was to discover while on assignment there in 1985, tape recorders and cassettes were used to help collect and disseminate valuable information. People could listen to them while working in the fields, at home, or in the library. Topics could include traditional medicine or the art of cultivating the land. The cassette library was an integral part of the Bamako library network and benefited from many different contributors.

The Library of the Poor World

Given the success of this first seminar in Leipzig, I was asked to organize several others. They took place in Caen, France, in 1990, with the participation of IBBY, and in Bangkok, Thailand in 1999, on the occasion of the IFLA congress. For the latter, I had asked Kingo Mchombu to kick off the seminar. I very much appreciated this eminent Tanzanian's perceptive and bold thinking. He had been trained in Great Britain at Loughborough and was now the Dean at the University of Windhoek, in Namibia, so he had a dual education and was dual-cultured—a genuine bounty.

What drove Kingo's commitment and thinking was his notion of the "Library of the Poor," which was the title of his major book. That was why I thought it was critical to entrust him with directing our debates. Like Raphaël Ndiaye, he said he wanted to put an end to the idea that an oral tradition would be an obstacle to the development of reading. On the contrary, a dynamic relationship could be established between orality and reading. Kingo then evoked those moments of reading in the library that are a source of connection and discussion. Reading could thus give new life to oral and local culture. He also mentioned that, more broadly, it was socioeconomic conditions and educational systems that hindered the development of reading in children, as well as poverty, the primary victims of which were women. It was not possible for librarians to address reading issues without actively participating in poverty eradication programs. We also had to learn to make the best use of the few resources at our disposal to avoid creating elitist systems based on what were erroneously referred to as international standards and that were costly, served a small number of people, and could not be developed in the long term, because these systems depended too exclusively on foreign donations and thus undervalued local resources.

Kingo presented us with our responsibilities as librarians to join in the fight against poverty. This made me think of Geeta Dharmarjan's work in India, which I discovered when I'd gone to New Delhi to give a paper at the Congress of the International Publishers Association. That had been in 1991. At UNESCO's request, I was to present some of the most significant experiences I'd had in Clamart and throughout the world. I followed the advice I got to meet with Geeta, and we've been in touch ever since. I spent a lot of time with her in one of the city's slums, where she'd hung up small plastic curtains on the branches of some puny trees. The curtains had pockets into which she had slipped some little books. In this way, she could observe whether the children showed any interest in them, which could serve as a guide for publications to come. She was just starting out on a project that was to develop widely and broadly, especially in the field of multilingual publishing and education. But can we get children to read without reforming the schools?

Thanks to various forms of aid, she had created a small school in this same slum, and I made a brief visit there one morning. I admired how it had been built—with simple materials, and beautifully designed. It was immaculate. I saw children there, attentive and happy to learn. Geeta asked them, "What do you want to be when you grow up?" Their answers were magnificent and full of generosity, revealing their hopes for a better future in the service of others. As I left the slum, I walked through a muddy, messy neighborhood where I saw children carrying heavy buckets of garbage. There was a child sitting in front of a small shop and reading a book to a group of children that had spontaneously gathered around him. Geeta's work was already bearing lovely fruits.

Liberated Speech

I've already mentioned how, at the conference in Leipzig, I greatly admired the elegance and depth of the thoughts shared by Raphaël Ndiaye, who was then Director of the Book in Senegal. I admired his desire to leave no one by the wayside. I found these same qualities in Marietou Diop Diongue who, years later, held the position of Director of the Book in Dakar. I always spoke with her a great deal about our experiences and thoughts. I invited her to participate in the Bangkok seminar. I had previously put her in touch with Kingo. They had, it seemed to me, the same notion of the library in parts of Africa that were linguistically and culturally different.

I was aware of many of her initiatives. There is one in particular that serves as an example of her dedication. World Book Day is celebrated in April around the world. Instead of cutting ribbons and making speeches, Marietou chose to simply go to the women's prison in Rufisque and spend time with the inmates. She was accompanied by two women who had written novels and poetry published in Wolof. At the start of the meeting, the prisoners hid their faces behind their large veils. They were ashamed.

But as they gradually entered the world of these texts, they felt seen. They uncovered their faces and began to speak with their three visitors. They realized that they frequently faced the same troubles: jealousy, severe husbands, the difficulties of women who have to juggle work and family. They also spoke of the problems arising from polygamy like the status of the first wife and fights between co-wives. The female guards approached and mingled with the prisoners and the three visitors. They participated in these exchanges with deep emotion. One of the women felt such an affinity with one of the poets that she burst into tears. The reading had created bonds beyond all expectations. In other years, Marietou organized similar meetings for the Book Festival (Fête du Livre), sometimes in hospitals with sick children or in prisons for young criminals. In this way, books became associated with notions of celebration, conviviality, and freedom.

Tales from Afar

In 1985, I was invited to lead a course for librarians in Bamako, Mali. They were all men, unlike in France. Dominique Vallet, a technical assistant who had chosen to settle in Mali and who had worked alongside the great Alpha Konaré, President of Mali (1992-2002), organized this remarkable week of training. In the morning we worked with the children, which ensured that we didn't remain limited to abstract pedagogical generalizations. We suggested that we read a small storybook from the Père Castor collection, *The Big Black Panther* (*La Grande Panthère noire*), written by Paul François and illustrated by Lucile Butel—a masterpiece. The text has wonderful rhythms that inspire reading aloud and dramatic play. It is the story of a hunt and it takes place in India. The big black panther is terribly hungry and mercilessly devours the animals it encounters along its way. We meet them one after the other over the course of the book. The villagers go hunting for this panther by following its tracks. At first, they find them in the sand. But then the animal leads them to the Himalayas, to Tibet, Mongolia, and Siberia, where the ground is covered in snow. The librarians' first reaction was that the story had to be changed. These children knew about sand but snow wouldn't mean anything to them. The children protested, "We must keep the snow." They'd either known about it or hadn't. It didn't matter! Now, thanks to the book, they knew. One of the librarians also firmly rejected the idea of changing the tale in any way, arguing that reading opens us up to the world. And so, the snow stayed put.

These reactions make me think of what Albert Camus wrote in his magnificent posthumous book, *The First Man*, about being a schoolboy in Algeria. "The texts were always those used in France. And these children, who knew only the sirocco, the dust, the short torrential cloudbursts, the sand of the beaches, and the sea in flames under the sun, would assiduously read (…) stories that to them were mythical, where children in hoods and mufflers, their feet in wooden shoes, would come home dragging bundles of sticks along snowy paths until they saw the snow-covered roof of the house where the smoking chimney told them the pea soup was cooking in the hearth. For Jacques, these stories were as exotic as they could possibly be. (…) For him these stories were part of the powerful poetry of school."[43]

Takam Tikou

During a training week in Mali, I had the opportunity to visit a few public libraries around Bamako. I was surprised to find that in the best ones, the books were very clean and slept quietly on the shelves. Apparently, they did not get loaned out. However, the contributions from the French ministry of overseas development had been well thought-out. At the request of Régine Fontaine, who worked at the ministry in charge of books in francophone Africa, they were comprised of books carefully chosen by the librarians who participated in our publication, *La Revue des livres pour enfants*. The African librarians received these books, and the most conscientious of them arranged them carefully on the

---

43. Albert Camus, *Le Premier Homme*, English trans. David Hapgood, Knopf, 1995, p. 65.

shelves. Others barely opened the boxes. What else should we have expected? The choices were made in Paris without the participation of our African partners.

I wanted to propose a project to the ministry that would fully involve African librarians in the selection process. We needed their opinions moving forward. Librarians and children would all be rallied and their written observations would be published. The magazine would be called *Takam Tikou*, which in Wolof means, "This is so good, I want more." Indeed, reading can be a true treat, and the goal of this program was to make it so for children as well as for the adults alongside them.

Back in Paris, I proposed my project to Régine Fontaine, who was enthusiastic about it and gave it her full support. The idea was to enlist help from African librarians and teachers. But what about the fact that they didn't have access to the full breadth of books published in French and Africa? It was decided that several times a year, fifty or so truly diverse works representing the best in publishing would be sent to ninety libraries in francophone Africa. The directors would be asked to send us their critical comments and notes about children's responses to each of the books. These would then be published. The children were also encouraged to express themselves. These observations from the field would then allow us to constantly make changes to what went into the batches of books. We didn't want to limit ourselves to books published in France. One of the first tasks was to gather information about African children's publishing and raise awareness about it in France as well as in the African libraries participating in our project.

To coordinate and support this collective work, I created a special department at La Joie Par les Livres. It was led by Marie Laurentin and Viviana Quinones. The analyses filled the "Critical Network" ("Réseau critique") section of *Takam Tikou* magazine,[44] which was and still is distributed throughout francophone Africa and France. Another section featured bibliographic selections of books published in Africa—and

---

44. For several years, this section open to children and librarians has no longer existed, unfortunately.

now, in the Arab world and in the Caribbean—which gives them broad visibility. This is how, in 1989, an annual review was born.

The *Takam Tikou* newsletter assisted in the development of high-quality African publishing, which now had the means to gain recognition. Great African artists started to become interested in the world of children's books. In France, readers also followed works that were being produced in Africa; long overlooked, they found a place in our libraries.

But what changes did this collaborative effort have on the ground? According to librarians I met, the change in African libraries had been radical. They were enthusiastically discovering a new profession that had nothing to do with the simple and passive role of distributors they'd had before. They read a lot and got closer to the children, greatly interested in how they would respond to books. The children, responsible for communicating their impressions, dove into their reading with enthusiasm and pride. Everyone's voice was heard, appearing in the widely distributed *Takam Tikou* newsletter. Everything was changing in the children's reading units in francophone Africa. I think of the words a young Malian woman who wrote to us: "The library has created more connections for us than the road that connects our village to Gao, the neighboring city."

I also think of a moving letter from a Congolese librarian, a member of the *Takam Tikou* network. It was written in the 1990s, in the midst of conflict: "I lament the disappearance of three members of the Reading Club, one of whom was shot in cold blood and two of whom died of illness, without any care, a situation exacerbated by malnutrition and the conditions of life in the forest (…) There is complete desolation, abject poverty. [...] At the moment, there is a kind of calm that gives us hope [...]. Hope for rebuilding our libraries. Many children from the regional library's reading club who found refuge in Brazzaville have asked me if it would be possible to review some books. [...] The children seem to have already forgotten all the abuses they have suffered. [...] What they want to do is to immerse themselves again in the world of books."[45]

---

45. Excerpt from an article by G. Patte, "Les bibliothèques pour enfants

A library that was open to the world: this had been Anne Schlumberger's intention when she'd had the idea of creating the Clamart library in 1965. Had she suspected that the project born in Clamart, in this Petite Bibliothèque Ronde, would have such an impact the world over? That I would never stop answering requests coming from every continent? Abroad and in France, I worked to bring people books. And my contributions were always simple. No lectures on library management. No lessons about what needed to be done. Only those who were there on the job could say. Our attention was focused on children, on sharing, and reading. I constantly spoke of what I'd seen and done in different places, and what lines of thinking they'd led to, and the power of these experiences to get institutions to change, regardless of the social, economic, and cultural contexts, and to create a new image of children and reading.

The Bunko

There has always been a special place for Japan in our library. This is because of our friend Tomoko Yamaguchi, who introduced us to the best Japanese books and to many aspects of the children's world. I've been invited to Japan on numerous occasions. My book, *Laissez-les lire!* was published several times and distributed widely. It is a country where I have benefited from enormous goodwill.

Thanks to my assignments there, I was able to travel extensively throughout the country to share my ideas about children's libraries. I even went to the farthest reaches of the Okinawa archipelago, just a skip and a jump away from Korea, where the Korean and Japanese cultures blend together.

I was very interested in *bunko*s, those little home libraries that seem all the more precious in a world that can seem too big, too stressed, and too fast.

---

dans les pays en développement," in *La Revue des livres pour enfants*, no. 191, February 2000.

Bunko libraries came about after the war. Momoko Ishii, a remarkable translator and literary director, had traveled to study children's libraries and publishing and discovered that in the United States and Great Britain, the children's sections provided an exceptional place to promote the best books, to give them a real place in the children's lives. *Bunko* libraries provide children with a limited but generally high-quality selection. They are places where it's possible to see what can happen when children and books come together freely.

I visited several of them, especially in Tokyo and Fukushima. In Tokyo, one of the most famous is Kyoko Matsuoka's. I went there on a Saturday afternoon and saw the children arriving on their bikes with their book bags on their backs. It was an idyllic scene in this quiet neighborhood. Nothing distinguished the library from the other houses in the neighborhood except for a discreet sign announcing the hours of operation. Each *bunko* has a name; the one here was called The Pinecone. Every Saturday, the office was transformed into a *bunko* for the neighborhood children. Kyoko told me that they had around two hundred regulars. There were more than a thousand books, organized according to a simple classification system. The children felt at home there and were at their leisure to read, to make their selections, to listen to stories. They would lie down on the floor to read, make themselves comfortable, and go home with a few books in their satchels. Kyoko offered them the books that she likes. It was like a family. Storytime on Saturdays were a real event, since the hostess was a celebrated storyteller.

I visited another bunko, the Lily of the Valley, and spent an afternoon there. I had met the hostess, Junko Watanabe, previously at a conference in Tokyo. Some of the children welcomed me in the Japanese way, with origami and other folded papers.

I've always kept in touch with Junko. In Japan, she is recognized as a great specialist of cloth books, and she gave me many of them for the library. This provided inspiration for La Petite Bibliothèque Ronde to offer a sewing workshop to mothers in the neighborhood, so they could make their own cloth books. Many of the mothers came from regions south of France, especially North Africa, and could wield the needles quite skillfully. Listening to a story would take on a whole new meaning with these books. Velcro strips were used to attach certain elements of the story. So, for example, I've seen children reading along with the story of Little Red Riding Hood and preparing her basket by carefully putting in a cake and a small jar of fresh butter. These activities are performed as the story is read out loud. Originally these books were designed for visually impaired children, but were quickly adopted by sighted children, too.

There was another bunko that caught my attention. One day we were enjoying some passages from Laura Ingalls Wilder's famous family chronicle, *Little House in the Big Woods*. To me, this book is like a naïf painting, a kind of art that children are particularly responsive to, looking searchingly to admire the details. The children enjoyed Wilder's detailed descriptions. It includes recipes for cooking that are so precise that reading them is like an invitation to put on an apron. This is why the children and the lady of the house prepared pancakes, following the author's instructions to the letter, during my visit.

According to my Japanese friends, there will always be a need for the bunko, even though Japan has good public libraries nowadays. They are probably the last refuge for children from overwhelming social pressure. In their own way, these small libraries create a family atmosphere, where it's enjoyable to take one's time without worrying about scholastic performance.

Guri and Gura

In Clamart, I had already read a few Japanese storybooks chosen by Maurice Cocagnac and published by Editions du Cerf. The storybooks by Kota Taniuchi he'd selected are like poems, evoking simple and profound sensations. They invite children to a kind of meditative silence that allows them to listen to their own emotions. They are exceptional books. The child in *Boy on a Hilltop*, one of my favorites, always appears from behind. We see him from one page to the next, identifiable in the midst of green meadows because of his big yellow hat. He seems to be attentive and silent, perhaps even contemplative. There is a subtle invitation for the reader to join him by his side. We climb a hill with him on his bicycle in the whiteness of the dawn. At the top, we sit down and wait for the sound of the train as it comes from afar, passes, then disappears. All the houses around, then, look like a succession of train cars passing by.

Tomoko introduced me to other great children's book artists. She put me in touch with them and I, in turn, introduced them to children as well as publishers. She wanted me to get to know the best-loved books, the ones that have a real place in families. The true classic is *The Giant Egg* by Rieko Nakagawa and Yuriko Yamawaki, which, fortunately, has also been published in France. When I read this storybook to children, they are irresistibly drawn to march along with Guri and Gura, the two friendly rats who are going to have a picnic in the forest. Carrying their basket of provisions, they're making good progress when they encounter a gigantic egg blocking their path. What can they do, given that they are so small? This is how the story, full of friendship, ingenuity, and generosity, begins.

Guri and Gura aren't exactly children, but they're not exactly rats either. There are two lines for whiskers, plus a hat and a child's outfit with holes to allow the ears and tail through. Thanks to this very subtle ambiguity, the children are able to identify with our two heroes in a meaningful way, not just physically but also more deeply. What a dream it is to have a picnic, to eat in good company, and to share a wonderful cake you prepared yourself!

As I write these pages, I recall the magical moments spent at the Clamart library with these two characters and the little ones who'd gathered around me to enjoy this story that so clearly spoke to them. We would sing along with them so as to truly feel that we were in their company. "We're Guri and Gura, the greediest field rats of all. Watch out! We're here, we're Guri and Gura."

Cabbage Soup and Goat Cheese

The Giant Egg was prominently featured in the exhibition we organized at the Centre Pompidou in 1978. I had suggested that the foreign cultural centers in Paris all organize exhibitions of children's books from their respective countries at the same time, and it turned out to be a great success. This is how I became familiar with Japanese publishers and some of their best artists.

Many artists and publishers came from Japan and brought the large space we'd reserved for them at the Centre Pompidou to life. Anno Mitsumasa was there. He was a big star in his country, and not just in the world of children's books. He was a cultural icon and had a great mind. It was a joy to meet him and spend time in his company. I had invited the artists from this exhibition, along with the small team from Clamart and a few friends, to my home for a home-made dinner. I knew they would appreciate visiting a private home rather than a public place for some cabbage soup and goat cheese. Everything was simple, and I think they liked that simplicity. Not enough seats? It didn't matter. They sat by the fire, on the floor, Japanese style. This was the reception that our friend Anno got. I had the chance to see him again from time to time, in Tokyo or in Paris. We'd always spend long evenings together. We didn't have any languages in common. On the rare occasions that we were one-on-one, without an interpreter, we communicated through little scribbled drawings, and we understood each other very well.

Turning the World Upside-Down

That evening, Anno had wanted to show me some of the many funny things in *Anno's Journey*, which L'École des Loisirs had just published. In this book without text, a man crosses cities, villages, and landscapes on horseback. Readers are drawn in by the game of finding famous paintings, scenes, and characters lost in the crowd or discovering the jokes that result from impossible plays of perspective. Indeed, Anno enjoyed merging contrary perspectives that combined to create worlds that had all the appearances of reality but were actually impossible. I enjoy suggesting this "reading" to children. They will ask me in surprise, "How is this possible?"

Anno gets us to turn the book and its worlds in all directions so that we can see subtle metamorphoses that are always surprising and funny. Most importantly, there are no words. They'd make this poet-painter's messages less clear and make it so the children couldn't explore these bountiful worlds at their leisure, depriving them of the pleasure of seeking and finding. There are so many victories to be had by visitors who wander through these images.

Anno offered us his artist's view of the world—a view that is extremely intelligent and witty. He was having fun. He never took himself seriously and invited us to laugh along with him. The books are true works of genius. To my knowledge, nobody else has used this medium so imaginatively. His works remind me of those by the woodblock artist Hiroshige, with so many small figures populating a lavish landscape. He was also a great scientist, in the tradition of Leonardo da Vinci. He was, among other things, a master of the art of anamorphic illusion.

I had asked the poet and mathematician Jacques Roubaud to give a lecture about Anno's for the BnF's major exhibition on the history of the Japanese book in 1993. He chose to discuss one of his picture books, *Anno's Animals*. He ended his admirable lecture with the simple words, "It's very powerful." For him, it was something entirely different from the game-books featuring Waldo, the character with the striped shirt hiding in the middle of a crowd, or the cerebral works of Escher, with whom he has often been compared. Anno was a great artist, and with *Anno's Animals* everyone could enjoy walking at their own pace in a shady forest inhabited by all sorts of animals hiding in the foliage. With him, we learned to look.

The Leamos Moose

Since the year 2000, I've been closely associated with a new initiative that originated in Latin America. It built on the numerous projects I was able to carry out while traveling throughout the continent over the course of more than thirty years.

When Maria Elvira Charria came to see me in Paris, I was about to retire. Even so, I was the one she came to ask for help in renewing and revitalizing the libraries that were open to children. She was the head of the reading division of Cerlalc, an intergovernmental organization linked to UNESCO, and as such had a prominent position in Latin America. She'd known me for a long time and knew me well. It was at her request that I spoke in almost every country in Latin America. For her, the time had come to launch a broad and sustainable project that could reach the least well-off. She told me that the libraries needed new blood. We'd need the help of young volunteers and would have to train them in the real work of passing on information. She wanted to get started as soon as possible and asked me to co-direct this network with her for the first four years. After that, we could reassess. With her agreement, I would always be accompanied by a member of ACCES, the lively organization created by René Diatkine that very successfully combines theory with practice. The project was called Leamos de la mano de Papa y Mama, or "Reading with Mom and Dad"; with this project, reading was a family affair. In truth, it is often children who help their parents discover the joy of reading.

And so, I got involved in this project. We corresponded by e-mail throughout the year, sharing observations, failures, successes, and the essential questions that arose. This was how we made progress. At the beginning, there were nine countries participating in this project, and we all met in Mexico once a year for intense reflection and to read with children and parents.

I was impressed by the imaginativeness of these purveyors of books. In addition, I was struck by how their consideration for the diversity of people and their situations resulted in highly diverse reading units.

In Guanajuato, Mexico, Liliana would take advantage of time spent in those rickety buses that are such distinctive features of the Latin American landscape in order to share the pleasure of storytelling. She would read picture books aloud and show the images. She also had a presence in a community where there were indigenous families that had suffered from segregation and rejection. A hut had been made available to her there, and she turned it into a vibrant library. Today, in León, she runs a remarkable library that is open to adults and children alike, every day and even late at night. Little children and their families get special attention there, as I was able to observe.

Odilia, an indigenous woman, was worried about all the young people in the Patzcuaro region who wanted to leave the country and emigrate to the United States. It was therefore important for life to be interesting in remote villages like hers. The small library in this community offered a selection of books alongside medicinal plants and close to places where workshops on the rich local traditions were held. These books had clearly been read and re-read and opened these young people to the world. The children took on responsibilities at the library and found a real place there.

In Mexico City, Nestor, who also worked as an accountant in a clothing store, would welcome parents, young people, and children from the neighborhood to his home once or twice a week. The reading space was set up in a room in his house and opened out onto the street. He wanted it that way. Many of his neighbors would come over and his whole family participated, from the grandfather to the young teenage brother. I admired the books he offered. They had come from publishers who'd sent them to get his assessment and the children's reactions. We'd tell stories, read aloud texts that moved us, and shared our impressions. The atmosphere was joyful. I liked to go whenever I visited Mexico City.

Not surprisingly, Nestor became an expert in children's literature and was sometimes invited to train people in this field.

My faithful interpreter Lirio also got swept up in the excitement and became involved. For years, she ran a small library at a juvenile rehabilitation center in the suburbs of Guanjajuato. A painter, musician, and poet, she would present kids with carefully selected art books and poetry collections as well as interesting non-fiction books and beautiful works of literature. It was a success. It inspired wonderful connections and shared experiences of reading, creating, discussing, and reflecting. She also ran a small library in her local school. Today, thanks to these experiences, she gets asked to give training courses for librarians in her region. She also participates in library programs in neighboring towns.

Experiences With Ripple Effects

Elsewhere, alongside the swings and slides of a public garden in Jinotepe, Nicaragua, there was a little shelter of sorts, made of odds and ends, where children would stop and read. They could sit at small tables and sometimes their parents would settle in next to them. The choice of books was remarkable, as was the children's ability to focus amidst the hustle and bustle of the surroundings. Large, illustrated signs pointed out this lively little stopping place to passersby. They featured full-length portraits of heroes from children's books such as Marcel, the irresistible chimpanzee created by Anthony Browne, and Max from Sendak's *Where the Wild Things Are*, with a crown on his head. There were also characters from well-known Latin American storybooks like Daniel Barbot's *A Bicycle for Rosaura* and Francisco Hinojosa's *The Worst Lady in the World*. These were a far cry from the Disney knockoffs too frequently associated with childhood. This city had no library, but the association Libros para niños, in its own way, was present everywhere—in the public gardens, in the squares, in the small rural schools, and in the health service centers. Everywhere, people were telling stories, reading, lending out books, and talking to each other.

I saw these modest trailblazers at work and admired them for their informality, their appreciation of excellence, and their rigorous judgment. I loved their cheerfulness and their enthusiasm was contagious.

This was how simple initiatives took root and developed in different corners of the globe. And they were spreading. Networking was essential for these small units. Without these contacts, the greatest of innovations ran the risk of growing weak and withering from isolation or discouragement. Leamos made it possible to track their progress step by step, to think collectively, and to provide mutual support and training.

These actions traveled easily, and the seeds they had sown were ready to sprout. In Mexico City, for example, a woman named Carola led a small team that offered weekly reading sessions in a large pediatric hospital. There, in the waiting rooms, time would drag on and people were often worried. As always, all it took was a few baskets of books and everything changed. We read, we told stories, we had fun, and we forgot our cares. The parents enjoyed themselves, too. This first initiative quickly spread to other hospitals and other countries.

Today, Carola is part of the small management team at the Vasconcelos Library, which is open to all. This recently established public library is the largest in Latin America and is particularly innovative. In spite of her weighty responsibilities, Carola remains close to children, especially toddlers. They are her priority. She refuses to stay in her office and prefers to be with them. She spares no efforts in training teachers and librarians in Mexico in this approach.

In Bogotá, I spent one morning in the pediatric ward of a large hospital where Patricia, a member of our network, would regularly lead a reading hour in the waiting room. The set-up was simple: a carpet and cushions. She would arrange the books on the floor so that each child could easily make his or her choice. I saw them settle down with their parents. One of them was hooked up to his oxygen tank. Like the others, he liked being read to and listening to stories. I saw more than one take a book of their choice with them to the doctor's office, clutching it to their heart as if it were a talisman or a comfort object, like a security blanket.

I had been invited to give a lecture that evening. At a crowded theater in the center of the city, I spoke of my visit to the hospital earlier that morning. In the audience were several people who worked in the pediatric ward. Doctors and health care staff spoke up and said they were impressed. They noticed how the children's and parents' anxiety had been transformed and soothed thanks to these moments of pleasure, trust, and intimacy. They wanted to see such actions proposed in other hospitals in the city, with priority given to those that served the most disadvantaged families.

There was also a person from a large pharmaceutical company in the audience. She was convinced of the importance of this initiative. In the weeks that followed, she wrote to me to tell me that her company was offering to finance such programs in Colombia. Very quickly, everything fell into place. Patricia became responsible for this project, which reached all the way to Peru. The allocated budget made it possible to purchase quality books and to pay readers so they could be there for children and parents during these moments of intimate sharing, which are so precious during long hospital stays. Patricia arranged to have the people she hired for this project to be trained. All this gave rise to astute observations that circulated throughout the network and inspired further reflection. A newsletter was widely distributed and a new concept of reading for children in the hospital was born. It was based on personal and trusting relationships between children and books, encouraged by sensitive adults who took the time to sit with kids and go along with them at their own pace.

Sowing Seeds Everywhere

In Bogotá, there was also the El Parque library, run by a woman named Graciela. I found it to be an exemplary library. Parents and children spent a lot of time there, in the company of books, as a family. They also got to know the young readers who participated seriously in the life of the library. The library played a central role in the neighborhood as a meeting place and point of reference for all, young and old. During one of my visits, I saw a child bring a small, sick bird that he'd just found in the neighborhood to the librarians. For him, there was no doubt that they'd know what to do. Unfortunately, this lively library had to close, but Graciela was able to do work raising awareness in the depths of the Amazonian forests, where she created small libraries and other places for reading. In the videos she showed me, I could see children who were spellbound as they listened to stories from marvelous books like those I'd introduced to the members of the network. Today, Graciela has important responsibilities at the national library in Bogotá. She travels throughout Colombia and neighboring countries to help public libraries become more dynamic.

I also remember the days I spent in Salvador de Bahia, Brazil, long before the Leamos program, with a former street kid who was passionate about music, dance, and especially capoeira, which he wanted to talk to me about. As was the case throughout this region of the world, there was the serious problem of children who, for the most part, would reject any form of schooling. Often, the only type of education that interested them was the arts. Having left a life on the streets behind him, this young man was committed to helping kids. Walking with him through the city, I saw how popular he was. He was a neighborhood personality and everyone greeted him.

I had the opportunity to show him some children's books, and he was immediately inspired to share them with these children. He'd invited me to spend an afternoon at a session he'd organized in an impoverished suburb. With the sun blazing overhead, we met in a shed and he spent most of the session showing the children how to build musical instruments to accompany capoeira by using metal rods recovered from the carcasses of old tires. I've rarely seen a class that was so focused, so eager to learn, or so diligent. And he had a lot of students. Thanks to him and the confidence he showed in them, these completely marginalized young people were ready to discipline themselves for the love of art. Under such conditions, were more than ready to discover magnificent picture books and texts of true beauty.

We were called on to carry out these actions everywhere: in unusual places, on the street, in hospital waiting rooms, in recreation centers, in public gardens, or in the homes of some of our network's members. It didn't matter if these young recruits had library training or not. What was essential was their support for the project, their dedication to quality, and the strength of their commitment. The idea was to sow seeds everywhere and to see together what needed to be added to the soil for plants and trees to grow and become firmly rooted.

A Productive Network

Over the course of my career, I've gotten many invitations from people across several continents. Things really started to shift, especially in Latin America, as dictatorships fell and exiles returned to their home country. They had experienced other realities elsewhere and wanted to bring about real change, especially in cultural life. They were interested in public libraries and children's services. Many knew about Clamart and wanted to learn from it.

They were especially impressed by the open-air library, the free interaction with children, starting with toddlers and their parents, and the exploration of the finest books likely to enchant the different generations. This involved an acknowledgment of the small, the intimate, the informal, and the surprising, combined first and foremost with the desire to reach those at a far remove form the world of writing and books, those who had been overlooked by the cultural and educational authorities: in a word, to reach out to the peripheries. Diatkine's thinking was always in the background, with the need to observe what was experienced on the job, to engage in serious reflection, and to act within a network. There was no need for big budgets and prestigious institutions. Everything was simple. Getting down to work was just a matter of being inspired to do so.

These seemingly modest actions have proven to be surprisingly rich. Whether with *Takam Tikou* in francophone Africa or with Leamos in

Latin America, these small, grassroots initiatives have developed in close connection with attentive intermediaries. They've proven enlightening to publishers, who have come to the realization that while children are demanding, they are drawn to beauty, to the imaginative, to others, and to windows on the world. It is enough to simply observe and listen. In Mexico, the ministry of education recognized the expertise of our intermediaries and asked them to participate in the selection of books for all the school libraries in the country. Every year the endowments are renewed, which provides tremendous support for quality publishing. In order to ensure that the ministry can offer these independently selected titles to all schools in Mexico, the print runs need to be very large. There is an illustrated catalog circulated to help each school make its choices. In the last few years, we have seen a real boom in publishing for young people in Latin America. In Mexico, the members of Leamos have contributed to this development in their own way.

The first seeds were sown here and there and the harvest has been bountiful. I'm writing this in 2015. In just the past few months, I've been approached about new projects. In my small international circle, people know my work. They recognize the importance of small-scale initiatives that are close to the people, so they invite me to work with them, as I did in Latin America. Marietou, a woman from Senegal, approached me about participating in a sweeping project for the development of public libraries. She asked me to step in for outreach activities like those facilitated by Leamos that bring children and parents together in the most varied of locales. All this was to be in French and Wolof, of course. Thanks to her, connections have already been established with an American who loves Senegal and children's books. We will work together to publish small bilingual picture books in French and Wolof, then distribute them broadly and free of charge to Senegalese children and their parents. Alongside simple non-fiction works, I've already come across a little masterpiece by our friend Steig, Amos and Boris.

Small is Beautiful

This is how these reading units found their places in Africa, Asia, Europe, and Latin America. They were made accessible to all and are, in my opinion, necessary for any project to promote reading. Most of them have arisen and developed in places far from the usual cultural institutions, though they have not been limited to such locales; they've grown and spread among the rich as well as the poor, in libraries large and small. They are valuable observation posts. One of their advantages is the variety of people engaged in service to children. This requires confidence in the ability of these "amateurs" to develop small structures and even to manage a little library. They are passionate about children's books and eager to expand young people's knowledge of literature and reading. I'm constantly sharing these experiences in countries that are embarking on large national projects. I remind them that these grassroots actions with children and families are like the solid foundations of any construction. According to the principle of economist E. F. Schumacher, "Small is beautiful."[46] In a world that is so big we risk getting lost in it, a smaller scale has become invaluable. "It is not the lack of wealth that is to be feared, but the absence of sharing." These admirable words, taken from the *Guanzi*, are quoted by François Cheng in *And the Breath Becomes Sign*.[47] They perfectly express what guides our actions.

All those who wish to enter our profession should go through the experience with small units that require closely working with people and that combine mediation with observation and reflection. Librarianship finds its rightful place in this way, with bureaucratic and technocratic temptations definitively forgotten; this places people at the core of our profession.

---

46. E.F. Schumacher, *Small is Beautiful: A Study of Economics As if People Mattered*, Blond & Briggs, 1973.

47. François Cheng, *Et le souffle devient signe. Portrait d'une âme à l'encre de Chine*, L'Iconoclaste, 2014.

Life Itself

All of these experiences get us thinking: Why, even in the farthest reaches of Armenia, in the Caucasus, do our beloved picture books elicit such enthusiasm? Why is it that in Stepanakert, in the harsh mountains near Azerbaijan still showing the ravages of a recent war, children dive delightedly into Philippe Dumas's *A Farm*? It describes a rather wealthy and old-fashioned English farm. But the details of these towering illustrations beckon them to discover and experience life itself, regardless of the time or place. These same children can't get enough of an old picture book, *Make Way for Ducklings*, which has antiquated, sepia-toned illustrations. It's a very Bostonian story about a family of ducks trying to find a peaceful place to settle in this New England town, which the book portrays with great accuracy.

Blue Dog, by Nadja, is also a universal favorite. Children everywhere love it. In a little colonial town in Mexico, in Guanajuato, there's a place for reading called "Blue Dog." In Nagorno-Karabakh, there's another reading place that also happened to choose the same name. Connections based on childhood favorites were forged in this way between Mexico and Armenia, as I've been able to observe.

Regardless of the country and traditions, I'm struck by the choices the children make and their fierce dedication to their selections. I notice they all keep coming back to Anthony Browne, Claude Ponti, Remy Charlip, Quentin Blake, Mario Ramos, Max Velthuijs, and Gerda Muller, not to mention Sendak, Ungerer, and Lobel. These books are classics. Some are new, some are old, but this is irrelevant. I like to share them for the rare and delightful experiences they can bring. I'm well aware of how important they can be in a child's life.

As I write this, La Petite Bibliothèque Ronde is getting ready to celebrate its 50th anniversary. Fifty years! It's not so young anymore—but honestly, it's hard to tell. It's run by a young team that has adopted, in its own way, what had always been my guiding principles: small scale, little people, being and doing together, reaching out to the margins, giving a rightful place to the spoken word, and beauty always within reach.

The library's new name says it all.[48] *Rond (round)* like the world, like the wheel, like the circle of the ascending spiral, like the circle of children delighted to be there. *Petit (small)* because reading is not a matter of crowds, of numbers and statistics, because it is best experienced through the intimacy and trust of relationships, in small and informal groups or one-on-one.

Today, this small library is constantly reinventing itself, while building on the beautiful legacies of the teams that came before it, legacies that assume new meanings in response to the challenges of the times. The library can't help but grow as it accounts for the great changes in our world, its riches and its weaknesses; this is the world in which our children will grow up. This is an exciting challenge.

Remaining Open to the World

The library offers exposure to all kinds of knowledge, skills, artistic expressions and creations, entertainment, and games. This is what the library has been offering since its inception. This is also what the Internet offers. The digital world is immense, putting us into contact with all realms of knowledge in all its forms. We can watch films and videos. We can listen to all the music of the world. We can play there, too. Every subject is covered. But you have to know how to choose or just flit from one subject to another. This tremendous abundance of information on all subjects makes it possible for the library, within its means, to open itself to a wide variety of modes of communication and expression. This is why the library is increasingly asserting itself today as the home of all the arts, all knowledge, all forms of cultural expression, and all recreational activities—without exception. Moreover, it chooses, advises, creates bonds with people and materials, provides guidance, and helps children to formulate their questions. It strives to respond to the many interests awakened by the Internet.

---

48. Until 2007, it was called La Joie par les livres, the name of the association that created and sustained it for many years.

Yet the library has not become a cybercafé. Some people are worried that libraries will disappear. On the contrary, the unique form of coexistence that they offer is more necessary than ever—even irreplaceable. Libraries' role as places of meeting and dialogue will only become more pronounced. Mediators have an essential role to play. Together with the children, they identify what is important to know. And this is of vital importance today.

Many of the suburban housing estates that are, like ours, classified as Priority Education Zones (Zones d'éducation prioritaire), suffer from isolation and poverty. With its programs and events, La Petite Bibliothèque Ronde enriches the life of the entire cité. It makes a point of inviting artists, artisans, travelers, and scientists of the highest caliber. In this way, it makes connections with the Les Siècles orchestra and the Cité de la Musique along with the little ensembles nearby. It also organizes musical workshops at the library, which are followed by visits to concerts at the Salle Pleyel in Paris. It is not uncommon to hear music resonating in the corridors. It's the children who are playing, and it's enchanting. This library thus positions itself in the cité as a cultural center that is open to all types of creativity and knowledge.[49]

It is not uncommon to see children filming the events— the workshop sessions, activities, receptions for our short- and long-term visitors, all the little celebrations. It's good to be able to look back on these happy moments and have records of them. Videos are edited in the multimedia studio so they can be posted on the library's website. There are also children designated as "special correspondents" who are invited to give their opinions on books, music, films, performances, websites, and software or video games that have come to their attention and that may be of interest the community. Any child can become a reporter or special correspondent if they so wish. Our website is greatly enriched by their contributions. In this way, a form of communal life takes shape, and it's especially precious today when our societies seem to be ruled by

---

49. It's possible that in the coming years, the library will need to close its doors for extensive repairs. But I know that it will persevere in its mission. The library's great strength is its flexibility.

consumption, mindless clicking, and individualism. Here, we participate in the community.

Taking Flight

I owe a lot to the very first librarians of L'Heure Joyeuse and I'm constantly reminded of this. It was only natural that I should, in turn, share with younger generations the beauty of this profession, which is a constant source of amazement to me. This is why I decided to write this book.

The library is a world of flight. In Paul Hazard's words, children only ask: "Give us books, give us wings…" It's like a wellspring where children come to drink from the source, where they can read and meet others, where they are acknowledged and where they can make their voices heard, where there is a unique way to all live together. Here, I see children making discoveries that awaken them to the world, and it's a pleasure for me to participate in this alongside others who appreciate the spirit of childhood.

I'm constantly answering invitations from people everywhere who want to reach all children and make sure that none are overlooked. Together, we work at the grassroots level so the intimate and celebratory joy of reading can be freely shared. And so we are all, in our own way, moved to the core.

I know that children's libraries have a bright future ahead of them. I meet passionate and imaginative librarians everywhere, always ready to consider how to best reach everyone, without exception. They know that the library, in its various forms, is a unique institution. Thanks to these librarians, there are thousands of little round libraries being created all the way across the world and just around the corner, to the great delight of children and those around them.

While finishing this book, I learned there is a serious risk that La Petite Bibliothèque Ronde may be diverted from its original mission with a change in status, supervision, and team members.

What will come of this place where bonds between children, families, and all generations are formed around reading?

What will come of this observatory of practices?

What will come of the creative energy of the teams dedicated to transmitting their experiences all throughout the world, to genuine sharing?

List of Titles Mentioned in Text

[Fables] (La Fontaine), 72
[Stories] (Comtesse de Ségur), 8, 27, 86, 113
[Tales] (Andersen), 15
[Tales] (Grimm), 89, 116
The Adventures of Hermes (Szac), 133
The Adventures of Petit Nicholas (Goscinny & Sempé), 21
Alice (Quine), 21
Alice in Wonderland (Carroll), 164
And the Breath Becomes Sign (Cheng), 205
Anno's Animals (Mitsumasa), 196
Anno's Journey (Mitsumasa), 195
Apoutsiak, the Little Snowflake (Victor), 136
Are You My Mother? (Eastman), 98
Around the World in Eighty Days (Verne), 79
Babar (de Brunhoff), 21
Baby (Manushkin), 115
Beautiful Books, Beautiful Stories (Gruny & Leriche), 59
Bibliothérapie (Ouaknin), 148
A Bicycle for Rosaura (Barbot), 199
The Big Black Panther (François), 187
The Big Question (Erlbruch), 133
The Bike Lesson (Berenstain), 98
Birth Without Violence (Leboyer), 115
Black Jack (Garfield), 70
Blue Dog (Nadja), 206
The Borrowers (Norton), 21
Boy on a Hilltop (Taniuchi), 193
The Brothers Karamazov (Dostoevsky), 62
Caroline (Probst), 21
Charlotte's Web (White), 81
Children are People (Hill), 25
Christmas Truce (Morpurgo), 135

Cosinus the Scholar (Christophe), 8
Crocodile Tears (François), 31
The Chronicles of Narnia (Lewis), 85
The Dead Bird (Brown), 99
Dominic (Steig), 128
Eloise series (Thompson & Knight), 121
Fahrenheit 451 (Bradbury), 175
A Farm (Dumas), 206
The Fenouillard Family (Christophe), 8
The First Man (Camus), 188
Frog and Toad are Friends (Lobel), 116
Frog and Toad Together (Lobel), 116
The Giant Egg (Nakagawa & Yamawaki), 194-5
Glory (Korczak), 142
The Good Earth (Buck), 8
Good Friends, 71
Holes (Sarchar), 95
Houpi the Kind Kangeroo (Roy), 31
The House of Happiness (Vivier), 15
How to Tell Stories to Children (Bryant), 9
Iliad (Homer), 41
In Search of Lost Time (Proust), 130
The Infinite Steppe (Hautzig), 82
Kati series (Lindgren), 98
Kensuke's Kingdom (Morpurgo), 136
Let's Go to the Market (Parain), 15
Little House in the Big Woods (Wilder), 18, 103, 193
The Little Red Hen (Galdone), 43
Make Way for Ducklings (McCloskey), 206
Martin Eden (London), 95
Moonfleet (Falkner), 70
Mother, Mother, I Feel Sick (Charlip), 93
Mouse Tales (Lobel), 73
No Kiss for Mother (Ungerer), 98

The Nuremberg Stove (Ouida), 42
Odyssey (Homer), 41, 88, 115, 160
Otto: The Autobiography of a Teddy Bear (Ungerer), 132
Owl at Home (Lobel), 116
Peasant Encyclopedia, 170
People and Stories: Who Owns Literature? Communities Find Their Voice throuh Short Stories (Hirschman), 153-4
Piccolo Circus (de Ginestoux), 22
Pippi Longstocking (Lindgren), 98
Rasmus and the Vagabond (Lindgren), 74
Reflections of a Frog (Iwamura), 133
The Robber Hotzenplotz (Preussler), 29
The Rolling Galette (Caputo), 112
The Rooster's Little Share (Pineau), 9
The Sapper Camember (Christophe), 8
Say Goodnight, Adelé (Hoban), 109
The Secret Garden (Burnett), 91
The Silver Crown (O'Brien), 90
Small is Beautiful: A Study of Economics as if People Mattered (Schumacher), 205
The Streets Are Free (Kurusa), 178
Sylvester and the Magic Pebble (Steig), 71
The Tailor of Gloucester (Potter), 42
Tales from Moominvalley (Jansson), 126
The Tales of the Ogress (Khemir), 88
Tales of the Rue Broca (Gripari), 88
The Three Robbers (Ungerer), 102
The Time of Our Singing (Powers), 35
Toby Alone (de Fombelle), 135
Tropic of Cancer (Miller), 33
Tuesday Siesta (Márquez), 153
Uncle Elephant (Lobel), 116
The Uses of Enchantment: The Meaning and Importance of Fairy Tales (Bettelheim), 24

The Vicar of Tours (Balzac), 11
Village in the Vaucluse (Wylie), 32
Watership Down (Adams), 134
We Need a Mother (Shepard), 15
Where the Wild Things Are (Sendak), 31, 71, 199
Why Are People Setting Fire to Libaries? (Merklen), 183
Willy the Champ (Browne), 110
Winnie the Pooh (Milne), 27
The Wolf and the Woodcutter (Bladé), 117
The Wonderful Adventures of Nils (Lagerlöf), 26
The Wonderful Farm (Aymé), 15, 101
The Worst Lady in the World (Hinojosa), 199
Zeralda's Ogre (Ungerer), 71, 102
Zig Zag Journeys (Töpffer), 21

INDEX

Aalto, Alvar, 69
Actions culturelles contre les exclusions et les segregation (ACCES), 145-6
Adams, Richard, 134
Africa, 21, 49, 54, 71, 177, 183-4, 186-90, 192, 203, 205
African culture, 124-5, 177
Akihito, Emperor of Japan, 105
Albertini, Michel, 86
All Together in Dignity (ATD), 106-7
Allouche, Wahed, 89, 111
Andersen, Hans Christian, 15, 41, 62, 127
Anouilh, Jean, 86
Antoine, Aline, 92-3
Armenia, 39, 206
Atelier de Montrouge, 53-4, 69
Aurenche, Blandine, 139
Aymé, Marcel, 15, 101
Aznavour, Charles, 86

Balthazar, 158
Balzac, Honoré de, 11
Banco del Libro, 178-9
Barbot, Daniel, 199
Barrault, Jean-Louis, 86-7
barrio, 178, 180
Barto, Agna, 104
Basdevant, Denise, 91
Batchelder, Mildred, 32

Bettelheim, Bruno, 24
Bettencourt, Virginia, 181
Bibliothèque des Enfants, *see also* Clarmart library and La Petite Bibliothèque Ronde, 16, 19, 53, 69, 99
Bibliothèque nationale de France (BnF), 16, 60-1, 63, 87, 99, 162
Bladé, Jean-François, 117
Blake, Quentin, 206
Blyton, Enid, 21
Boimare, Serge, 129, 134-5, 155-9
Boivert, Patrick, 92
Bonnafé, Marie, 145, 149
Boston Public Library, 40
Boubat, Édouard, 66
Bourrelier, Michel, 15, 20
Bradbury, Ray, 175
Brazil, 163-8, 202
Breuer, Marcel, 54
Brown, Marcia, 43
Brown, Margaret Wise, 99
Browne, Anthony, 110, 199, 206
Brunovský, Albín, 30
Bryant, Sara Cone, 9, 40
Buck, Pearl, 8
Burnett, Frances Hodgson, 91
Butai (street theater), 118
Butel, Lucile, 187

Caillié, René, 20-1
Cain, Julien, 16, 52, 161

Campbell, Harry, 62
Camus, Albert, 188
capoeira, 202
Carné, Marcel , 47
Cerlalc, 197
Cevin, Evelyne, 115
Chaplet, Pierre and Kersti, 125, 127
Charlip, Remy, 43, 50, 99, 206
Charria, Maria Elvira, 197
Chatain, Christine, 51, 56, 59
Chauveau, Léopold , 117
Cheng, François, 205
Chiland, Colette, 131
Christophe, 8, 15
Ciranda dos libros, 168
Clair, René, 47
Clamart library, *see also* Bibliothèque des Enfants and La Petite Bibliothèque Ronde, 48, 54, 57-8, 61, 64-72, 75, 86, 102, 105, 119, 134, 143-4, 161, 191, 194
Claveloux, Nicole, 103
Clément, François, 57-8
Clozier, René, 20
Cohn, Emma, 45, 82
Colombia, 78, 167, 200-202
Comte, Pierre, 162
Congress of the International Publishers Association, 185
conscientization, 154
costumes, 122
Couder, Paul, 20
Couratin, Patrick, 103
Cousinet, Roger, 17, 51

cultural center[s], 66, 182, 195, 208
Cultural Intervention Fund (Fonds d'Intervention Culturelle), 87

Daane, Janetje, 127-8
Dapper African Art Museum, 124
Dasté, Catherine, 85
Dauzat, Albert, 20
de Brunhoff, Jean, 21, 44
de Brunhoff, Laurent, 100
de Dearden, Carmen Diana, 179
de Fombelle, Timothée, 134-5
de Fontenay, Elisabeth, 133
de Ginestoux, Madeleine, 22
de La Salle, Bruno, 88, 114, 160
de Ségur, Comtesse, 8, 27, 86, 113
delinquency, 40, 95, 107, 156
Delpire, Robert, 30-31, 102
Demy, Jacques, 122
Dharmarjan, Geeta, 185
Diatkine, René, 93, 109, 129, 197, 143-52, 160, 197
Dickens, Charles, 15, 22, 113
Diongue, Marietou Diop, 186
Disney, 98, 199
Division of Small and Medium-Sized Libraries (Section des petites et moyennes bibliothèques), 58
Doisneau, Robert, 123
Duhême, Jacqueline, 31
Dumas, Philippe, 206
Dumazedier, Joffre , 59
Duras, Marguerite, 103

Eastman, P. D., 98
École des loisirs, 31, 98, 102, 195
Ecuador, 174
Ediciones Ekaré, 179
Éditions de l'Atelier, 163
Editions du Cerf, 193
Éditions Nathan, 98
Edy-Legrand, Edouard Léon Louis, 43
El Parque library, 201
Elzbieta, 129
Erlbruch, Wolf, 133
ethnology, 45, 47, 136
Euvremer, Teryl, 93-4

fairy tales, 24, 41, 130, 156
Falkner, John Meade, 70
favela[s], 168, 175, 181
Ferreiro, Emilia, 144
Fischer, Hans, 31
Fleury-Mérogis prison, 154-5
folk tales, 9, 41, 78, 94, 117
Foncin, Myriem, 60
Fontaine, Régine, 188-9
Foucambert, Jean, 165
Franck, Martine, 66
François, André, 30-31
François, Paul, 187
freedom, 19-2056-7, 70, 105, 129, 141, 144-5, 149-50, 172, 181, 187
Freinet Modern School Movement, 13, 119, 140-1, 151, 155, 165
Freinet, Célestin, 13, 17, 119
Freire, Paulo, 154, 170, 180

Gaessler, Christophe, 124-5
Galdone, Paul, 43
Gallimard Jeunesse, 104, 163
Gandhi, Mohandas Karamchand, 174
García Márquez, Gabriel, 153-4
Garfield, Leon, 70
Gestapo, 10
Gilard, Madeleine, 31
Gilbert, Claude, 107, 140
Givel, Gilberte, 14
Gripari, Pierre, 88
Gruny, Marguerite, 15. 24, 26, 76
Guérin, Pierre, 119, 141, 155

Hachette Publishing, 44
Hassenforder, Jean, 58-9, 165
Hautzig, Esther, 82
Hazard, Paul, 22-4
Hermite, Charles, 130
Hill, Janet, 25-6, 42
Hinojosa, Francisco, 199
Hirschman, Sarah, 152-4, 160
Hoban, Russel
Hoban, Tana, 123-4
Horiuchi, Seichii, 117

Illiteracy, 183-4
immigrants, 35-6, 38-41, 112, 139, 144
Inca, 169-71
India, 54, 182, 185, 187
Inner Theater, 130-31
Innovation, 48, 58, 200
intelligent heart, 160-61

International Board on Books for Young People (IBBY), 55, 105, 163, 168, 172, 176, 184
International Federation of Library Associations (IFLA), 161-2, 172, 184
International Youth Library (Munich), 28-9
Ionesco, Eugène, 103
Iwamura, Kazuo, 133

Jan, Isabelle, 62-3, 103, 136
Jankélévitch, Vladimir
Jansson, Tove, 125-7
Japan, 50, 84, 104-5, 117-8, 177-8, 191-3, 195
justice, 11, 107, 122, 166, 170, 172

kamishibai, 118
Keats, Ezra Jack, 100
Khemir, Nacer, 88
Knight, Hilary, 121
Komagata, Katsumi, 83-4
Konaré, Alpha, 187
Korczak, Janusz, 137, 142
Kurusa, 178

L'Ecole des loisirs, 31, 98, 136, 195
L'Heure Joyeuse, 15-25, 28, 31, 33, 36, 44, 47-8, 50-52, 54-6, 59, 76, 78, 86, 90, 97, 103, 209
La Fontaine, Jean de, 72
La Joie par les Livres, 48-52, 59-60, 63, 87, 161, 189, 207

La Petite Bibliothèque Ronde, *see also* Bibliothèque des Enfants and Clarmart library, 58, 110, 183, 192, 206, 208, 210
La Urbina library, 178-80
Lagerlöf, Selma, 26, 154
Lamblin, Simone, 61, 86
Larsson, Carl, 18
Latin America, 150, 163, 167, 178, 197, 200, 203-5
Laurentin, Marie, 189
Le Cacheux, Geneviève, 61-2
Le Théâtre du Soleil, 85
Leboyer, Frédérick, 115
Lee, Ho Baek, 84
Leipzig, 50, 172-3, 175, 177, 183-4, 186
Lentin, Laurence, 103
Lepman, Jella, 29
Leriche, Mathilde, 15-6, 76
Leroi-Gourhan, André, 20
Levinas, Emmanuel, 110, 133
Lévi-Strauss, Claude, 163
Lewis, C. S., 85
Library of the Institute (Bibliothèque de l'Institut de France), 100
Library of the Poor, 184-6
Lindgren, Astrid, 74, 98, 125
Lobel, Arnold, 50, 73-4, 100, 102, 116-7, 125, 206
London, Jack, 95-6, 157
Lortic, Elisabeth, 83
Lory, Véronique, 103

Madame Kowaliski, 122-3
Madame Pêtre, 70-71

Mado, Michio, 104
Mahfouz, Naguib, 154
Maissen, Leena, 105
Mali, 184, 187-8
Malot, Hector, 15
Manushkin, Fran, 115
Marchand, Colette, 141
Marchand, Pierre, 104
Marouzeau, Jules, 17
Matsuoka, Kyoko, 192
Mazeaud, Henri, 17
Mchombu, Kingo, 184-6
Medcalf, Juan, 171
mediation, 57, 121, 148, 151-2, 155, 159, 167, 170, 172205
Merklen, Denis, 183
Merlet, Marie-Isabelle, 89-90
Mexico, 132, 166-7, 197-200, 204, 206
Michiko, Empress of Japan, 104-5
Mikhalkov, Sergey, 30
Miller, Henry, 33
Milne, A.A. (Alan Alexander), 27
Mitsumasa, Anno50, 104, 195
Montreuil Children's Book Fair (Salon du livre jeunesse de Montreuil), 104
Moomintroll, 103, 125-6
Moore, Anne Carroll, 35-6, 44
Morocco, 181-2
Morpurgo, Michael, 134-5
Muller, Gerda, 206
Munari, Bruno, 50, 121
Munich, 12-3, 28-32, 49, 52, 55

Nadja, 206

Nakagawa, Rieko, 194
National Center for Children's Literature (Centre national de littérature pour jeunesse), 63
National Institute for Pedagogical Research (Institut national de la recherche pédagogique), 58, 165
Ndiaye, Raphaël, 183-6
Neutra, Richard, 54
New York Public Library (NYPL), 16, 30. 32-3, 35-6, 16, 30. 32-3, 35-6, 38, 44-7, 55-6, 96
Nicaragua, 199
Norton, Mary, 21

O'Brien, Robert, 90-91
observation, 64, 123, 148-9, 151, 205
Okinawa, 191
oral culture, 114, 169-70, 177, 183-5
Ortiz, Alfredo Mirez, 168
Ouaknin, Marc-Alain, 148

Papy, Jacques, 27
Parain, Nathalie, 15
Paris Fair (Foire de Paris), 57
Parra, Evelio Cabrejo, 149
Pauvert, Jean-Jacques, 113
Pennac, Daniel, 90, 132
Perrault, Charles, 86, 122
Peru, 168-9, 171, 201
Pétain, Maréchal Phillippe, 11-12, 16
Petit, Michèle, 156
Piaget, Jean, 123, 144
Picasso, Pablo, 112

Pineau, Léon, 9
Pippi Longstocking, 98, 125
Ponti, Claude, 206
poverty, 13, 106, 163, 166, 172, 180-1, 184-6, 190, 208
Powers, Richard, 35
Preussler, Otfried, 29
Prévert, Jacques, 30
Probst, Pierre, 21, 44
Public Information Library (Bibliothèque publique d'information), 87

Quine, Caroline, 21
Quinones, Viviana, 189
Quist, Harlin, 103

Radenac, Jean-Pierre, 127
Rageot, Tatiana, 61
Ramos, Mario, 206
reflective activity, 61, 150, 197, 201, 203, 205
refugee camps, 176
Renaud, Bruno, 178
Renaud, Madeleine, 87
Resistance, French, 10, 12
The Revue of Books for Children (La Revue des livres pour enfants), 61
Ricoeur, Paul, 148
Robbe-Grillet, Alain, 164
Rose, Jean, 163, 168
Roubaud, Jacques, 196
Rouch, Jean, 47
Roy, Claude, 22, 30-1
Rushdie, Salman, 135

Ruy-Vidal, François, 103

Sachar, Louis, 95
Saint-Dizier, Marie, 95-6
Salgado, Kusum, 174
Salomon, Katia, 153-4
Sarvodaya movement, 174
Satie, Erik, 36
Sawyer, Ruth, 41
Scherf, Walter, 28, 55
Scholl, Hans and Sophie, 28
Schumacher, E. F., 205
Secularism, 48
Seguin, Jean-Pierre, 87
Sendak, Maurice, 31, 50, 71, 100, 102, 116-7, 206
Sennaji, Houria, 181-2
Shakespeare, 41, 88
Shedlock, Marie L., 130
Shepherd, Colin, 15
Shining Path (Sendero Luminoso), 169
Simenon, Georges, 12
Singer, Isaac Bashevis, 89
Singkamanan, Somboon, 175-6
Sonnet, Martine, 92-3
Steig, William, 138-9, 204
storytelling, 7-8, 23-7, 43, 71, 88-90, 93-4, 103, 114-5, 136, 160, 166, 198
storytime, 23, 25-6, 36-8, 40-42, 44, 47, 88-90, 93, 129-30, 192
Szac, Murielle, 133

Takam Tikou, 189-90, 203
Talibon-Lapomme, Edwige, 103

Taniuchi, Kota, 193
Taquet, Philippe, 120
Tévoédjrè, Albert, 181
Thailand, 182, 175-6, 179
Thompson, Kay, 121
Thurnauer, Gerard, 54
Töpffer, Rodolphe, 21
tradition[s], 25, 38-40, 44, 54, 85, 89, 91, 115, 162, 177, 179, 184-5, 198, 206
Trnka, Jiří, 50

UNESCO, 30, 66, 172, 197
Ungerer, Tomi, 43, 50, 84, 98, 102, 132, 206
Union of Writers for Young People (Union des écrivains pour la jeunesse), 104

Vandalism, 183
Vasconcelos Library, 200
Velthuijs, Max, 206
Venezuela, 178-81
Verne, Jules, 80, 135, 157
Victor, Paul-Émile, 136
violence, 41, 80, 113, 133, 155-7, 169, 171, 179
Vivier, Colette, 15
Vuilleumier-Encrevé, Lise, 56

Watanabe, Junko, 192
Waumgana, Ellen, 177
Weil, Simone, 126
Werneck, Leny, 163

When Books Connect (Quand les livres reliant), 146
White, E. B., 81
Wilder, Laura Ingalls, 18, 103, 193
Wilkon, Josef, 91
Williams, Garth, 18
Wolof language, 186, 189, 204
Wresinsky, Père Joseph, 106
Wylie, Laurence, 32

Yamaguchi, Tomoko, 191
Yamawaki, Yuriko, 194

Zimbabwe, 177
Zimet, Ben, 89
Zimnik, Reiner, 31

www.ingramcontent.com/pod-product-compliance
Lightning Source LLC
Chambersburg PA
CBHW070828300426
44111CB00014B/2490